NINETY BROTHERS
AND SISTERS

Lenore De Pree

NINETY BROTHERS

AND SISTERS

Lenore De Pree

To order additional copies of this book, contact:
Xlibris Corporation
1-888-795-4274
www.Xlibris.com
Orders@Xlibris.com
21058

To my ninety brothers and sisters wherever life has taken you. May you remember the laughter and good times we shared as well as the tears and despair. Bless you all, even those of you I never saw again. And to our mother, Anna, who is celebrating her 90th birthday in 2004.

Lenore

CHAPTER ONE

So many worlds, so many circles where lives intersect . . . How can I begin to tell a story that is past when nothing is ever past, but comes around again and catches one at the next turn of the circle? There have been times when I have tried to believe the past was done, that it was forgotten and gone; and then the wheel swings, and there it is again, warm, fresh, laughing, bleeding in my mind.

When it all began, the summer they opened the orphanage in the hills of Kentucky, I was only six. John, my father, and Anna, my mother, were young and deeply committed. I doubt if it ever entered John's head that what he was about to do was dangerous. Anna might have known. She was a short pretty brown-eyed woman with a hearty laugh and enough common sense for both of them. John was not blessed with common sense, but he was a dreamer of dreams and a seer of visions, a thin intense man with a bush of dark hair, a little mustache, and bright blue eyes behind rimless glasses.

Looking back, the point in the circle that stands out as the beginning was the evening before the orphanage opened. It was the end of a hot summer afternoon, the kind of mosquito-filled heat that settles over the Cumberland Mountains in July. The sun was beginning to head down behind the jagged black edges of the pine trees, and the first cool stirring of breeze carried the song of jarflies and tree frogs. For weeks the woods, from our cabin to the Laurel River, had echoed with the pounding of hammers and the shouts of men, but now the final night had come and there was an almost expectant hush over the forest.

In the log cabin facing the dirt road, I sat gloomily on the kitchen floor watching Anna prepare supper. She stood over the squat cooking stove, turning fried potatoes in a black iron skillet and humming to herself. There were things I wanted to say to her, but I didn't know how to say them without appearing to be mean and selfish. The notes of Anna's humming, the buzz of the flies in the kitchen, and the sizzling of potatoes in hot grease made a droning sleepy sound, a sound that kept pulling me into it like a strong current, dragging me against my will to float along.

I curled my arms around my knees and sniffed hungrily. The potatoes frying in the skillet smelled good. John would probably be late. He usually was, which bothered Anna, who was always on time. She was already glancing out the kitchen window and up at the red clock over the table, wondering where he was.

"Mother, when is he coming?" I asked impatiently.

Anna kept on humming for a moment. "When he's ready," she said finally.

"But . . . , why do we always have to wait?"

"That's just the way it is. Rome wasn't built in a day."

I didn't know much about Rome, I thought dismally, but that sure was the way it was around this place. I watched the last glow of the sun touching the redness of the sliced tomatoes on the table. In its own good time the sun would go down and the lamps would be lit and the tomatoes would be eaten. Everything in the world seemed to take such terrible amounts of time. Nothing ever happened as it should, quickly and clearly. Everything was a mystery and took forever, while potatoes sizzled and flies buzzed and people hummed mysterious tunes.

I almost jumped when the door jerked open and John strode in. He was covered with sweat and sawdust, and he reached for the dipper to pour wash water into the basin.

"Supper ready?" he asked, rattling the dipper in the empty pail.

"Half an hour ago," Anna said, glancing at the clock.

John took the bucket and went out to the back porch to draw fresh water. I trotted after him, anxious for the usual treat of placing my hands just below his on the chain and letting it slide between my fingers to the gurgling water in the well.

"Not tonight," he said, pushing me aside hurriedly. "We have to eat and run. Do you want to go along?"

I turned the chain loose and glowered indignantly across the hollow to where a glint of the new building was showing through the trees. I was right. Now they would be too busy for me. I wanted to call the new monster some scorching name picked up from the country school playground, but thanks to Anna and her mouth scrubbing for dirty words, all that came to mind was the slightly bitter taste of Fels-Naphtha soap. Instead of risking saying anything, I changed my approach and planted a kiss on the highest part of John I could reach, his sweaty white shirt sleeve. He patted me absentmindedly on the head, and we went in to eat supper.

It was already dusk, and the whippoorwills and tree frogs were singing up a storm when we left the cabin and headed for the new building. We must have been a strange procession winding through the woods and down the hollow, over the creek and up the hill. John was in the lead, taking determined strides up the rough slope, his bundle hoisted on his shoulder. Anna followed, barely able to see over the load clasped in front of her, stumbling now and then in the half-darkness. I trudged along behind, tightly clutching my package of bath towels tied in a string. No one said much; for one thing the climbing took our wind, and for another thing there was not much to be said at this point. It had all been decided.

At the top of the hill the new building crouched in the shadowy trees. The woods had been cut down in front of it, leaving the yard dotted with tree stumps. The sloped gables had green asphalt roofing bought from the country store, and the new siding had a coat of brown creosote. White building tags were still stuck to the windows, proud reminders that they too were brand-new and store-bought.

Inside the entryway we dumped our loads and went on into the living room. It had a rough stone fireplace in one corner and several rooms opening off it. The whole place smelled new, raw, and woodsy.

Someone was already in the building, a young woman whom John and Anna had known in Chicago. Miss Edna had appeared at our house several days before, much to my consternation and surprise. I had found her asleep on the couch early one morning, and for a long horrified moment I thought that my mother had grown a big nose and thick eyebrows. I was terribly relieved when she opened her eyes and I saw that she was somebody else. She had come to help John and Anna start the orphanage. She was a quiet woman with sad dark eyes and black hair pulled back in a bun, and she moved about almost noiselessly.

Now the three of them set to work sorting piles of clothes, washing the windows, putting hinges on a door, and making beds. When it was too dark to see, John lit a gasoline lantern and swung it from a nail, where it hung casting dancing shadows on their serious faces.

They worked far into the night. I sat in the corner watching, half dozing, half worrying what tomorrow would be like. Twelve brothers and sisters, they had said. They had said it like they were doing me the greatest favor in the world, but I wasn't so sure about that. If they wanted to be bothered with twelve kids, it was okay with me, but I didn't want a load of kids shoved under my nose as brothers and sisters. Brothers and sisters took a long time to collect. They weren't just something you could rush out and get a dozen of, like doughnuts. I could see them already, kids with snotty noses and scabby knees, grabbing everything in sight. Why did they have to come? Why didn't they stay in their own homes anyway?

A feeling of hopelessness and anger swept over me, of having been tricked. What could I do if I didn't like it? John would look sad and scold me for being selfish and unchristian, and Anna would look the other way. What, actually, could I do?"

There was only one way out. As soon as things settled down, I would collect up my clothes and go to Gram's house in Chicago. She was one person I could depend on, because her own family was more important to her than all the troubles of the world.

The lantern glowed and hissed, and the whippoorwills and tree frogs droned their summer song. The feeling came again, powerful this time, of strong currents flowing through continuous sound, sound that reached from the beginning of time to the end of the sky. The blanket of sound curled around me, and I drifted off to sleep.

Even in sleep the worries and fears hounded me. So much had happened to John and Anna before I was born that it was hard for me to understand what made them the people they were. I had been able to piece together a good amount by listening, prying, eavesdropping, and guessing, but I seldom got anywhere by making a direct inquiry. Anna had to be careful of what she said in order not to anger John, and John's answers never seemed to fit the questions. There was one person who was a good source of information, however, and that was Gram, John's straight-as-a-pin little mother.

When we visited Gram's house by the railroad tracks in Oak Lawn, Chicago, I would wake up early in the morning to watch her lace up the one-piece corset that made her back so straight and her stomach so stiff when I hugged her. But there was nothing stiff about Gram's stories. They were not only the best, they were dangerously true. One story that Gram told was so true she would glance around to see that no one else was listening, especially Grandpa Will, whose feelings she would never have hurt for the world. Grandpa Will was a dear. He worked on the WPA and ate windmill cookies dunked in coffee, he loved Gram's vegetable soup because he only had two teeth that didn't meet, and he prayed in Dutch because he secretly doubted that God understood English. But he was the second grandfather, not the one that was related to me. It was the unknown one who stirred up my curiosity.

Gram and I had a private ritual, understood only by the two of us, and that was the way the story was always told. It never changed; in fact, if she had changed so much as a word of it, I would have been upset. It was the repetition that gave it strength.

I would wait until just the two of us were alone in the kitchen at her house after a meal or a teatime, then I would climb on a chair and offer to dry the dishes for her, and she would tell me about him.

"You must be nice to your Grandpa Will," she would begin, "He's a good man, and would do anything for you."

"I will, always."

"But your daddy's own father, Grandpa Frank . . ." She would grow quiet, a faraway look in her Siamese-cat eyes. "He was an artist, a painter of portraits and beautiful scenes. I remember one scene he painted of a pasture and sheep. I wanted more than anything to keep that one, but we had to sell it because we were hungry."

"What was he like, my real grandfather?"

"Oh, he was a handsome man, tall with dark curly hair and deep blue eyes. And how that man could sing! One day I was standing in another room listening to his voice while he painted and sang, and then I tiptoed in very quietly to see how his work was coming, and I found the funniest sight. Without knowing it he had wiped his brushes in his hair, and his dark bushy hair had red and yellow streaks in it!"

That was the point at which I clapped my hands and laughed, always freshly delighted with the surprise.

"But how did you meet him"

"My folks owned a large house down in southern Illinois. In fact, my grandmother lived in Kentucky, like you do, only she lived up in the Bluegrass section and owned slaves. But my folks, they moved to Illinois, and there's where I lived when I met your grandfather. He was from the old country, from Holland, and had come over with his family. But not long after he got here, his wife died, and my folks took his three little ones as foster children while he studied art in Chicago. He used to come and see the children . . ."

She went on dreamily as I struggled to dry the cups and glasses.

"I don't know when it happened, but I started counting the

days until his next visit. I was a young music student, and my folks wanted me to study piano professionally, but then everything changed."

"Why?"

"One day we realized we were in love. He was thirty-six and I was nineteen. I knew my folks would never give their consent, but I loved him more than anything in the world. I couldn't forget him. So one day I packed a bag and we met in a secret place and were married. My folks never spoke to me again."

"How sad! Were you sorry you did it?"

"Never! A year later we had a baby, and that was your father. We had four babies, but your father was the first-born, the only son."

These last words were always spoken proudly, and I knew the story was over; and I would stand clasping the dish towel as though it were a wedding veil, in love with the past and the future. Then I would kiss Gram, and we would both pretend nothing had been said. He was an invisible bond between us, this Legendary Grandfather who was all the more powerful for his absence.

I picked up the rest of the story from my father, John, because Gram could not bear to talk about it. But John's stories always came out strangely, like bits of lightning he remembered from dark nights in the past, and he seemed to tell them when he needed to, not when he was asked.

We had a chicken house in the yard behind the log cabin, and in the spring John bought fifty baby chicks to raise. There was a heavy rain one day, and before anyone thought to check, the rain had swooped down into the chicken pen and washed the tiny chicks into a flooded corner, and they drowned.

I went to the chicken pen with John and helped him put them in a box to bury them. Suddenly in the middle of picking up the baby chicks he began to cry. I thought he was crying because they cost so much, or because he felt sorry for them.

"Oh, don't," I begged. "Poor little things are dead now. They can't feel anything. See, their eyes are shut." I was close to tears myself.

He wiped his eyes with a big handkerchief and blew his nose. "Just like the chicks that got burned to death right after he died, on the farm-my father," he said slowly. "I remember picking up the little charred bodies and cradling them in my hands and wondering if their souls went to heaven, like they said my father's did, or if they were just wasted for nothing. Everything seemed so unfair, and I wanted to throw them down and scream at God, but I had the feeling that He wouldn't even hear me."

I glanced at his face and saw he had forgotten me. He was crying for something that had happened long ago, and he hardly saw me or the baby chicks.

It seemed he'd had more fire than most people as a child, and the way he told his stories puzzled me. Several years after John's father died, Gram went to do housework for Grandpa Will, whose wife had also died and left him with five children. Young John had been living in many different foster homes while Gram worked, and all the other children had been adopted out; but when she decided to marry Grandpa Will, she included John in the new family. John had dreamed of living with his own mother for many years, and now that he was finally home again he resented having to share her with a new husband and his five children.

Then one night there was a house fire, and all the children sleeping upstairs were burned to death. John somehow scrambled out of the flames unharmed. The fact that he was the only child who survived awed him, and he took it as a sign that God had spared his life for a special purpose, while allowing the others to be destroyed.

I always felt sad for the five children who died. John seemed to have forgotten that part of it, but Grandpa Will hadn't. There was a picture of them on the dresser in his bedroom.

No one exactly told me about the big quarrel between John and Grandpa Will, but I heard Gram and Anna joking about it. Grandpa Will was a very honest earthly little man, and he was definitely put off by this young son who had such grand ideas about himself. For a few years after the fire there was silent dislike between them, and then John committed the one sin that to Grandpa Will was unpardonable. First he criticized the teachings of the Dutch Calvinist Church that the older man took so seriously, and then, right in front of his psalm-reading stepfather, John called the Reverend Dominie VerBeek an old fart.

Purple with anger, the usually tolerant Grandpa Will grabbed his stepson by the collar, whipped him soundly, and threw him out of the house.

"Out mitt you!" he shouted. 'Get out of mine house! Get out in the onion fields and vear the skin off your knees, and lurn an little vat it is to be humble before Gott! I vill not feed an young heretic who calls the dominie an old fart! Ach!"

John was taken out of school and made to work in the onion fields for two years.

Around and around they whirled that night, all the worrisome things, a tumbled assortment of snapshots in Anna's album, of things picked up by listening when nobody noticed, half of them understood and half of them only sensed as the scrambled blur of an adult world.

Anna had a snapshot of her wedding day. She wore a long print dress and held a bouquet of roses, while John stood beside her biting his bottom lip and looking embarrassed.

They had met in high school, when Anna was fifteen and John nineteen. She was quick and popular and felt sorry for the shy young boy who had come to school two years later than anyone else. She helped him with his work, and he grew to depend on her.

He had saved money and bought a model-T Ford of his own. He took her for long drives and claimed her as his girl. He was fiercely jealous of her, and fell into black moods of anger if she spoke too long to anyone else.

The wedding picture had been taken in the back yard of the Kingma house. Dr. Kingma, Anna's father, was a veterinarian, and his brood of ten sturdy Dutchmen were a close, warm family. Before Anna was married, her five beer-drinking brothers had taken one look at John and told her to forget him. Her four sisters had thought him peculiar, and her parents had refused to give permission before she was eighteen. But the week Anna was of age, she and John were married. She was as stubborn as she was pretty, and no amount of advice could change her mind. Deep down she knew better than anyone else that John had a dark strange side, but it was this quality that set him apart. She felt he needed her and, like her father, she loved healing wounded creatures.

But John hated Anna's family.

It was a puzzle the way John felt that everything was bad. He had gone to college and he'd even wanted to study medicine, but it had been a bitter experience for him. Times were hard, and there was no way to borrow money. Anna became pregnant, and he knew he had to find some kind of work so they could eat. Ever since the fire, he had believed in his divine calling, and he even thought of being a minister, saying that his quarrel was not with God but only with the stuffy traditions of the Dutch Calvinist Church. He began to search for other ways to find his calling, ways that would not need years of schooling. He took to saying that all official titles were a farce and that a formal education was a waste of time. During the summer before I was born, he and Anna joined a group of young people who called themselves Independent Fundamentalists and began to attend classes at a Bible school in Chicago.

I was born that August, a fat sassy infant who howled so lustily I woke up the whole neighborhood. There was no money for Anna to go to the hospital, and I was delivered at her sister Della's house, in the front bedroom. Anna was in labor for hours, screaming with pain, and John was frightened, thinking something had gone wrong. Then suddenly I emerged with an indignant look on my face, bald as an onion, and howling heartily. John wanted to name me Gladis after his mother, and Anna wanted to call me Lenore, so each gave me a different name and each called me by that name. I wished they had waited to ask me what I wanted to be called.

One of the pages in Anna's album had a picture taken the day we left for Kentucky. I was two years old, standing on the running board of an old car, sticking my stomach out. In their new circle of friends in Chicago, John and Anna had met a Mr. Baker who was scouting for young recruits willing to do mission work in the backwoods of Appalachia. John and Anna had gone to hear him speak one night, and afterward they had gone forward and offered their services. Within a few weeks they had packed their few possessions in a secondhand Chevy, said goodbye to their families, and begun the then-difficult trip to Kentucky's mountain area.

The south, as I first remember it, was rutted roads and old snuff signs. It was people who wondered why we, northerners, had come. It was the mountain behind our house, and the brown water of the Laurel River. It was Whippoorwill Creek bubbling over the stones under the footlog, and John happier than he had been before, John saying that he was a Kentuckian on his mother's side and that he had come back where he belonged. He began to wear overalls over his dress shirts and to talk like the mountain people.

At first we lived at Mr. Baker's compound. They were all supposed to live together in peace and brotherhood, but John was restless. He wanted to be alone, with no brothers, no one to bother him. He started looking for a place in the hills, out between Corbin and Williamsburg, in the backwoods off the Falls Pike.

But it was not easy to find a place to live. John might have fooled himself that he had turned Kentuckian, but he had not fooled the mountain people. One day we found a house that Anna liked and went to ask the old lady who owned it if she would rent it to us.

She came to the door and looked John over carefully. "Are you a Babtist? she asked.

"Well. I guess I'm sort of a Baptist." he answered.

She sucked on the snuff in her lip and nearly spat on him. "If you was a Babtist" she said, "you'd know there ain't no such critter as a sort-of-a-Babtist!" She closed the door and refused to rent to us.

Finally we found a man who fished on Sunday instead of going to church, and it didn't matter to him what we were. He rented a house to us, a one-room log cabin set in a sage-grass field and surrounded by tall pines. A dirt road connected it with the highway eight miles away, and behind it a path ran through the hills to the river.

"How much is the rent?" John asked.

"Two fifty." the owner said.

"How much?"

"Two dollars and fifty cents a month, unless that's too much."

"Oh, fine!" John smiled. "I'll take it."

The cabin was no prize. It had no electricity, no running water, only one window, and there were cracks between the logs, as the owner pointed out, big enough to throw a cat through. But the fisherman was a good landlord. He helped John build a fireplace out of road clay and fieldstone and chink up the cracks with more of the sticky mud. John tacked up building paper inside to prepare for the winter, and Anna carried water from the Indian spring in the hollow and cooked over the open fire. There was only one bed, and John and Anna slept at the head and I slept at the foot. I felt snug and secure, sleeping with their warm feet on either side of me. For all its ruggedness, the cabin was home.

During the next two years I must have been too busy to notice that things were going wrong. For me, life was an adventure, running through the sage grass and watching the clouds drift above the tops of the pines. I grew to have a strong sense of self, a love of wandering alone through the woods and climbing trees where there were no watchful adult eyes. I poked sticks at the lazy snakes stretched across the paths, and then ran like the wind with a breathless sense of having stirred up danger. I learned to be caught up in the song of the crickets and the whippoorwills, and to feel the soft velvet fear of the darkness. From old Jim Earls down by the river I learned about the boogerman and from the constant church services I learned about God. There seemed to be two kinds of gods, the god-in-the-woods who was friendly and green, and the god-in-church who was angry and killed his son for everyone. I thought that was a dirty trick, and it scared me to death. A world where gods killed their children was not a very safe place to live.

Yet the world seemed safe enough. John was a good man, who took me with him on his mule when he went to visit the sick or to get mail from the old gray post office by the river. Some people stared at us suspiciously as we jogged along in the saddle, wondering if John were a secret "revenoor" come to spy out their moonshine stills; but as time passed and there were no raids on stills, people began to relax. Sometimes all three of us were invited to a neighbor's house for a dinner of squirrel or rabbit, or a breakfast of fried chicken. John became Brother Vogel, and Anna Sister Vogel. In the country schools and in the churches where the Baptists would allow it, John preached and Anna played hymns on the little folding pump organ. I was shined and polished and stuck up on the platform to sing and recite verses like some wind-up toy. Because ministers were scarce, Brother Vogel was often called on to preach funeral services, and Anna usually went along to help the family wash and lay out the body. In the hills it was enough if a preacher was called of the spirit, and no one minded that John was not a regular minister. The only time it made any difference was when couples came and asked him to marry them. He always refused, saying he was not licensed to marry and they would be living in sin.

Someone had given Anna a snapshot taken the summer the men came from Mr. Baker's compound to help John add four rooms onto our log house. What I was doing, strutting around over a log pile in the middle of summer in a big pair of overshoes, goodness only knows. But then that was the summer that anything was possible to me. I had a pair of striped coveralls and a shaggy mop of curls, and felt absolutely invincible. I decided not to be either of the names they had given me but to call myself Jimmy. I was Princess Jimmy, and the world was my kingdom.

But at four, kingdoms are fragile things. For some reason beyond my control, everything began to fall apart. It all started as a good time, a trip back to Chicago with its clanging streetcars and blinking lights. We went to Grandma Kingma's house and sat in the warm kitchen eating soup and Dutch rye bread and cheese. The doctor had died of a heart attack several years before, and Anna's mother was alone in the big house. Her face was smiling and glad to see Anna, but she had wary eyes on father John.

"What do you live on?" she asked. "Do you have a job with those people? How do you eat?"

"We have a garden, and chickens," Anna said cheerfully.

"We live by faith," John corrected her seriously, "We do God's work, and He feeds us."

Grandma Kingma's high-cheek boned face went red. Her mouth was open and her dark eyes were half shut. "I don't call that faith," she said. "I call it an insult to those of us who have to work to earn our daily bread . . . , and support those of us who don't."

No one said anything, and it was so quiet in the kitchen my throat squeaked when I tried to swallow.

When it happened, we were in the car on the road to Aunt Ida's house in Wisconsin. It was night, and there was a cold wind and ice on the road. A sudden screech of brakes and a flash of light, and then there were screams in the darkness and a terrible feeling of falling. Flashlights shone on us, and strange people were saying, *Here they are . . . They're still alive . . . Get the old woman out from under the car, she's pinned . . . There's a child here. She seems all right, just a little skinned . . . Is the older lady dead? . . . Who was the driver?*

Strangers were taking us to the hospital. John was stretched out on a table in the emergency room moaning, and Anna was holding her mother's hand. They were covered with blood.

The next day at Aunt Ida's house everyone was crying. Grandma Kingma had died.

Back in Chicago, Gram took care of me so Anna could go to the funeral. John refused to go with her.

"Do you know how I would feel having all your family glowering at me, accusing me of killing her?" John asked. "They've always hated me, and now they have something to blame on me. How can you expect me to go?"

"Why do I always have to think about how you feel?" Anna said, covering her face. "Couldn't you just for once in your life think about how someone else feels? Remember, it was my mother who was killed."

"And I did it, I suppose!"

"Oh, for goodness' sake, don't complicate things. My mother is dead. It was an accident. Please go with me."

But John refused. When Anna had gone, alone, I heard Gram talking to John. "You should have gone, for Anna's sake," she scolded him. 'What kind of a man are you?"

"Why should I go to her funeral?" John mumbled. "That old battle axe never liked me anyhow. I'm sure she wouldn't be shedding any tears if I were dead. And anyhow if she was supposed to have lived, she would have lived. They have nothing to blame on me. It was God's will."

When we went back to Kentucky, things were not the same. Anna brought back a kettle and an iron skillet that had been her mother's, and they were important. Sometimes I touched the black iron skillet and thought of Anna's mother and remembered her beautiful high-cheekboned face. It was hard to believe that she was dead, and that John didn't care.

The cabin seemed ghostly. Anna cried quietly at night when she lit the kerosene lamps and John went outside. Sometimes he stayed out half the night. When Anna asked him where he had been, he said he was out in the woods praying.

Perhaps it was because of the tensions between my parents when I was four, or maybe it was just because I was a silly kid, but I honestly could not decide if I wanted to be a man or a woman when I grew up. As far as I was concerned., anyone named Princess Jimmy was a bit of both, at least until one could make the decision in decency and order.

Then one day Anna went to visit Mrs. Hopper, one of her friends from the compound group, and took me along. The women were in the house chatting, and Harry Hopper and I, both four, were playing in the back yard. He had on very short shorts, and as he was climbing over the back-yard fence I noticed something hanging out.

"Excuse me, Harry," I said politely, "but I think you've got a little clothespin caught in your pants." Without waiting for any further explanation, I tried to pull it off.

The little boy let out a shriek and headed for the house, clutching his groin as he went. "Ma, Ma!" he screamed. "She pulled my weewee!"

I could hear the mothers coming, thundering across the porch like a herd of cows. Anna was trying not to laugh.

"Lenore, what did you do?" she asked sternly

I really didn't know. I was still in a state of shock that it was stuck on him. There was nothing like that stuck on me. And then in a sudden leap of intuition I knew that one of the most important decisions in life had been made for me, without my consent. Harry was a boy, and I was a girl. We were different.

I hid my face in Anna's big skirt and cried.

Anna might have suspected that we were no longer enough for John, that he needed something else beyond us as his family, when he showed her the postcard that came in the mail one morning. It was from Harlan County, and had only a few words scrawled in pencil, asking John to come and get a baby that needed a home. But if Anna did suspect such a thing, she never let on. She was as excited as John about the idea of taking in a new baby.

The postcard came from a mining town to the northeast of us, and John had to find someone who knew the area to go along and act as a guide. When they reached the town, they discovered themselves in the middle of a feud between the baby's father and grandfather, who claimed the young man had ruined his daughter and ought to marry her. At the risk of being shot, John and his guide took the baby from the teenage mother and roared out of town, hoping no one was on their trail.

Anna and I were waiting at home. We prepared a basket and watched the road for two days before we finally saw them coming over the hill. The road was muddy, and they had had to park the car and sleep awhile before walking the last six miles

Anna took the little bundle from John and opened it. Inside lay a small red-haired blue-eyed baby, sucking its fingers hungrily. Anna let me hold it, and I stood stiffly, afraid I would break it. When we reached the cabin I watched her change its diaper and give it a bath, hoping it would be a boy so I could get a good look at what they were like. But Christina was smooth on the bottom, like me. Along with being happy. I was rather disappointed.

Then we found out that the new baby couldn't drink. Every time she took a bottle., the milk ran out of her nose. The doctor in Corbin said she would have to have surgery or she would never learn to talk properly, and might even starve to death.

"Surgery !" Anna worried. "Where will we get the money?"

"God will provide." John said calmly.

But in the end, it was Gram who came through with the solution. She took Christina to her house in Chicago, and they found a plastic surgeon who was willing to donate his services to a charitable cause. Christina stayed with them for almost two years.

With Christina gone. I was alone again and dying to go to school. The property next to our cabin belonged to the county, and on it stood a white clapboard schoolhouse. Every weekday morning in the fall and winter, children from the mountains gathered outside to play tag and marbles until the bell rang to "take up books." Every recess I sat longingly on the rail fence between the properties wishing I could join them. Anna had already taught me to read and write, but school was so much more than that.

I was not quite five when Anna convinced John that I should go. The first day was terrible. Anna dressed me up in a navy blue dress with a white collar, brushed my curls around her fingers, and put white shoes and socks on me. When I walked into the schoolyard, no one would come near me. Everyone else was barefoot and in overalls. After the first day, I took my shoes off and left them in the bushes by the rail fence and made sure I got at least respectably dusty before I got to the schoolyard, and things were better.

The school itself was an experience never to be forgotten. All the classes were in one room. Each row was a class, with the teacher's desk up front. The place had the smell of paper and chalk, and of kids who ate a lot of raw onions. There were two crackled blackboards, a purplish potbellied stove, and a water bucket with a common dipper. Anna insisted that I bring my own drinking glass, but I hid it in my desk and never mentioned it. One was considered snobbish if she didn't want to drink out of the dipper.

There were three other people in the primer class, the grouping before first grade. One was a boy of thirteen who still could not read. He came only the first weeks of each school year and for the Christmas program.

Outside on the playground there was nothing but bare dirt with a few tufts of grass, a wooden well and two toilets. At recess lining up at the toilets was the main activity, complete with a whole set of unspoken rules. There were two holes cut in the seat inside the privy to speed the line-up, which made it important to stand in line next to a friend. It was considered to be downright mortifying to have to pee in front of someone who hated you.

It became a matter of survival for me to be able to sort out which things were tolerated at home and which things were expected at school. In the classroom, knowing how to read was as clumsy as having shoes, so I pretended to stumble along in the reader like the rest of the class. But I still had to learn what not to say at home.

The sweet potato trick was an example. It had probably been played on everyone else in the schoolyard but me, but being the youngest, it was my turn. Many of the boys carried sweet potatoes for lunch, and instead of packing a lunch pail simply stuck the gooey baked potatoes in their baggy overall pockets.

One day at recess one of the big boys called me over to his group. "Would you like a bite of my sweet tater" he asked generously.

"Sure!" I said gratefully.

"Reach in my pocket and get it," he invited.

Trustingly, I stuck my hand in his pocket. What I grabbed was definitely not a sweet potato. I hastily took my hand out, and the boys hooted with laughter.

When I told John about it, his face turned a dark red. "That's a damnable public school for you!" he said accusingly to Anna. "You'd better get her out of there or one of those big hillbilly morons will rape her next!"

"Come on now," said Anna, laughing a little. "I thought you were the one original true and loyal Kentuckian. You have to take the bitter with the sweet"

But I was scared. John was angry, and for a few days I thought he was going to keep me out of school.

Christina must have been the seed of the idea, but during that winter the notion of starting an orphanage seemed to grow full-blown out of John's head. He had his mind made up before any of the rest of us knew about it.

I heard him discussing it with Anna one night.

"But where would we get the money?" she asked, looking

startled.

"By faith. If we took in a group of children, I believe the Lord would feed them like He feeds us. We haven't gone hungry yet, have we?" He glanced at Anna's round figure, puffy from a diet of fried potatoes and biscuits.

"No . . . I guess not," she said slowly. "But what you're talking about is a different thing. People would be trusting their children's lives to us. And how about the legal side? Would the welfare system allow you to take in children with no regular source of income? I know they're very strict about those things in Illinois."

"The welfare department!" John snorted. "They don't even know these kids exist! What do they do when Joe Blow gets his throat slit at a moonshine still and leaves a dozen kids to starve in some hollow? Tell me that! You've seen them as well as I have, the kids left after the funerals. They're castaways!"

"I know, but they're still human beings, and I don't want to try to help unless we can do so responsibly."

"I've been doing a lot of thinking," John said, as though he were talking to himself. "If we bought some land. I could hire men-"

"Where do we have money to buy land?"

"It'll come."

"Even if it does, we still owe for last month's groceries, and the car payment is overdue. I think we should pay our debts before-"

John stood up hastily, as though he could not listen to one more word. "I've already made a deal for a hundred acres of land," he said stubbornly. "I paid a dollar down yesterday, and need two hundred and forty-nine more by September first."

Anna stared at him for a moment, then shook her head. "God help us," she said.

"He will." John answered.

After that, events moved along swiftly.

The day before the money was due John still owed $100. All summer every penny had been saved and used to pay the first

$150, and now if we did not have the remaining $100 in one day we would lose all we had paid and the land would go back to the owner.

John was understandably tense as he walked to the post office that Saturday morning. He allowed me to take his hand, but barely heard when I tried to talk to him.

We walked up the steps and across the vine-covered porch of the post office. Along the wall, a row of chairs was filled with community people, visiting, gossiping, and spitting snuff. They looked at us curiously and nodded as we went on through to the dark inner room. It was a close, thickly papered room, with a fireplace hung with dried beans on one end and a partitioned-off postal office on the other. Tall skinny Jack Decker handed out the mail.

"Howdy, Preacher." he said as we entered. "I don't reckon as there's anything here for you-all today."

John's hand went limp. He turned suddenly to leave without saying a word.

"Hey. Wait a minute." Mr. Decker called. "I do believe you have got one here, from a place called Holland, Michigan. You know anybody up thataway?"

John turned and reached for the letter. I could see his hand shaking as he tore it open. In it there was a $100 check from a Mr. Brower and a note that John should use it for whatever he happened to need.

"My God!" John said, staring at the check.

We ran all the way up the hill to tell Anna.

With the land paid for and his first proof that he was on the right track, John began to plan. He went to Charlie Roaden, who owned the country grocery store on the Bee Creek road, and asked if he were willing to make a deal.

"Like the coal mines," John explained. "I'll hire men and pay them a dollar a day in scrip, and you honor the notes when they come to buy groceries and supplies from you."

"How soon could you pay the notes off?" Roaden asked.

"Soon as I cut enough lumber, Ill take it to town and sell it for cash and settle up with you."

"I'll stand it as long as I can," Roaden agreed.

John began hiring men. A crew of four cut trees, and two others hooked heavy chains around the logs and pulled them behind mules to the mill site. When a large pile was collected, John found a sawmill man who was willing to come in and set up his equipment, saw the logs, and be paid with a part of the lumber. The rest of the wood John divided up into piles, one to sell and clear his debt at the country store, and one to use for his own buildings.

That winter, since I only went to school mornings, I followed John around through the logwoods, watching the giant trees toppled into the underbrush and dragged to the mill by strong-smelling mules and men. I stood openmouthed as the pine logs screeched through the circular saw of the mill, shedding a spray of sawdust in a growing mound and coming out the other end as smooth new lumber.

When spring came and the deadness of the brown forest changed to a yellow-green, the new building had begun to take shape on the next ridge. I climbed over the floor joists and swung from the rafters and learned the difference between number-eight and finishing nails. I sat and watched John in his overalls and white shirt, planing boards by hand for the windows and doors, sweat streaming down his face in great rivers.

That summer the hired men worked from sunup to sundown. They were paid a dollar a day in used clothing. Friends in Chicago had begun to send us boxes of secondhand clothes to give to the poor, but John said people would appreciate them more if they had to work for them. Besides using the clothes for wages, he also set up a swapping system that helped him get building supplies.

A pile of ordinary clothing was worth a chicken, or a dozen eggs, and a good coat was worth a bag of potatoes. Then he would take this produce to the country store and swap the eggs, chickens, and potatoes for nails, roofing paper, and hinges. By the time the whole house was up, it had cost less than a hundred dollars in cash.

While John and the crew of men built the house, Anna planted a bigger garden and started raising more chickens. She canned wild berries and anything left over from the garden, and set the jars in the dirt cellar under the cabin. She wrote to her sisters in Chicago asking them to collect overalls, dresses, pajamas, shoes, and coats in children's sizes instead of the outmoded evening dresses, plumed hats, and corsets that filled so many of the boxes. When the clothing arrived, she washed and sorted it, sewing on buttons and replacing zippers that not-so-cheerful givers had ripped out.

Then suddenly it was July, the hot humid July evening before the orphanage was to open. Only the finishing touches were left to be completed while the whippoorwills and tree frogs called on their endless song.

In some ways, it was a beautiful beginning. But with a small child's nose for danger, I was worried. There was a lot for someone who was only six to think about. During that night, slumped in the corner and sleeping by the light of the lantern, I had a terrifying dream. John was going to take his only son, Jimmy, to the top of a mountain and kill him to save the world. I woke up screaming, and found Anna searching me from head to toe to see if I had been bitten by a spider.

CHAPTER TWO

We all had so much to prove that first day. John was trying to prove that God was in heaven and would hear his prayers. Anna was trying to prove that she loved John and would comply with his wishes. And I was trying to prove that I hated all these intruders and wanted them to go to hell or back up the creek or wherever they had come from.

It was nine o'clock in the morning when the first carload arrived. A man with a sheriff's badge dropped them off and drove slowly back down the sandy road. There were two girls and a boy. Loretta was twelve and well developed, R. C. was ten and skinny, and Virgie was nine and quiet. To me they all looked huge and terrifying, dirty and mean. R. C. climbed a tree in front of our cabin and refused to come down. Loretta and Virgie were angry about having to come, and talked only in whispers to each other.

John wanted me to entertain them, but I wanted to go with him to get the next batch. I hoped they might be better than these. But the Wilcox family could only be reached by traveling for several hours up a creek bed on the other side of Williamsburg, and since it was a bumpy ride and I got carsick, it was decided I should stay home. Entertaining the first three was fairly easy. They didn't say anything, and neither did I.

It was almost noon before John returned, his blue eyes sparkling and a look of pure bliss on his face. In the car were four small shapes, two boys and two girls. They piled out, and I eyed them. A tiny girl, a boy about my age, a girl of eight or nine, and another bigger boy. R. C. came down out of his tree, and the two older boys began to talk.

The boy about my age looked friendly.

"What's your name" I asked.

"Stumpy," he said, grinning. "My real name's Ross, but they call me Stumpy. And this here's my little sister Betsy, and that one's Hallie, and the other one over there is Lewis. We got another sister at home, but she's tetched in the head, and my ma reckoned she'd better keep her. Are you his kid?"

"Yep." I nodded. "Where's your father?"

He looked at me, cocking his head questioningly. "You mean my daddy?"

"Yeah." I saw I was going to have to use schoolhouse lingo.

"Well, he got busted over the head with a shotgun butt. Him and my uncle was arguing over a saddle, and they was both drunk, and he got his brains knocked out."

"Oh," I said, not knowing quite what to say. "But why didn't your mother keep you?"

"We didn't have much to eat." Stumpy said. "She didn't have no help raisin' us, and there was somebody else wanted to marry her, but he didn't want us kids, so she was glad when they said Brother What's-his-name wanted us."

I looked at Stumpy. He was only seven, not much older than me, but he seemed to know so much more. I had never thought of my father or mother marrying someone else.

Hallie came over and joined us. She was big and rawboned for eight, with a starved look. Shaggy brown hair fell over her eyes.

"Is Hallie your real name?" I asked her.

Stumpy grinned mischievously, his freckles spreading across his broad nose. "Naw her name's Toe-belly." he said.

Hallie reached to push him. "It ain't either. My name's Hallie."

"Its Toe-belly!" he teased, ducking the blow.

"What does toe-belly mean?" I asked curiously.

"There wasn't nobody to tie her belly button when she was borned and it sticks out like a big toe. Come on, Hallie, don't be unfriendly. Why don't you show her?"

Hallie had on overalls and decided to oblige. She unfastened her suspenders and stuck out her belly, round and strangely hard. In the middle of her abdomen a huge navel protruded.

"See?" she said. "It ain't nothing."

After that Stumpy, Hallie, and I were friends. I showed them the sage grass in the back yard and the worms that bored up out of the ground in the sewer, the chicken pen, and the long grassy hill one could roll clown and get dizzy. We spent a long time getting dizzy and falling down, until Hallie threw up and then we quit.

That afternoon three more boys came. Their father and mother had both died of TB and they had been living with an aunt. They were good-looking boys, tanned, well fed, and fairly polite. Homer was around six. Troy about twelve, and Ray, who looked a bit simple, was fourteen.

I liked Homer. He had wicked little eyes and rosy cheeks.

The other two children never came. That night everyone slept at our cabin. The dorm was ready, but it was decided it would be better to let everyone get "homed in" at our house. By dark we were all chasing around the yard catching fireflies in a fruit jar, sneaking up on tree frogs, and acting as if we'd known one another for years. It wasn't as bad as I had expected, and I decided to postpone running away.

Bedtime was a war. Anna and Miss Edna filled a washtub with hot water heated on the cooking stove, and one by one the children were dunked and scrubbed. Anna brought out the pajamas she had so carefully hoarded, and some of the boys refused to wear them.

"I ain't wearing them sissy things," Stumpy said. "What are they, anyhow? They look like girls' britches!"

Homer decided to model a pair. With his sparkling eyes and rosy cheeks, he looked adorable in the blue and white striped pajamas. I decided he might be okay for a brother.

I looked at him closer, and saw something crawling in his hair.

"Do you have ants in your hair?" I asked companionably.

"Naw" He shook his head. "Them's boogers."

I ran over to where Anna was scrubbing Betsy. The little girl was screaming frantically for her mother.

"What's boogers?" I asked Anna.

"What about boogers?" she shouted over the screaming.

"Homer's got them," I said. "Walking in his hair."

Anna suddenly let go of Betsy, who ran across the floor naked and screaming. Hallie caught her, and Anna examined Homer's hair.

"Oh my Lord." She sighed. "These kids are full of lice."

A lot of people had them at school. I had always thought they were ants.

For once John heard what Anna said. He whipped out the tin box in the kitchen where the scissors and clipper were kept, and lined the boys up in a row. One by one he shaved their heads completely bare. Then the boys were doused in kerosene from the tank outside and scrubbed again. The girls' hair was trimmed short, dipped in kerosene, and tied up in rags.

Finally, around ten o'clock, we were sorted into two piles on the floor, the boys on one end and the girls on the other, and the lamp was blown out. For the first time in our cabin the song of the whippoorwills and the croak of tree frogs were mixed with the rustle of giggling, pinching, fighting kids trying to get to sleep. Stumpy's little sister was still sniffing and crying for her mother.

I got up and went into the kitchen to say good night, but Miss Edna was there, and I felt embarrassed. Anna said I could sleep in their bedroom if I wanted, but I didn't. I found an old rubber doll that belonged to Christina and gave it to Betsy., and she finally stopped crying and fell asleep.

By the next night the kids had moved into the dorm. Miss Edna had a room on the left front corner, a mysterious place where no one was allowed to go unless invited. The girls had the front bedroom, the boys the back one. Big iron beds, two in each room, easily slept everyone. There was a dining room, a room for washing up where a row of towels hung on the wall, and the center room where everyone could meet.

Anna and Miss Edna cooked the evening meal. There were fourteen of us when we all sat around the long table on the rough benches.

After the meal John stood up and read from the Bible about

God taking care of the birds. Then he prayed, asking that food would be sent for the next day.

Stumpy was sitting next to me at the table. He had eaten a huge plate of pork and beans and six slices of bread, and still looked hungry. He leaned over and whispered to me, "Ain't he got nothin' to feed us neither?"

"Of course he has." I said, hoping it was true. "He wouldn't let you go hungry."

Stumpy looked worried. "My big sister is tetched in the head," he said. "And she's always gettin' religion. Every time there's a revival up the creek, she gets religion. Is your daddy tetched in the head?"

The way he said it, I knew it was nothing to be.

"Of course not." I said. "And if you say he is I'm going to punch you."

"Well," Stumpy said, "you can't never be sure about nothin' like that."

Sometimes Stumpy looked like a little old man, like Grandpa Will. Most of his teeth were out in front too.

It was good we had been friendly with the people of the community before the children started coming. Although we never had anything to spare in our cabin, whenever he could John had always helped anyone who needed him. When people were sick, he took them to the doctor or brought medicine to them. When people died, he buried them and assured the family of a better life in the hereafter. When people were poor, we gave them clothes even without trading, or if they came to our house while we were eating, we shared what was on the table with them. Everyone in the surrounding hills and valleys seemed to owe John for something, not to be paid in kind but in good will. Now that Anna and John had taken the extra children, the community felt responsible for them.

People came with sacks of potatoes and wagonloads of pumpkins. The neighbors showed us how to dig a hole and line it with hay to store the potatoes for winter. They helped John build a smokehouse on the flat ground behind our cabin, and butchered a pig to smoke for winter. Money and clothing came in the mail from people in Chicago and Michigan who had heard about the children. Anna's family sent all they could spare from raising their own broods, and John's mother sent loving packages of Dutch rye and Edam cheese. The country store extended credit and agreed to have the bill paid once a month. We were not quite as dependent on God as the birds were.

It was too late in the year to grow anything else, but John barteted with a nearby farmer, trading lumber for part of his molasses crop. The green glass jars were lined up neatly for the winter, filled to the brim with rich dark brown sorghum molasses to be mixed with butter and spread on corn bread.

We never had meat, except on Sundays and then we had Jell-O as well, chilled in the cool spring behind the dam and dolloped with cream from the neighbor's cows. Nobody went hungry, but we ate a lot of soup beans and pumpkin.

But no matter how it came to the table, we were taught that our food came from the hand of God.

In the evenings, when we had our pajamas on, everyone had a spoon of cod liver oil. Then, fishy-smelling but otherwise clean, we sat on the floor and listened to John or Anna or Miss Edna tell a story from the Bible. Miss Edna was precise and correct, and we all sat still because we were in awe of her. Anna told the stories with a motherly make-believe flavor, the same way she told about Hansel and Gretel. But John! When John told them we listened, drawn into him and fascinated. To him they were real. There was a pure light in his eyes and a warmth in his voice that inspired us. What he said, we believed.

Then we knelt down, itching and scratching, poking and coughing and farting from too many soup beans, and imitated one another's prayers. We went to bed feeling clean and holy.

Life might have gone along very peaceably, and John and Anna might have learned to work together, might even have learned something from each other, if Nada had not come. Nada, the Frenchwoman, with her flashing smile and slender ankles, who seemed to think and talk like John. But was it really she who made the trouble, or was it already there in my father, who was driven by some dark strange hunger that none of us could ever understand?

The day she came it was fall. The oaks and sassafras trees were red and gold against the blue October sky, and the air was crisp and cool. Bees droned lazily in the last summer sun, and squirrels scampered up and down the big oak in front of our cabin, storing acorns for winter. Under the oak, John and a group of the older boys were sawing logs for the winter fires while a cluster of younger children watched.

A blue car lurched and bumped over the hill just beyond the neighbor's house and eased smoothly over the sandy ruts to our cabin. It stopped under the oak tree, and a young woman got out.

John laid the saw aside and walked over to meet the stranger.

She held out a small well-manicured hand and flashed a brilliant smile. Her eyes were black, shadowed with luxuriant brows and lashes.

"You must be Mr. Vogel?"

"That's right. And you?"

"I'm Nada Rivore, working over in McCreary County as a Bible woman in the schools."

"Bible woman?" John stared, taking her in. She did not fit the picture of the typical mountain Bible teacher.

"Yes, my home is in St. Louis, but I've been working in the hills of Kentucky this summer. I and my co-worker, Miss Simmons"-she motioned to the car-"have just completed a summer of work in the rural schools, and we've heard good reports about your work."

John glanced inside the car and nodded. Miss Simmons was the typical knot-in-the-back gray-faced mission type.

He had his eyes on Nada's face again, listening to her.

"We've heard exciting things about you, Mr. Vogel."

"Please, call me John."

"John." She smiled slowly. "Thank you, I will. I think what you're doing here is absolutely marvelous. Imagine someone brave enough to dare to prove what we all believe, that prayers can actually be heard and answered."

A crowd of us had gathered around by now, picking apart the newcomer. Strangers of any sort were a phenomenon, and a striking young woman in a tailored blue suit was unheard of. We stared at her hairdo, her white teeth, her olive skin with the tiny mole above the upper lip, her plentiful bosom, her small waist, her narrow ankles, and the tiny feet in high-heeled shoes. She was a wonder to behold.

"Lord, she's purdy," Stumpy mumbled.

"I think she's too fat on top," Hallie whispered.

"That ain't fat, that's tits," Homer said too loudly, and we all giggled.

But John didn't even hear him. His eyes were on Nada, soaking her in, watching her mouth when she spoke, her eyes when she smiled. His face looked strange.

Suddenly I felt panic, a need to call for help, to tell Anna something dreadful was happening. I dashed into the cabin breathless and shaking.

Anna was in the kitchen washing clothes in the sink.

"Somebody's out there." I said. "A lady!"

Anna looked up from the washing and brushed the hair from her eyes, leaving a ridge of soap across her forehead. Her slip was hanging and her bare feet were stuck into flat shoes. She looked white and tired.

She glanced out the window and saw Nada Rivore and John coming toward the cabin. "Oh. My Lord" she said. "What shall I do?"

That night, before the story, John told us that Miss Nada was coming to help us. She would be busy until next spring taking care of her father in St. Louis, but after that she would come and be a part of our family.

I glanced at Anna sitting quietly in the corner. I had never seen her look so tired.

Mornings were getting cold, and frost lay over the ridges of what had now been named the Galilean Children's Home. The land spread out in a wide fan behind our cabin to include a large rolling pasture area, the top of the next ridge, the crest of the ridge down to the dorm, and the hollow beyond. Straight behind the dorm a steep hill led down to another grassy flat where John began to dream of constructing a second building.

There was always a building in the plan now. A barn was put up between the cabin and the county school, and two Holstein cows were brought in. By swapping, John got rid of his mule, which he had discovered was half blind, and gained a mean plow horse named Ted. Smells of hay and manure vied with the county school outhouse. The mooing of cows and the tinkle of cowbells was added to the school bell calling us to class.

The ten immigrants had come to the community so suddenly that the balance of nature was upset. Only nine were old enough to line up in front of the white schoolhouse in the morning, but nine new students in a one-room school was a high rate of increase. Even without their coming, school would have been confused enough. Last year's teacher had left. Mr. Hill was new, and there were no records of who was in what grade. It was left up to the students to place themselves. Harried Mr. Hill walked up and down the dusty rows waving his white handkerchief and asking questions. When he came to a student whose nose was running, he wiped the nose first, then asked the question.

"What grade are you in?" he asked when he came to me.

I thought quickly. This was my chance. The primer class had been such a drag last year I might as well step it up a little.

"Second grade." I decided.

He wrote me down for second grade. Hands shot up all over the classroom.

"She ain't either, teacher, she's lyin'. She's in first!"

"I don't want to be in first!" I protested. "Nobody in first even knows how to read."

Mr. Hill looked at me and nodded. I was glad my nose wasn't running, because I dreaded the risk of getting someone else's snot rubbed all over me.

"We'll try it," he said gravely. "You can stay in second as long as you can do the work."

I had a crawling feeling I would get it at recess.

We were lined up at the outhouse when the Eliot girls came and stood on either side of me. They were sixth and seventh graders, tall, and in command of the girls' side of the playground. My heart started beating fast.

"Hey, little orphan lover, ain't you gettin' a little big for your britches?" one asked.

"I am not a orphan lover," I started to say, and then saw Hallie standing behind me, and felt confused. "Orphans are as good as you!" I shouted. "And anyhow, what are you going to do about it?"

"You're getting the big head," said the other one. "You snotty little preacher's kid. You think your shit don't stink."

We were getting close to the outhouse, and I was trembling from head to foot. They stood on either side of me, not letting me move. I tried to run, but the biggest one grabbed my arm. "Come on," she said. "We'll teach you something."

They forced me into the outhouse and stuck my head down the hole. Two feet from my face lay a pile of human waste crawling with white maggots.

"So what?" I shouted, struggling to run.

"So there, that's what. Just get a good look and remember that's what happens to yours the same as anybody else's, smart aleck!"

I ducked under their arms and ran out, the laughter of the lineup ringing in my ears. I decided not to tell Mr. Hill. The next time they might throw me in.

Being called an orphan lover almost made me angrier than getting my head stuck down a toilet hole. I was no such thing. I hadn't even wanted them to come, not at all. But once they came, what could I do? They were Stumpy and Hallie, Homer and Troy, Virgie and Lewis. They were my friends, almost my family. It was very confusing. They hadn't wanted to come either, but here we all were. What could we do about it?

Mr. Hill did his best to enrich our spartan lives. He was a kind, gentle person, devout and dignified. He had a watch with a gold chain and the air of a gentleman. In spite of the hassle of teaching eight grades, he managed to find time for some form of art. One day he told us to copy a picture out of our reader, any picture we liked. I copied a boy and a jumping dog. Whether part of it was traced or not, I don't remember. It wasn't important until later. I wasn't even sure what tracing was.

When I brought the drawing home, I showed it to Anna. She proudly took it to John. "She drew it," she said excitedly. "Isn't it good?"

John looked at it closely "She couldn't have drawn that." he said. "You mean you traced it, don't you?"

"No. I drew it," I said stubbornly.

"You couldn't have," he insisted. "It's too well proportioned for someone your age to have drawn it. You traced it."

"I did not!" I said, becoming more and more entrenched in holding to what I said was true, feeling my honor was at stake.

"You're getting to be a little liar, just like the rest of these kids." John said angrily.

One spanking later, I sat in the back yard sniffing and rubbing my buttocks and searching my mind for some consolation. I tried desperately to think of something that was mine, something that no one could take away from me. After an appropriate amount of rubbing and sniffing it appeared, like a genie, out of my head. The Legendary Grandfather. He was mine. He did not belong to any of this. He painted beautiful pictures . . . he sang songs . . . I was related to him.

I decided that day to become an artist, and I buried two smooth stones and a piece of string in the back yard to seal the promise.

The Legendary Grandfather would be my secret friend, my magic protection against ugliness and stupidity. None of this mess would ever touch me.

It was with an unbelievable sense of relief that I heard snatches of a conversation between the county superintendent and John a few months after school had started.

"There've been a number of complaints from families in the area," he began slowly and politely. "It seems as though other taxpaying families are objecting to their sons and daughters being exposed to the sort of children you're taking in-you understand, bad backgrounds and all-and also some complaints of lice. Would it be possible for you to start a branch of the county school on your own property? We would do everything we could to help you—books, desks . . ."

John was uneasy with government officials and wanted no involvement with the county seat at Williamsburg. On the other hand, there was nothing he wanted more than to establish his own school so as to control absolutely the education his charges would have. Now since the county superintendent had suggested it, the state education department could give him no trouble. A small smile spread from his eyes over his face.

"I believe we could do that." he said agreeably. "There's a building up on the ridge that the sawmill crew put up for shelter. I think we could fix it up to use temporarily. Of course, we'll provide our own teacher in time, but would there be someone who could help us out until our new teacher comes?"

"I'll see who's still available this time of year," the man promised. "Of course, you realize all the choice teachers are already signed up."

The next morning there was more building, more hammering and sawing. The mill shed stood only a few hundred yards from the dorm, straight out from the front door. Below it was a huge mountain of sawdust, and around it the forest pressed in, not large and lush as it was before the cutting, but dense again with spindly trees and undergrowth. Here and there a thick oak had been left at random, hollow perhaps, or too twisted to be cut into planks.

The shed itself was only four walls with a front step, a sloping roof, and a stovepipe stuck out the front wall. Outside, John and the older boys stripped the cracks, and inside they lined it with building paper. Nothing was done about the wind coming up through the wide floor cracks, but a potbellied stove was connected to the pipe, and two blackboards were put up. A few windows were set in, and two bookshelves. The county came through with beat-up desks and secondhand books, and we were all set, except for a teacher.

The teacher the county sent us looked as beat-up and secondhand as the rest of the deal. She was a slovenly square woman with greasy bangs, and we had to hold our breath when she walked past us. She kept a brown bag with a bottle in it under her desk and carried a willow switch in her hand as a matter of habit. The only way she knew how to teach was to give us lists to memorize—states and capitals, multiplication tables—either learned letter perfect or down came the switch. She swigged from the bottle often and slept with her feet on the desk, drunkenly exposing her huge bottom side. The older boys would snicker, throwing paper wads, trying to hit target. Suddenly a paper wad would zero in, and she would be on her feet switching left and right with the willow lash, yelling, "Who did that, who did that, who did that?"

At recess we would imitate her, rolling with laughter.

Perhaps John could have a overlooked these minor shortcomings temporarily, but the teacher had one fatal flaw. She criticized the orphanage for its constant Bible reading. She was not religiously inclined, and it infuriated her to be forced to read the Bible before each day's classes. John, on the other hand, felt that no child could ever hear enough of the Bible. It was read after breakfast, after lunch, after supper, before bed, and in school. He felt that the more he submerged us in the lyrical language and historical beauty of the Bible, along with its moral teachings, the more educated we would be. A personality clash began to build up. John and the teacher became mortal enemies.

Move number one was the teacher's. She bribed Ray and R. C. with a box of crackers and a jar of peanut butter, and they agreed to be picked up by car and taken to the county seat. There they were told to swear before the judge that they had been beaten and starved at the home.

The problem was, it was half true. The boys who stood before the judge were thin. We were all thin. We weren't starving, but we were hungry enough to sell our souls for a jar of peanut butter. The beating was half true as well. John was a believer in "spare the rod and spoil the child." and any misdemeanor met with sudden and strong armed spanking-whipping for some of the tougher older boys. They might have had a bruise or two to show the judge.

For once in his life John's anger was greater than his fear of the authorities. He went to the courthouse and threatened to swear out a kidnap warrant against the teacher unless she returned the boys. There was a long fight, and in the end the teacher left.

It wasn't the fact that she left, but the way she left that troubled me. Faced with what he considered an ultimate threat to his dream, and without funds to fight a legal battle, in spite of his threats, John retreated to the woods and prayed for God to smite the teacher. The next Monday morning she came to school feverish, with a bandage wrapped around her hand. She took it off and showed us a large festering sore.

I saw it, but I didn't believe it, not the way John did. None of us could afford to believe it. The implications of believing it were too frightening. Could we, if we opposed John, be smitten by some festering disease?"

At any rate, we were out of school again.

Work teams were organized to keep us busy. The older boys were responsible for milking the cows, feeding the horse, cleaning the barn, and cutting firewood. The smaller boys had to chop stove wood and carry water from the spring. The older girls helped with the dishwashing and the laundry, while the younger ones peeled potatoes or sorted the small rocks from the ever-present soup beans. The most detested job of all was emptying the pots. With no indoor plumbing, it became necessary to set covered pots in the bedrooms at night for those who needed them. In the morning some unlucky soul got the job of taking the whole reeking mess and carrying it down the hill to the privy, washing them out, and lining them up at the back of the house to air. In time this became Lethie's job, because she was the only one who didn't mind. She walked along every morning carrying the slop jars, singing her tuneless song as happily as ever.

Lethie was Stumpy 's "tetched" older sister. The new husband had decided he didn't want her around either, but she seemed harmless enough, and we all tolerated her. She had come with the second wave of children. Every few weeks another car would come humping and bumping over the road, bringing more of them. Word was spreading that the orphanage would take anyone, and every community for miles around began dumping its troubled and unwanted on us.

Ray and Homer's little brother Duncan came to join them. Janey and Dean came, a nine-year-old girl whose little brother clung to her back like a baby monkey. Wilma and Mary Ellen came, and Winnie and Tessie. Over on High Top a woman died, and the father brought us Otis, Evelyn, and Shirley.

The dormitory began to bulge at the seams. The iron beds, big enough for three, now had three at the head and three at the foot. Luckily it was winter, and crowding helped keep warm in the icy bedrooms.

I seldom slept at the cabin any more. The dormitory was much more exciting, and as often as possible I snuggled into the squirming, giggling pile of girls in the bedroom at night.

Christina had come back from Gram's house in Chicago, and she swelled the ranks by one more. Even though I felt responsible in a way to all the children, Christina and I had a special relationship. She was my first sister, mine to protect. And Christina needed a lot of protection. Although the surgery on her mouth had made it possible for her to eat, and she had grown into a plump little red-haired toddler, she still had trouble speaking. Air leaked through the roof of her mouth, giving her words a mushy sound. With the easy cruelty of children, the others made fun of her, especially a coward like R. C.

"Hey, Christina, why you talk so funny, huh? You got something stuck up your nose?" he taunted her one day.

She was too little to know what he meant, but the tone was cruel and she started to cry.

"You'd better shut up or you'll get something stuck up your nose." I said threateningly. My days at the county school had taught me to fight.

"Like what?" he jeered. "Like what?"

Before he knew what was happening, I made a fist and came crashing up at his nose. He howled and stuck up his hands, and blood started pouring down his face.

"I'm going to tell on you. I'm going to tell on you," he wailed.

"Go tell, you stupid scaredy-cat!" I shouted.

He did tell, and I was properly whipped, but he never teased Christina again, at least not where I could hear it.

Still, I had my own problems with Christina. She was three going on four, and I was six going on seven, and it exasperated me to have her dogging my footsteps wherever I went. Privately I called her a little pest and was cross with her, but she didn't seem to mind as long as I let her tag along.

John had spread the word in the circles where he was becoming known that the orphanage needed a teacher. Every night during the story and prayer routine we prayed for one. Finally a letter arrived from a Miss Smith, inquiring about the opening. John told us about her in the dining room after the noon meal, and we all shouted and cheered. She was a graduate of Wheaton College in Illinois, came from Massachusetts, and was eager to come and live with us. We could hardly wait to see her.

Meanwhile, the bulging dorm was creating problems. Anna and John finally decided to move in and help Miss Edna at night because it was impossible for her to control the squirming and profane mass crowded under one roof. Most nights she didn't even try. She simply went into her room with a lighted candle and a little mystical smile, shut the door, and went to bed—or at least so we thought.

Then the real activity began.

The notes would be passed at supper, under the table and behind hands. Few of the adolescents could read or spell, so the messages were rudimentary: MET IN HOLER TONIT.

And after a certain fake and unusually quiet bedtime, most people twelve or over would silently disappear out the window. There were whispered warnings to the small ones left behind not to tell or they would be killed.

The tetched sister, Lethie, was fifteen, but she never went. I never knew whether it was because she was crazy and they didn't want her, or because she was religious and thought it was wrong. She was gentle and sweet, and lay in bed rocking and singing herself to sleep. It helped her get to sleep, but it drove the rest of us crazy, mostly because she sang all on one note.

About midnight they would all come crawling back in the window, whispering excitedly about who was the best, and who they were going to go with again. It was all very mysterious. I tried to ask then what it was all about, but they laughed.

"Why should we tell you, you fuckin' little preachers kid?" Tessie laughed. She was one of the new ones, and wild as a jackrabbit.

"You're not allowed to use that word. You'll get your mouth scrubbed out with yellow soap!"

"You tell," she said, holding the pillow over my head until I struggled for breath, "and I'll kill you!"

I really think she would have.

The first week John stayed in the dorm he began to get wise to what was happening. One night big clumsy Ray was passing a note and dropped it. John picked it up without anyone seeing him and put it in his pocket.

That night when the boys crawled out the back window, John was waiting for them. He marched them over and lined them up against the house. Then he ordered them to drop their pants, and went down the line giving them each a solid thrashing with a stick of stove wood.

They crawled back in the window too sore to do much but lie down. The girls heard the commotion on the other side of the building and hurried back inside, boosting each other frantically up through the window. When Anna came in with a flashlight, they were all in bed.

It was quiet and oppressive in the dining room the next morning. Four or five boys were sitting sideways, eating oatmeal without saying much. After breakfast John read us a passage from the Bible about immorality and told us that everyone who committed sins of the body would suffer forever in hell. Furthermore, in this world they would be whipped and locked up for three days with bread and water, and be subject to all kinds of horrible diseases.

It was all a shady mystery to me.

Not only the people were increasing, but the animals as well. Now we had three cows for milk, two horses for pulling the wagon in winter when the road to town was too bad for the car, raunchy-smelling pigs in a pen down by the creek, and a yard full of fluttery black, white, and brown chickens. There were two dogs, a couple of cats, and even a pet possum the boys had caught. Along with twenty-two children and three adults, we were getting to be quite a family.

The laundry for so many people was staggering, and there was nothing but the most primitive equipment—an outside fire in a pile of stones, a tub, a scrub board, and bars of yellow soap. As winter closed in, the only way to get water from the creek was to break the ice and scoop up frigid bucketfuls. The boys built a fire and filled the tub, and Anna and the older girls scrubbed out the clothes. We only changed clothes once a week, or the piles would have been sky-high. On Saturday there was a line-up of water pans, and Miss Edna and Anna scrubbed all the hair. The older girls helped the younger ones comb and braid their hair. In the louse purge I had been spared and still had braids, but a few of the newer girls had long hair as well, so I didn't feel too different. Once a month the boys sat on a stump in the front yard with a towel hung around their shoulders, and John ran the clipper up the sides of their hair. The lice were gone now, so he left the hair on top.

A man named Cal, who had been in the Army, moved in to help with the boys. Every morning he lined them up for exercises in front of the dorm. He had one eye and a big stomach and bellowed out commands as though he were in charge of a regiment. The boys listened to him. Between morning exercises, hard work all day, and the fear of God at night, the gang began to calm down, and things became more peaceful.

The matter of Miss Nada's coming was still hanging in the air. It was seldom brought up, but it was always there under the surface. John hired a new crew of men, and the frame of a new building began to appear in the grassy flat beyond the hollow. A path ran down to one side of the dorm, across the creek, and up to the new building. It was similar in style to the first dorm, but, following the slope of the hill, it had an upstairs and down. Miss Nada was going to become the secretary, as well as dorm mother for the boys.

"Don't you think it would be more normal to have some boys and some girls in each house?" Anna asked. "It would be more like a real family."

John ran his fingers through his hair. "If you had normal kids, maybe," he said. "This pack is like a bunch of animals. We've got to crack down, and hard, or we'll end up with a pregnant teenager. That would give the community something to wag their tongues about."

Anna looked thoughtful. "How soon is Nada coming?" she asked.

"Not until after Christmas.' John said. "But I do hope Miss Smith will get here before that. I live every day in fear of that county superintendent poking his nose in here and finding out that we don't have a teacher yet. Sometimes I have the feeling that gang in the Williamsburg courthouse is out to get me."

"Why is that?"

"Well, for one thing, I'm from the north. I'm taking care of welfare cases they've neglected, and it shows them up. I'm not a Baptist, and I'm not a Democrat. I'm a horse of the wrong color all the way around, and I can feel the ice every time I walk into the courthouse."

"They can't get you for any of those things," she said carefully. "Just be sure you never give them anything valid to pin on you."

John looked angrily at Anna, as though she were accusing him. "What do you mean by that?" he asked.

In the evening around the fireplace John would spin his old web of charm, but now his tone was more threatening.

"We are a family, a family of God's children." he would begin. "And we must behave as the children of God. I will not tolerate filthy language or any kind of immoral relationships on these grounds. We have taken on the name of the great Galilean, and our lives must be an example to the world. Great wonders are going to happen here, and we must keep our lives pure so we do not block the flow of the power. Someday this simple place will be known over the nation and around the world, but those who do not cooperate will be asked to leave. If there is sin here, God will not hear us. We cannot afford that risk."

He talked on, hypnotizing us with his vision of the future. All of us listened, and thought we understood. There were choices to be made, and we could line up on one side or the other. It seemed fairly simple. Of course, we would all line up on the side of right, where there was food and approval and a happy future. No one wanted bread and water and dreadful diseases, let alone hell in the hereafter.

Then, just before the first white snow, just before all the excitement of Christmas in the air, the scandal broke. Miss Edna— prim, stiff, and unbending Miss Edna—had been discovered in a parked car along the Bee Creek road, snuggled up with one of the building crew. John had been on his way home from town one night and caught her in the act.

The news ran through the group like a shock wave. Miss Edna, of all people, and with a native. She had broken the faith, had committed the unpardonable sin. No one could look her in the face. No one spoke to her.

She left for Chicago immediately, and the dark secret room in the corner of the dorm was emptied and scrubbed clean for the next occupant.

I felt a little sorry to see her go. Just recently she had started smiling and even invited us into her room for a piece of candy. And it was very puzzling. How could she have done such a terrible thing and look so happy?

Perhaps things were not going to be so simple after all.

CHAPTER THREE

That December, snow fell over the hills, thick and white. The pale blue of the mountains looked even lighter against the gray sky, and the pines huddled in padded clumps, weighted down with snow.

In the brown dormitory on the hill we shivered with cold. The barn boys had to get up early, but the rest of us waited until the adults had a crackling fire built in the fireplace. Then we took turns, first the boys and then the girls, standing around the warm blaze hurriedly pulling on long underwear. Breakfast was steaming bowls of oatmeal, cooked on the wood stove in the kitchen.

But not even the cold could chill our spirits. Christmas was coming, and an order was placed in town for thirty chickens. We were going to have a Christmas dinner with all the fried chicken everyone could eat. The thought of it made even the bowls of oatmeal taste better. Christmas, everything would be happy.

After Miss Edna left, John and Anna had to manage the dorm alone until the Meeks came. When they arrived from Chicago, quiet and gentle as their name, they moved into the empty space in the front bedroom. The Meeks were nothing to set the world on fire, but they were well-scrubbed honest-looking young people, and very sincere. Mrs. Meek helped Anna with the cooking and washing, and Mr. Meek went with the boys to milk cows, chop wood, and carry water.

The week before Christmas the older boys chopped down an evergreen and fastened it to a base on the floor of the main room. Mr. Hensley, a neighbor, gave us popcorn, and we popped it over the open fire, strung it, and roped it around the tree. The smell of the corn combined with the pine was warm and clean. The holly berries we had gathered from the woods gave a touch of red, and the extra pine cones hung on the tree completed the homey look.

A mysterious box of presents came from the post office by the river and was stored in the closet. The excitement soared.

"What do you hope you get?" I asked Stumpy.

"I don't know." he said, staring at the tree. "I ain't never had nothin' for Christmas."

The cold December nights were perfect for snuggling six in a bed and telling horror stories. There were tales of rawhide and bloody bones, and of the bear who wanted his toe. There was the tale of the golden pear: "Oh mother, oh mother, don't pull my poor hair, for you have killed me over one golden pear." Every new girl had a new story to add to the collection, and the stories were told over and over, growing in intensity until the little ones crawled deep under the covers, shivering with fright. At some point the storyteller would provoke sheer panic and someone would begin to scream. A flashlight would come shining in the door.

"What's happening in here?"

"Nothing."

"Then be quiet."

The door would bang shut. After a brief pause the storytelling would continue until we grew bored with scaring ourselves to death and went to sleep.

One of the best storytellers was Jessie, a swarthy eleven-year-old newcomer who claimed she was a quarter of a quarter of a Injun. Her grandmother was a half-Injun, and her mother was a quarter-Injun, so that made her a quarter of a quarter-Injun. We argued several nights about the mathematical correctness of this, then settled down to hear Jessie's collection of tales. She told whorehouse stories.

According to her, there was a place on Depot Street in Corbin that was called a cat house. She described the place in detail and told us men came there and paid money to go into the rooms with the women. They all had to wear something called rubbers (I envisioned overshoes) because the women in the cat house didn't like having kids. The men always tried to go without their rubbers, because it felt better. There was this woman who accidentally started having a kid. One day a man came in and she said no, she wasn't working, so he knocked her down on the floor and forced her, and her kid was born dead. They put it in a big matchbox, it was so little, and buried it in the woods outside town so no one would know about it.

I listened to this story, chilled with a horror deeper than the fear of rawhide and bloody-bones. What did men do in the rooms, and why did they pay money?

And what did a dead baby have to do with it? And if women wore overshoes, did it keep them from having babies too?

Then one night all the mystery and illusions were gone, torn away with a suddenness that left me both enlightened and shattered.

It was one of those nights when we were just talking, everyone saying what was on her mind.

"Hey," I began, "I know the mother part of how babies get born, but there's something I don't understand. I know this kid, and she looks like her father. Why is that? Is it because they live in the same house and eat the same food? And how do you get a baby started? Does it just happen to you?"

A roar of laughter rose from the crowded beds.

"Oh, Lordy!" Jessie laughed. "You kill me! Don't you know nothin?"

"Know what?"

"Don't you even know how you got borned?"

"Yeah, but . . . No, how?"

"You sure you want to hear? Your ma get mad at me?"

"Yeah, No, I won't tell her."

"Okay, I'll tell you. You sure?"

"Yeah."

"Okay." The bedroom was deadly silent, waiting," "The man gets on top of the woman, and he sticks his big whacker in her, and some stuff comes out, and then she gets a big belly and has a baby."

"But why do men do it if they don't want babies? Why do they pay money?"

"Because it feels good. It don't feel so good to the woman, but men like it."

I lay quiet in the tangled mass of legs and arms, a series of images floating through my mind. It was still fuzzy, hard to picture.

"But how?" I persisted. "Where does he . . ."

Jessie was getting impatient. "Have you ever seen dogs mate?" she asked bluntly.

I had. The male dog chased the female, and then she howled and shrieked while the male dog mounted her.

I shuddered. "Like dogs?" I said, starting to feel sick.

"Like dogs." She yawned.

It was a long time before I went to sleep that night. I could see it all. My father had chased my mother until he caught her, then he had done it to her. I wondered if she shrieked and screamed, and he stood there with his tongue hanging out, panting. The thought of it was horrible and I hated him. I hated all men.

And then a new thought came, an even more disturbing thought. Even though he had done it, now he thought it was wrong. That was what the kids had been doing in the hollow, what they had been beaten for. That was what he meant by immorality. I could understand it now. Yet he had done it to Anna, and the proof of it was that I had been born. Was he ashamed now? Was that why he disliked Anna? Did he think of it when he looked at me? Was I bad?

In the cabin Anna put up our family tree. John said we did not need a separate one, but Anna insisted. It was decorated with tinsel and colored balls from former Christmases and had patches of cotton snow. Under the tree there was a box for Christina and me from Gram. I knew my present was a doll and hoped it wouldn't be too different from the presents under the tree at the dorm. Life was getting complicated between the households. When Anna suggested I sleep at home, I didn't argue with her. If there was anything else to be learned in the world I didn't want to know it, at least not right away.

True to promise. Christmas did bring the big fried chicken feast. In the town of Corbin the grocer who had reserved the thirty chickens found out about the children and loaded a box full of treats. There were oranges and walnuts, things some of the kids had never seen. We sat around two long wooden tables, gorging on chicken and dressing, corn and peas, sweet potatoes and gravy. For dessert there was plenty of pumpkin pie, and the Hoppus came with a five-gallon can of ice cream for a special treat.

Anna scooped up the pumpkin pie, laughingly quoting an old poem:

> We have pumpkins at morning and pumpkins at noon,
> If it were not for pumpkins, we should be undoon!

After the meal John stood in his reading corner by the door and told the Christmas story. I noticed when he told it that the Bible story said that Mary had no husband, that she "knew not a man." Last year that hadn't mattered. This year it did. How did her baby get started?

And then I remembered his birth was supposed to be holy. If he had to get born like the rest of us, with his parents mating like dogs, he wouldn't have been very holy. That was why he had to be born a different way. It was a relief. At least someone was still good.

The presents had been under the tree since the night before, and it was finally time to open them. They were all the same size and shape, wrapped in different colors of tissue paper. Everyone listened nervously until his or her name was called, then rushed up to clutch the package with relief. Even the big boys like Lewis could hardly wait, although they tried not to show it.

Stumpy's eyes were shining. "I ain't never had nothin' for Christmas before." he repeated excitedly.

When the last person received a package, we had permission to open them. We tore at the paper eagerly, and then the room was strangely silent. Each packet contained a metal soap box, a bar of soap, and a comb.

"Shit," Lewis said softly. He was biting his top lip.

I looked at Stumpy, and could see it was the only thing in the world he wouldn't have wanted. He hated washing his face, because the more dirt he got off the more freckles showed.

"This afternoon," John was saying. "anyone who would like to write a thank-you note . . ."

Nobody could hear him. Kids had started swapping with each other to get the color soap or comb they wanted. Being good Kentuckians, they knew that as long as a thing could be swapped it was at least worth *something*.

The new dorm under the hill had been built that winter, and now it stood, wet and bare, peeking through the last rainy starkness of February. The rooms were roughed in, and it promised to be ready for occupancy when Nada came in March.

She arrived one day during the noon meal, and we all left the table and rushed out to meet her. She unloaded the luggage from her car, good luggage. We stood and stared. John and the boys picked up her bags and her hatbox, and she walked toward the new dorm with all of us in tow. She was not large, but the earth seemed to tremble under her small feet.

The next day the boys left the original dorm. We had all eaten a lot of pumpkin and beans together, and somehow through all the cod liver oil and stories, all the mornings dressing by the fire and eating oatmeal, they had really become like brothers. The thought of a dorm without boys seemed dull and lifeless. I had even forgotten I hated boys and started liking them, at least temporarily.

But they were going now. Loaded with bedsteads and boxes of overalls, they filed down the trail to the new house. Miss Nada would be their dorm mother, with help from Mr. Meek. They would come back to the girls' dorm only for meals. All the girls cried, and a few of the little boys. The older boys set their faces and marched down the hill carrying the iron bedsteads.

After that they seemed different. Their coming to meals was an event, and the older girls primped and preened for the occasion. The soft metal soap boxes were put to another use. Jessie was the first to do it, and one by one the soap boxes disappeared from the bathroom. The girls cut them into strips and covered them with waxed paper from old bread wrappers and wound up their hair with the homemade curlers. Every night their hair was wound up, and every morning the big girls came to breakfast in frizzy splendor, ready to impress the boys, who were no longer brothers but inhabitants of the boys' dorm.

With all the moving, Anna insisted that I come home to sleep at night "You never know what ideas she might pick up in those bedrooms sleeping with all those kids," she said.

I wanted to tell her that she was just a little bit late.

In the evenings that spring, John worked until the wee hours of the morning helping Nada set up the office in the new building. For many months unanswered letters had been piling up, and this had been a constant source of contention between John and Anna. He was angry that gifts had not been acknowledged, and she, worn senseless with the grinding physical labor expected of her each day, could only apologize for not doing it.

Now Nada had come, and she was in charge of correspondence. John liked her efficiency, her style, her knack for business. To him she was not only a charming woman but one who fitted perfectly into his dreams for the future. In addition to her other more obvious talents, she was an expert in typing and shorthand. In John's opinion, she was a godsend.

But as the days passed, it got harder for Anna to agree. Everywhere Anna went, tired and shoddily dressed, she was confronted with the specter of the smiling, polished Nada. Nada sat with John and Anna at meals, monopolizing the conversation, and when she gathered the boys around her after the meal and tramped down the hill with them, she seemed to have mobilized the whole male contingent behind her. When evening came, John spent long hours at the boys' dormitory, and Anna sat in the cabin with Christina and me, feeling angry and lonely. Halfway through the night John would come home, absentminded and in no mood to talk, and fall happily asleep.

Late one night I heard them talking in the other room, first as though I were dreaming, but then wide awake.

"I'm sorry I'm late. There was a lot to do."

"Like what?" Anna's voice was tight.

"We finished the new filing system tonight. Nada knows how to set all this in order. And then I didn't want to leave right away. Nada's someone I can have a deeply spiritual discussion with. She understands me. She doesn't think like you do. Every time I try to tell you something of my plans for this home, all you do is remind me of our debts, or give me reasons why things can't be done. You're always asking me where the money will come from. I don't know where the money will come from most of the time, but for God's sake I know I believe it will come! Nada understands living by faith. It doesn't seem crazy to her, and *she's* certainly nobody's fool."

It was quiet for a few moments, and then I heard a choked sob.

"What did you say?" John asked.

"I said I'm just beginning to wonder how heavenly these discussions are."

"You dirty-minded bitch!" John said loudly. There was the wet thud of someone being slapped, and Anna screamed.

"Get your dirty hands off me, you skirt chaser. Why don't you go over and live with her?"

I heard a chair go flying across the floor, and the front door slammed. Anna was outside the window, crying in the dark.

I sprang out of bed and ran into the living room. John was standing in his pajamas.

"What did you do to my mother?" I asked furiously.

He looked at me without saying anything. I flew at him, pounded him with my fists, and sank my teeth into his hairy arm.

"Let go of me, you little beast! Now get to bed. This is none of your business!"

I ran outside in the dark to find Anna. She was choking and sniffling and needed a handkerchief. I didn't have one and didn't know what to do.

In the middle of the anguish and confusion of that year, Miss Smith came. She was not trouble, like Nada. She was Wonder Woman suddenly appearing in our world, enlightening us, encouraging us, setting us in order, bringing sanity and fairness, cleanliness, patriotism, and music, whether we wanted them or not. Besides all this, she became Anna's friend.

She had sent a letter saying she would come as soon as she was released from another obligation, but we had no idea when she would arrive. The day she appeared, a group of us had gone down into the hollow where John was planning to dam up the creek to make a better water supply. The older boys were collecting stones for a possible dam, and the younger children were poking around the edge of the creek trying to catch water dogs.

Suddenly Hallie's voice could be heard from the top of the ridge. "Yoo-hoo, Are you down there?"

"Shhhhh." John said. "Somebody's calling."

"Yooo-hooo, hey! Anybody there?"

"We're here!" John said, cupping his mouth.

"Come on up to the dorm! Miss Smith's here! The new teacher's here!"

Here . . . , here . . . , here . . . Hallie's voice echoed down the hollow. We looked at one another for a second, and then it hit us.

"The new teacher! She's here!"

We began scrambling up the side of the mossy hill, grabbing at bushes and slipping on rocks. Everybody wanted to be the first to get a glimpse of her.

When we reached the top of the hill, we suddenly fell back in a shy circle and let John go ahead. She was there, standing in front of the dorm, and no one knew what to say. She was a slender young woman with an almost boyish figure and short curly brown hair. The brown eyes smiling behind glasses were friendly, yet there was a firm set to her mouth and strength in the way she stood. We knew at once that she would be a strict teacher.

Since the boys had moved out, the Meeks had taken the middle bedroom to be closer to the smaller girls at night. The front room was empty again, and Miss Smith moved into it. She decorated it quietly with materials she had brought, and in one day she was ready to go to work.

John must have tried to include her in his soul community of the Truly Spiritual. He knocked on her door one day, bringing a gift. She allowed him to come in, but in a very short time he came out with a red face, present in hand. After that there was a definite coolness between them.

On Saturdays Miss Smith washed her hair, put it up in a scarf, and brought out a bag of whole-meal flour mixed with wheat germ. She went into the kitchen, dissolved dry yeast, and mixed up a batch of dark brown bread. All morning she let the bread rise by the cook stove, then baked it, the fragrance spreading over the house. She refused to eat white bread, cornbread, or biscuits. We were astounded. To us food was food, and white or brown, no one ever asked any questions.

Her first attempts at educating us were linguistic. Every time we said ain't, she said ain't isn't in the dictionary. John liked the musical, grammatically atrocious mountain language patterns and had encouraged them, since he enjoyed using them himself; but Miss Smith would stand for no corruption of the English language.

In the morning when groups were assigned to potato peeling

or bean sorting, we sang. We droned the slow mountain tunes, complete with mountain harmony, slurring and dragging the music as everyone around us did, or changing to a quick tempo and patting our feet to the swinging rhythms.

Miss Smith cocked her head and listened. "It certainly is indigenous," she said.

Nobody dared ask her what indigenous meant.

There were flies in the dining room, and she badgered John until he put up screens. She stripped the beds and sprayed them with insecticide, suspecting that there were bedbugs. She went out into the woods and gathered wild greens from the edges of the pasture to supplement our pre-garden diet. They were cooked, bitter dark green and greasy, and we shivered getting them down while she assured us they were good for us.

The confusion of names bothered her. Some of the children called John Daddy, some called him Preacher. Miss Nada was variously called Miss Rivore or Miss Nada (and, out of hearing, Big Titt) Anna was Mother Vogel or Mrs. Vogel. Each person had his or her own name for various individuals, and no one knew what to call anyone. A meeting was held, and a new system was established. All women would be called Aunt, except by those whom they served directly as housemother. Miss Smith was to be called Miss, because she was the teacher. John was to be called Daddy by everyone, while each dorm had its separate mother. The adults laughed, and said it sounded like a harem system. Daddy Vogel blushed bashfully and stared at his feet.

Along with the name system, a salary system was agreed on. All adults who worked full time were to receive a salary of ten dollars a month, plus room, board, and medical care. All the other money sent us was to be pooled in a common fund, and it was understood that the ten-dollar salary would only be paid out of any surplus above the amount needed to feed everyone.

Politeness and manners were discussed. No one was allowed to say Huh, or What, but rather. I beg your pardon, or Pardon me please. All children would say sir and mam to adults, and anyone who did not say Please pass the food could go hungry.

After the social structure was set up, Miss Smith helped organize our summer. She wrapped her head in a blue bandanna and marched us out to the fields to plant potatoes and cane seed. When berry-picking time came, she lined us up and tied lard pails to our waists and led us off to the berry fields down by the river. Only this time she had to follow us, because we knew where they were, and she was a stranger from Massachusetts.

Berry picking was fun. We went early in the morning, down through the dewy woods and the caves damp with early mist, down over the golden sage-grass fields and past old tumbledown shacks to the broad lush plain bordering the river where the blackberries grew. Mr. Meek took the boys, and Miss Smith took the girls; and the whole day had the competitive feel of an athletic meet. We filled our lard buckets and dumped them into the larger milk pails left standing in the cool shady creek. At noon, when the sun beat down overhead, we stopped and lay in the shade, drenched with sweat and stiff with sunburn, to eat slices of raisin bread and drink creek water. By two o'clock the pails would be full, and Miss Smith let us jump in the creek, clothes and all, to cool off. When we were cool, we started up the hill, soaked and strange-looking, scratched and sunburned, but sure we had more berries than the boys. Sometimes we did, and at dinner the winning team was given three cheers as the victor of the day.

When the cane seeds grew and ripened, Miss Smith went with us into the cane fields, lining us up in pairs of one tall and one short. Up and down the rows we went, stripping off the long green leaves, one from the bottom and the other from the top. The boys came behind us with machete knives, chopping the canes and loading them on the wagon to take to the sorghum mill. She led us in singing as we went along, sometimes the songs and choruses John liked, sometimes the "outside songs" she brought with her.

Occasionally she sang,

> "I love you in the morning, and I love you in the night.
> I love you in the evening,
> When the moon is shining bright . . ."

We were always a bit wary about singing such songs in John's presence. He had begun to insist that our voices should be used only for psalms and hymns and spiritual songs, and we became apprehensive about singing about the moon or eensie-weensie spider. It got to seem disloyal, even heretical.

But heretical or not, Miss Smith wanted us to know what was going on in the world. She set her battery radio in the general meeting room in the mornings and let us listen to the world news. She gathered us around her on Monday nights to hear the *Bell Telephone Hour*, and on Sunday we could use her radio to listen to the *Old-Fashioned Revival Hour*. The latter had been a Sunday afternoon must before she came, but now we had a choice of where to hear it.

Although I preferred the Bell Telephone Hour, the Old-Fashioned Revival Hour stirred deep wondering feelings in me. These feelings were too complex and private to share with any adult I knew, especially my parents. Ever since I could remember, running through the woods singing songs made up on the spot and forgotten a moment later, staring up through the leafy trees and the jagged pines, I had had the feeling there was a God somewhere and we were friends. This friendship did not depend on anything. It was comfortable and deep, like my relationship with the Legendary Grandfather. Yet every time I listened to a preacher on the radio, he was sure that God was angry with everyone and that people had to repent of their sins. I didn't feel that God and I had any quarrel, but the preacher always said that if one wasn't converted he would burn forever in hell. In the end, I decided to get converted because I didn't want to burn forever in hell, but I always felt that somehow by going through that formality I had insulted a friend. I explained it to God by telling Him I had to listen to the grownups and do as they said, but I knew that was a lie. I had done it to avoid the possibility of burning forever in hell, and, for the first time, I felt I was being false. The green goodness was spoiled, and confusion set in.

But that was not Miss Smith's fault. It was more a general climate of guilt that was developing.

When fall came, Wonder Woman began to organize the school. She and a team of girls scrubbed the dusty mill shed clean, polished the scruffy desks, and nailed up pictures cut from the National Geographic. She got John to install a water cooler, a crock with a spout and bubbler that had to be filled with spring water. This did away with the old habit of drinking out of the communal dipper, but it was considered by some to be very northern and unfriendly.

Then she privately interviewed each child and classified us in grades. I was sure I had been in school long enough to be in the third grade, but she disagreed.

"Last year none of you went to school for a regular period of time," she said. "And since you're only seven, I think you'd better start second grade over again."

"Not over again!" I wailed. "I read the whole second-grade reader in a week last year! I read all the second-grade books in my spare time! I can tell you everything that's in them!"

"Yes, but you read with your nose in the book. You slouch when you read, and your writing is not neat. You do have things to learn, you know. You're not perfect, miss."

"Then who is going in third grade?" I asked.

"Winnie. Troy, Lewis—some of the older children."

"Those kids can't even read the label on a milk can! Troy calls evaporated milk eva-ported!"

Miss Smith looked at me sternly. "I would like you to know that *I* am in charge of this classroom. Those children are older than you, and it would be good for them to be placed a little higher. I think you need to watch yourself. You're a very conceited little miss at times. Just because your father runs this place, it does not follow that you are going to have any special privileges in my classroom or anywhere else. You need to see yourself as one of the group, and curb your tendency to show off and dominate. That is very ugly in you, and certainly not behavior becoming to a young lady."

I had always seen myself as a good kid, fighting everyone's battles and being a good Samaritan (and doing a little bit of wheeling and dealing on the side), but now I began to feel loud, bossy, aggressive, stupid, and unsure before people and guilty before God. It was the beginning of my education. I wished to goodness I were an orphan like everyone else, or at least a boy. Being a loud, bossy, aggressive, stupid boy would be better than being a girl who was all of these things.

I began to understand that even though I hated boys, they had all the power, all the strength. A group of women clustered around one man. It would never be the other way around. A man gave orders, and the women followed. In the mountains around us it was the women's faces that were ground down by poverty and hard labor, by childbirth and superstition. The men could wash and shave and put on a shirt and trousers and go to town, and no one could tell if they were poor or superstitious or had fifteen children. Their faces were firm and their hair was cut and they looked strong. But the women's faces were soft, were impressionable and shapable, and the proof of all these things showed in the weariness of their eyes, the sagging of their skin. Their hair was unkempt, and their skirts dragged, and they looked poor and afraid.

Even Mother Anna—it was beginning to show. Who wanted to grow up to be like Anna, weak and afraid, caught in a frightening trap? Who in their right mind would ever want to be a woman?

With the shred of faith I had left, I began to pray to God to change me into a boy. But it was a forced prayer, a new kind of making-deals-with-the-deity prayer. *If you really can answer prayers, as my father says you can, prove it to me by changing me into a boy. And do it by tomorrow morning, so I'll know you're real.*

In my deepest heart I knew such a prayer was very impolite, but it was urgent. As things stood, I would grow up to be a despised woman.

But if God was in heaven, He was not interested in proving it to me as He was to my father. Morning after morning I awoke, still a doomed female. I began to brood about taking matters into my own hands.

John no longer slept regularly with Anna, but had built himself a study-bedroom on the back of the cabin. Behind the door there were assorted strange things, including an accordion, a guitar, and a white china platter that had belonged to Gram's family. Inside there were rows of shelves containing old *Reader's Digests*, medical books, and other wonderful sources of knowledge. I secretly pored over the medical books, devouring pictures of human anatomy.

One night, I dreamed I discovered a cactus plant behind the study door, but it was a strange plant. Instead of leaving cactus flowers on it, there were a variety of penises. All one had to do was to pick one off and attach it to the front of one's body, and the magical transformation would occur. I tried to pick one, but it wiggled and squirmed away from me, and I spent a hot guilty night trying to pick and attach it without anyone knowing it.

All this compounded my sense of sin because of my thoughts and frustration over being a girl. I wheedled John into buying a pair of high-top boots for me at the country store, complete with a knife pocket in them. I scrounged a jackknife from somewhere and a whistle and a compass from a cereal box, and these went into a tin and were buried in the back yard of the cabin, near the two stones and the string. My secret knowledge of this box, the boots, and the certainty that I would someday be an artist sustained me.

But my prayers at night became a farce. Who would have dared to tell God about feeling guilty because I'd been conned into getting converted, or that I was terrified of growing up to be a woman? Not me. We weren't that good friends anymore. I yawned and scratched at prayers and waited for my turn, then prayed rapidly for the "worn-torn" countries in Europe which were far away and unembarrassing. Miss Smith said a war was going on between the Germans and somebody else. It didn't matter who, since I didn't know them anyhow.

In September school started, crisp and efficient. Enough used clothes had come in the mail to provide dresses for the girls, and, much to my sorrow, overalls were banned. Going barefoot was banned too, because the townspeople were saying those pore little orphans didn't even have shoes. So we stood in line in front of the mill shed, starched and skirted, shod, hot, and miserable, ready to be educated. I looked at the line of boys, still in soft overalls, and felt a dark hatred.

There was no fooling around in Miss Smith's school. The classes clipped along, the lessons were assigned on the board, math was taught, geography studied, health pounded in, English drilled, and spelling memorized. I had to admit that second grade had never been like this. She moved like a whiz from first grade to fourth, teaching all subjects at all levels. At recess she marched us out and organized games, blowing a police whistle to call turns and order. No one stepped out of line.

In a few weeks a pine flagpole was set in a hole in the ground, and rigged with a rope and pulley. An American flag, bought with Miss Smith's own money, was hoisted. Every morning we filed out to the flag in formation, saluted, said the pledge of allegiance, sang the national anthem, and marched back into school to begin classes. On rainy days someone held a flag indoors, and the routine was unbroken.

Bible classes in Miss Smith's school were taught as knowledge. I never minded knowing how many pieces of furniture there were in the tabernacle, or how many times Israel was marched across the desert and back again as long as it wasn't my fault, as long as it did not add to the guilt I had begun to associate with religion.

On Friday afternoons Miss Smith concentrated on music. Patiently she squeezed out songs on the little pump organ, teaching us harmony, melody, counting, and chording. She took our rough untrained voices that slurred during potato peeling and began to shape them into a clear harmonious sound. The first time we sang a table blessing in three-part harmony John was so surprised he opened his eyes to look around and see who was doing it.

"Keep that up." he said excitedly. "and you'll be in demand all over the area!"

It was true. As we learned song after song, harmony after

harmony, the news spread that the orphans could sing. The first time there was a community sing, we were invited.

The "all day singin'" was held at the High Top schoolhouse, much like the one next to our cabin. The trees in the schoolyard were hitched full of mules swatting flies and dropping piles of manure. Long wooden tables were set up, lined with cardboard boxes and fruit jars, ready for the picnic.

The meeting lasted all morning, with various local groups getting up to sing. The favorite was the Four and One Quartet, four male voices in barbershop gospel led by a high-voiced woman with a low neckline. She swayed and bounced as she sang the piercing soprano lead. The music had a good beat to it, and everybody patted their feet and rocked in time.

When we stood up, our harmony sounded different. We had lost the mountain beat and the nasal twang that Miss Smith disliked, but here in the schoolhouse our clear correct northern notes sounded strange. No one stomped or clapped or whistled when we were finished, but stared at us with a kind of mistrust.

We rushed to our seats, our ears burning. Something had gone wrong. There were half-whispers.

"Ain't them Whitley County kids?"

"They're makin' furriners out of them younguns."

"You never know what queer things they're teachin' them."

"They might even be Nazzies, come in here to start one of them Hitler youth things I heard about on the radio. You never can tell."

On the way home in the horse-drawn wagon, John and Miss Smith had a long hot argument. They finally agreed that we should learn more mountain tunes, correctly and harmoniously, but songs that would be right for the Kentucky environment.

The next time we were invited to sing, it was for an all-day grave decorating.

Stumpy grinned when he heard it. "We're down to singin' for dead fellers now." he said. "I guess they ain't about to stomp their feet nohow!"

Whenever John started getting nervous about something *he* was doing, he would find an excuse to crack down on the rest of us. It didn't have to be a big thing, and sometimes it was nothing at all except a kind of wild look in his eyes that had to find an object.

"I do not want to hear any kind of dirty talk," he warned one day. "or see it written on the wall of any building. This includes all kinds of swear words, even gosh, golly, gee, darn, or whatever. The Bible says not to swear by anything, but let your yea be yea and your nay nay. Any breaking of this rule will be punished with a whipping. In fact, I want you to remember that any writing on any wall is forbidden."

I listened, thinking how many things were punishable by whipping. It was hard to remember them all, and new ones were being added all the time. With my luck. I was usually whipped first and the rule was made afterward. The punishments were getting ahead of the crimes.

But the gang whipping that grew out of this rule was something new and terrifying. There was an irrational element in it, and instead of inspiring truthfulness it drove us to be devious in self-defense.

One day the wall of the girls dorm outside the dining room had words and symbols scribbled on it. The word scribbled was HELLO and after it were four stars. It was probably inspired by the current cornflakes blurb on the back of the box, but John saw it as a sign of hidden rebellion.

"You can't tell me that means hello," he said. "Who would defy me just to write hello on a wall? Inverted it says o hell. Someone is trying to be funny at my expense."

"Oh, come on!" Anna laughed. "Yesterday you saw a stranger walking in the woods and thought the FBI was on your trail, and now you think hello is o hell. Isn't there enough to do around here without making up trouble? Let it go!"

But at lunchtime John stood up in the dining room and made an announcement. "This scribbling on the dorm wall is in direct defiance of the latest rule. I will give you until four o'clock this afternoon to come and tell me who did it. If no one admits it, there will be no dinner tonight, and you will be whipped until someone does confess."

All afternoon we stood around in clumps talking about it. Someone suggested we get Lethie to admit doing it, but then we remembered she couldn't write, so that wouldn't work.

"It looks like the way you make stars," Hallie said to me, and I was so frightened I nearly choked. Nothing was making sense, and I had the feeling that I might even have done it in my sleep or sometime when I didn't know it, and they would find out about it. Everybody was guilty. I was guilty, whether I knew it or not.

By four o'clock there had been no confessions. John rolled up his shirt sleeves and stood in front of us. "All I want is the truth," he said sternly. "Does anyone want to tell me?"

We stood huddled together like sheep, too confused to figure out what was happening. Most of the time John was gentle and affectionate, and we were baffled by this sudden fierceness; but before we could collect our wits we were taken one at a time into a room, interrogated, slapped, whipped, and put back in line. The smaller children stood around crying, and the larger ones were too stunned to react.

The third round of whippings started, and we began to come to our senses. With the long interrogations it was getting dark. We had had no dinner, and some of us had raw welts on our backs and buttocks. In the inside room we sensed that the adults were quarreling with one another, that the others wanted to stop but John was insisting on getting at the truth.

"I'll find out who did that if I have to break every bone in their bodies!" we could hear him shouting. "I'll not be surrounded by a foul-mouthed bunch of liars making a fool out of me!"

We looked at one another. Somebody had to stop him.

There was a quiet buzz of whispers in the line-up. Lewis, Stumpy's brother, was a big kid with a rough backwoods sense of justice. He had learned to survive worse things than this and knew what to do. He motioned to R. C. and took out his pocketknife, the one treasure he had brought from his former life.

"Hey R. C.," he whispered, "you like this pocketknife?"

R. C. eyed the knife greedily. "Yeah!"

"Then tell them you done it, and I'll give it to you."

"They'll kill me!'

"They're aimin' to kill all of us thisaway. You want it or not?"

"Yeah!"

"Then go and tell them you done it."

R. C. put on a dour face and went blubbering to the whipping room. He knocked on the door and told them he was sorry. He had a name for being one of the bad boys, so of course they believed him. He was praised for telling the truth, whipped soundly, and we were all let go. When it was over. R. C. came for his knife.

Lewis stood smiling, sharpening the blade on a rock. "Come and get it, you little yeller-bellied idiot." he said quietly. "Where do you want it?"

R. C. stood staring at the sharpened blade for a moment, then turned away. For once he couldn't even tattle to defend himself.

We all laughed. R. C. had it coming.

The Meeks had been quiet people, living among us but not accepting as gospel every word that John said. The whipping incident shocked them deeply, and they were not able to laugh it off. When the next scandal broke, they themselves were the accusers.

Mr. Meek confronted John with specific accusations about Nada. He said he refused to be part of a group where the leader set one standard of behavior and lived another. He handed John a letter of resignation in which he said that it was against his conscience to continue working at the home.

John, fiery with anger, called Meek an instrument of the devil sent to destroy God's work, a filthy-minded beast who had evil designs on every woman on the place, and a liar fresh from the pit of hell. And so the Meeks left the only way there was to leave, in disgrace. No one looked at them, or said goodbye or thank you, or wished them well. They were to be forgotten, like so many after them.

We heard later from John that God was punishing Mr. Meek, and the only job he could get was making cheese in the Kraft factory in Chicago. The punishment did not seem all that clear-cut to me. In fact, the thought of a whole factory full of cheese made my mouth water, and I wished for such a curse to fall on me, any day.

One fall night, while the evenings were still warm, Anna finished her evening work and went outside the girls' dorm. I was playing indoors with some of the girls and didn't see her leave. When I did notice it, I went out and found her sitting quietly on the hillside. Miss Smith was with her. I crouched down to hear what they were saying, with an uneasy feeling that I should not be doing it.

"What action are you going to take?" Miss Smith was saying.

"What can I do? It's all hearsay. I can't prove anything."

"I would venture to say its more than hearsay. Meek doesn't lie, and he told me that he was shocked out of his wits. He walked into the office one night after they thought he was gone, and there they sat. I hardly dare to repeat such a thing aloud for fear of being struck dead, but he swears John was sitting there reading the Bible with his hand tucked in Nada's bra!"

"Maybe it's some new pledge of allegiance." Anna began laughing, and then the laugh suddenly turned into crying. "John vows it's all a lie, that Meek only made it up because he wanted an excuse to leave, that he wasn't getting enough money."

Miss Smith sat with her arm around Anna, letting her cry. "Do you believe that?" she asked quietly.

"No, but the problem is. I think John does. He will not face anything head-on. I guess the most I can do is wait and hope that he'll get over it."

"I know how you feel," Miss Smith said. "But let me tell you, I was once in a situation similar to this, and time didn't help. Time is not always on our side."

They sat quietly in the dark, saying no more for a moment. I moved, and a pebble skittered down the hill.

"Who's there?" they both said, looking startled.

"Me." I said. "When are we going home?"

I knew Miss Smith wanted to correct the me to I, but for once she didn't.

Anna was sick, and the shades were pulled down in the bedroom. She was vomiting into a pan, and the house smelled like despair and green bile. I was angry and wished she would get up and hit John instead of vomiting and being sick.

I got a cloth for her head and tried to hold her hand. In the back of my mind there was a tangle of fear and curiosity. He had done it to her again, and now he hated her.

"Are you going to have a baby?" I asked.

"No. I won't have any more babies."

"But why?" I still want a real brother."

"You almost had a brother once." she said, with her eyes covered with the wet cloth. "He was born too soon and was already dead. He was very tiny, but I could tell he would have been a little boy."

"Ohhhhh . . ." I said, stung with disappointment. Why . . .?"

She swallowed and turned her face to the wall. I put my arm across her soft bosom and tried to hug her. She was quiet, and I kept wondering if she had buried my brother in a big matchbox like the baby in the whorehouse.

John came in. "Let your mother rest now," he said.

I went into the kitchen and John followed me. "Your mother has to go to the hospital," he said.

"Why can't I ever have a real brother:" I asked angrily.

"Don't worry about that. You have a lot of brothers now. Our family is not just you and Mother and me anymore, it's many people. You have to get used to that."

As soon as she was well enough to travel. Anna caught the

train to Chicago. John and Christina and I were left alone in the cabin.

Christina was sent to the girls' dorm, but John took me to the boys dorm to be cared for by Nada, whom I hated. I was getting too big to bite and kick her as I felt like doing, but whenever she came near me I ducked out of the way to keep her from touching me. To me she was poison, and her flashing smile was like the baring of a snake's fangs.

At night I lay on the Army cot in the dorm kitchen where I was told to sleep, wondering what my father was doing upstairs, and planning how to run away. If Gram knew what was going on, she wouldn't like it. I wondered where Anna was, and if she would die, and if John wanted her to die. I lay seething with hatred for the white-toothed woman upstairs who shook her big tits and talked so loudly about God, the woman who was so pious and so evil.

Then one night as I lay awake listening to every sound and squeak in the floor upstairs. I knew I could not bear it any longer. I got up in the dark and walked out the front door, through the quiet of the hollow and the shadowy black trees, and slipped into the girls' dorm. In the morning John found me there, and he was decent enough not to force me to go back. That day he took me to town with him in the car. He talked about his plans for the future, and how Nada was the only one who could help him carry out those plans. It was the first time he had taken me into his confidence, talking about things that were important to him. I knew I should feel flattered, but I was still too confused about everything.

"Why did you make Mother go to the hospital?" I asked.

"I didn't make her go. She was sick, she needed surgery, and her sisters are going to take care of her. Its as simple as that."

"When is she coming back?"

"I don't know" he said, looking out the car window. "Tell me, if she decides never to come back, will you leave me too?"

For a moment I was shocked speechless. Would Anna decide never to come back? She couldn't do that! If they all started running away, how could I? There wouldn't even be anything left to run away from.

"You were my first baby, the only one born to me," John was saying. "If you left me, I would feel very alone."

I had no idea I was so important to him. It complicated things even more. Did he still want Anna and me as his family, or not?

"Will you leave me too?" I heard him repeating.

He looked directly at me and smiled sadly. He did have nice blue eyes. He was my father, the only one I would ever have. For a moment I forgot all about Nada, about Anna, about all the things that made me angry. I wanted to please him and say no, that I would never leave him, but it seemed a terribly unsafe thing to say.

He stopped the car in front of the Krystal Kitchen in Corbin and bought two hamburgers. He ate his in a few big bites, but I nibbled mine all the way home, afraid that if I finished it I would have to answer him. I finally threw the last bite away.

It was winter again, and bitterly cold, and I did not want to risk having another Christmas with all the disappointing things that could happen. Virgie offered to teach me to tap-dance on a stab down at the sawdust pile where no one could see us, but I refused, certain I would die before spring.

CHAPTER FOUR

How is it that in the face of all the pain and disillusionment of life, human beings still have the courage to love? John and Anna were unofficially separated, their marriage a farce, one of the older boys had just been sent away from the home for doing something obscene in the barn with a cow . . . and I was in love with Homer. He was nine and I was eight, and we were in love. At least I was in love with him. He was probably in love with somebody else.

It was spring and everybody was in love with somebody. Jean was in love with Troy. Winnie was too, and they pulled hair and fought over him. Troy was nice to everybody and paid no attention to either of them. A whole new crop of kids had come, and there was a scramble for who was whose. It was all purely academic. The boys and girls never played together any more, not even in the schoolyard, which made them seem even more mysterious to each other.

I dreamed of Homer before falling asleep at night. He would come to my gate, in some mysterious place, and bring me a single flower. Dressed in a long white gown, I would look up at the moon, and it would all be very touching.

I hated seeing him at breakfast, though, because he would barely glance at me and sniff his nose, which was usually running a long yellow string. But his cheeks were nice and red.

Now that Anna was gone. John began to see the necessity for better laundry facilities. Every week Nada had to scrub piles of overalls by hand, and John noticed what a hardship it was. Her manicured hands were getting as rough and red as Anna's. He began to make plans for a laundry building.

In the hollow, between our cabin and the girls' dorm, the creek ran full and deep. Winter and summer there was a plentiful supply of water. A bridge had been built over the creek during the summer, and now it spanned the deep gorge, standing fully twenty feet high over the stream. It was slightly raised in the middle, making a graceful arc under the dense trees. A tall smooth-barked tree leaned over the bridge, its huge umbrella leaves casting cool shadows. The tree was a constant source of argument between Miss Smith and her students. We had always called it a cowcumber tree. She said it was a catalpa. The name embarrassed us. It was a sore point, especially with the older boys.

"Them northerners, who do they think they are, comin' down here and tellin' us what to call our trees, how to sing our songs, how to spit and kiss their ass," mumbled David, a newcomer who had not yet absorbed the no-dirty-language code. He was curly-haired and surly and a great favorite of the girls, as was his brother Eugene.

But, a central laundry to serve all the dorms had to be built, and the hollow by the bridge was chosen for the site. It was staked out several hundred yards upstream from the bridge so that the trees hid it from view.

Every day John worked on the structure with the help of a local man who was paid a dollar twenty-five a day. The man's name was O.B., and between them they had a simple three-room structure roughed in within a few weeks. There was a washing room, an ironing room, and a room for a live-in laundress. Of course, there was no laundress yet, but a detail like that never bothered John. If he built the building, a laundress would come, like a bird to a birdhouse.

One day when John and O. B. were on the roof, a car came easing over the ruts and down the sandy road. The driver parked in front of the cabin and made his way down the path to where the sound of hammers could be heard. I was perched on the lumber stack watching them.

John looked down from the roof. "Howdy!" he shouted, spotting the man as an outsider, and deliberately putting on his best southern accent. "What can I do for you?"

"Hello!" replied the man.—Are you John Vogel? Nice place you've got here, if the road wasn't so bad." John climbed down the ladder and shook hands. The two of them began to walk and talk, leaving O. B, to hammer by himself.

The man was from the north, a friend of a friend from whom John had borrowed money he had never repaid, and John was nervous. He showed the visitor the school, the girls' dorm with its flock of chattering girls, Miss Smith with her brisk good-natured efficiency, the boys' dorm with its sturdy pack of polite overalled boys, Nada charming as ever in the office. He showed him the cabin, closed and a bit musty from days of being shut. Then they sat down under a tree and talked.

"Where is your wife?" the man asked. "Your friend Bob especially wanted me to send her his greetings."

John blanched. "She's not been well.' he said quickly. "I've sent her to her sister's house in Chicago to rest up for a while. It's a rugged life we live here, and she's not too strong. Sometimes I worry."

The man nodded sympathetically. "I see," he said. "It must be an enormous strain just to feed this whole group. If you don't mind my asking, where do you get the money?"

John had told him about the land deals, about the daily prayers and the whole idea of trusting heaven for daily food. He considered the question redundant, but for the sake of courtesy he struggled to hide his annoyance.

"It takes almost a thousand a month to keep us operational right now," John said slowly, "and I only have pledges amounting to thirty dollars. You tell me where the rest comes from!'

The visitor had waited patiently to come to the point of his business, and now he laid it before John carefully.

"Your friend Bob is worried about you." he said. "You have a good idea here, but he's afraid you're going to fail for lack of funds. Now, I'll tell you what he's offered. Bob has done well in his business, and he has a surplus he'd like to invest. He sent me to find out if you'd be interested in a deal. If you would decide to form a board of managers and make him one of your men, he'd see that these kids never go hungry a day. You need a thousand a month, you'll have it."

Silence. John picked a leaf and slowly tore it to shreds. I glanced at his face and saw that look of stubborn anger I was beginning to dread.

"That's very generous of you." he said, slowly, his face reddening down to the white collar that Nada had ironed, "but I don't think Bob and I could work together. I've never thought of him as a friend. I made the foolish mistake of borrowing money from him once. He made a public issue out of it when I owed him a few hundred." John's face was getting redder. "You say Bob's business has gone well. He doesn't fool me. Bob was born rich, and he's a spoiled rich snob who's never done a day's work in his life. He knows how to bow and scrape to the right people, but he sucks the blood out of anyone he considers the underdog. I've played the underdog to him once, and you tell him I said he can take his damnable thousand bucks and go to hell!" John was so angry he was shaking.

Soon afterward the man from the north left.

"Board of managers!" John said with a forced laugh. "It would take them less than six months to vote me out! Tells me he didn't know Anna wasn't here! She and dear friend Bob have probably been plotting this whole thing behind my back!"

When the laundry building was finished, Lethie moved in until a laundress could be found. John talked the Norge dealer in town into selling him a gasoline washing machine on credit (telling himself it would soon be paid for and not become a bad habit like the grocery bill), and the machine's loud putt-putt-putt could be heard up and down the ridges twice a week. Each dorm had a washday, and Lethie was assistant to whoever washed. She was in her glory, and kept the place immaculately clean. When the sun shone, she was sure heaven was smiling on her and the "crothes would gry," and when it rained she was sure the netherworld had won out, and she sang "Heavenly Sunshine" hour after hour, trying to coax the sun out and scare the devil away. Anyone with less gall than the devil would have run.

Finally a real laundress came. Her name was Alice, and she looked like the pictures of Eleanor Roosevelt Miss Smith put up in school. She was crippled, and wore one tall shoe. She and Lethie worked together during the day, and Alice slept in the laundry building at night.

The crippled woman fascinated me. She sat on a stool while she ironed, her short leg up and her long leg down, and talked of many things. She sensed that our world was limited, and she liked to challenge our thinking, to shake our assumptions. She taught me a Dutch song about a crow, and a song about Solomon Levi, both of which were contraband. She also taught me the words and music of "Faniculi. Faniculai," and I was delighted. It was the first completely happy devil-may-care song I had ever known, and I ran up and down the hill and across the bridge, singing it full blast:

> "For me. I like to spend my time in singing
> Some joyous song, some joyous song.
> To spend my time in music gaily ringing
> Is far from wrong, is far from wrong.
> Harken, harken, echoes sound afar.
> Harken, harken, echoes sound afar.
> Tra-la-la-la, tra-la-la-la.
> There is joy, oh there is joy,
> Oh there is joy, oh everywhere!"

It seemed to me like a promise not even qualified by getting my sins forgiven, like a secret message from the Legendary Grandfather.

The procession of adults kept coming, people who had heard what was happening in the hills near Corbin and wanted to join the group. A woman named Clara, a tall freckle-faced girl from

Indiana, offered her services as a dorm mother. She was the sort of devout person who could laugh easily; she was patient and gentle with the shortcomings of others, and she made delicious Dutch apple slices.

But I was lonely for Anna.

After what seemed an interminable time. John got a letter saying she was coming home. He opened up the cabin and aired it out. He swept and dusted and made up the beds and told me to bring our things home. He brought his clothes from Nada's and scattered them around to make the place look lived in, and I wondered if he was trying to fool Anna for her sake or for his.

The two of us drove to Corbin and parked on Depot Street, waiting for the train. I glanced around the infamous street, wondering where Jessie's whorehouse was, and what terrible kind of men went there. I was almost sure my father would never . . . He might like one other woman, but he would never do that sort of thing, not to just anyone.

The train rumbled in, and we stood on the dusty platform watching the white steam and black iron roll past. Then came the dusty blue cars, and Anna, looking rested and more beautiful than I had ever seen her in my life. She was slender and pink, her hair was done, her eyebrow plucked and her nails manicured. I squeezed her soft gentle beauty with a hunger stored from nights of crying, days of loneliness. She was my mother, and she was back.

John kissed her lightly and took her bags. She was dressed smartly, and had new luggage. He seemed afraid to touch her. "New things?" he asked.

"From my sisters." She smiled. "But how are you? How is everything?"

We climbed into the car and I wanted to push them together, to make them hold hands, to help them cut across the polite silence between them.

"Did you miss me, John?" Anna asked softly.

"I did," he said uneasily.

"Will things be any different?" she asked slowly.

"What do you mean by different?"

"I don't think I have to draw you a picture."

He was silent, the stubborn look coming across his face.

"I asked you a question." Anna said. "Will things be any different?"

It was quiet in the car. The train was being called over the loudspeaker, then was pulling out of the station with a roar and a hiss. I huddled in the corner of the seat, afraid of his answer, wishing the overpowering noise of the train would never stop. I could see him thinking things through. Now the noise was dying down and he would have to say something.

"I suppose you saw our good friend Bob," he said.

Anna looked puzzled. "No," she said, "Was I supposed to have?"

A look of annoyance crossed his face, as though she were lying.

"You still haven't answered me," she said. "Will things be any different?" He stuck his key in the ignition and turned his head.

"We'll try," he promised.

He started the car, and we drove home. Somewhere along the road between Corbin and home I decided that I didn't want a family anymore. They were too much trouble. They could do as they pleased, as long as they didn't kill me . . .

Some things were better when Anna returned. With more adults, the work load was lighter. She no longer went to the dorm, but concentrated on making the cabin home. She papered the walls, ordered new white curtains from the catalogue, painted the kitchen linoleum red, and made the place fresh and cheerful. The barn boys brought the milk to our house, and Anna turned the back porch into a dairy room. For the first time in months life at least seemed peaceful.

Into this seeming peace Mr. Powers, a kind-faced young man whose wife had died in childbirth, brought his two daughters. Pearl was five, and Carlita seven. They were not hangdog or louse-eaten, but well cared for, clean, and dimpled. Pearl looked like a spoiled brat, but Carlita was a sweet child, and pretty. She had dark curls and china blue eyes, and she laughed a tinkling little laugh that went straight to John's heart. Besides being fascinated by her, he was flattered that we were finally being given children that someone cared about. The Powers children were a sacred trust. Special permission was given Mr. Powers to visit the girls once a week instead of twice a year, as the case for the other parents.

"I'd like to raise them myself." Mr. Powers said. "but with no mother around and me working, I can't stand to see them batted back and forth from this relative to that one. I'll come back every Sunday. I know you'll bring them up right."

He shook hands and left quickly, his eyes full of tears. It was the beginning of a new era.

I watched Carlita, trying to decide whether or not to be friends with her. She was sweet enough, but she soon struck me as being brainless, even though she got good marks on her first day at school. I had the feeling that if she were ever faced with a snake on the path or any other emergency, she wouldn't have the sense to get out of the way. This was, at least, my excuse to myself for not liking her. The real reason was that I was jealous of the attention John paid her. She was like Nada without tits, my competition instead of Anna's. He could not resist picking her up or ruffling her dark hair, and she clung to him in a way I considered disgraceful for a seven-year-old. After all, her own father had walked away with tears in his eyes only the day before. Had she no sense of decency? I decided I definitely did not like her.

When John and Anna had come to Kentucky, they had all but forgotten their Dutch religious heritage. John had been somewhat ordained by the laying on of hands in their loosely organized fundamentalist group, but even that tie was dissolved by now. He and the other members had disagreed on some fine point of the second coming, and that had been the end of the alliance. For all practical purposes, he was autonomous.

Then the letter came, marked urgent, from a man in Grand Haven, Michigan. He was a leading dominie in the Dutch Calvinist Church organization in which both John and Anna had grown up.

Their parents had belonged to this church, and their parents' parents, and so on all the way back to the Protestant Reformation in Holland. It was a powerful organization and exerted a firm control over its members. All persons born into the church were baptized as infants and regarded as communicants unless they proclaimed themselves otherwise or were excommunicated.

The letter from Michigan put John on guard. In itself it contained no actual threat. It was a polite invitation to John to come to Grand Haven and speak to a group who were interested in his work. They wanted slides and a full presentation of his ideas.

For some reason, John accepted the invitation, perhaps to show them that he had done very well without them. He and Anna decided that she would stay and be in charge and I should go with John. I was deliriously excited at the prospect of a trip.

Up through the towns and cities of Kentucky we wound, John's precious projector and slides resting on the back seat. The wonders of the outside world were not strange to me because of our frequent trips to Corbin, a city of five thousand, but it was still interesting to go out and see how other people lived. When we drove through towns and cities I saw children skating on sidewalks and riding bicycles, and I did envy them a little; but I told myself we had creeks and woods, and that I preferred the soft glow of the lamplight to the brightness of the cities.

As we drove along and talked, John tried to entertain me, chatting about presidents and politics, about the war in Europe and the communists who were trying to take over the United States. I was fascinated with his knowledge, but most of it went over my head.

The second night we stopped at a small diner for our evening meal, and John bought a newspaper. He glanced at the headlines and scowled. "That Roosevelt is selling us down the river!" he complained.

"Why don't you like President Roosevelt?" I asked.

"He's selling the country down the river to socialism!"

"What's wrong with socialism?"

"It's too much like communism!"

"What's communism?"

"You know that, don't you?"

"No."

"Well, very simply stated, it's a form of government under which people who have things are forced to share with the people who don't have things."

It sounded to me exactly like what was going on at home.

"I wouldn't like that." I agreed.

"And all children are taken away from their parents and stuffed with propaganda. They're taught to reject their parents and love the state."

I looked at him wordlessly, wondering what other parallels there were.

"And there is no individual freedom. The individual must give up his rights for the sake of the group. People are told what to do, what to become. They have no *freedom*."

I listened to him, feeling uneasy. "Well, what do we have?" I asked.

"We live in a democracy . . ." He began to explain.

We drove through the flats of Indiana, skirting the city of Chicago with its complicated family ties, and on to Grand Haven on the big lake.

Almost two hundred people were present at the meeting. They watched the slides projected on the screen and listened to John for an hour and a half, letting him speak without interruption. Then we were invited to the dominie's house for coffee.

The room was smoke-filled and heavy with stocky Dutchmen. Women floated about serving slices of rich cake and pouring steaming black coffee. It looked like a gathering of Anna's clan, but the men were older, gray-haired, dignified.

There was a steady drone of voices, and I felt very small and sleepy.

A fat lady was trying to give me a doughnut but I decided not to take it. The sight of so many grandfatherly adults made me feel safe and protected. The noise in the room droned on.

Suddenly it was quiet. An important-looking gentleman called for attention, and they began to question John.

"Would you tell us once more in your own words, Mr. Vogel, what your basic reason was for starting this children's home?"

John sat a little apart from the rest. He looked very alone. "As I stated, my only reason was to prove the power of prayer, to show the world that the Lord God of Elijah still rules in the heavens."

The men looked at one another and nodded.

The leader began to speak again. "Do you ever take in children out of a sense of the child's need? In your mind, is not the welfare and happiness of the child the primary concern?"

"Of course I'm concerned about the children. I think my lifework speaks for itself. Children are the greatest in the kingdom of God. What greater medium could we use to prove that God hears and answers prayer?"

There was a buzz around the room, a murmur of voices.

"I didn't ask if you felt it was right to *use* the children," said the leader. "I asked if you were concerned about a child for the child's sake."

"Of course I care for all my children. They are my life."

"Then how can you submit them to your fanatic whims? It is not for men to demand things of God, holding innocent children as hostages. What if God punishes your arrogance by withholding money and food? Will those children suffer?"

"You have no right to judge me. I stand before God."

"And who among us can claim to live so perfectly before God that we need no human counsel? The Divine also reveals Himself in the collective . . ."

The voice went on. A feeling of excitement was coming into the room. Men sat on the edge of their chairs. Their faces were thoughtful and keen.

The speaker turned away from John and toward the others.

" . . . what I mean to say is that this young brother, sincere in heart and God-fearing as he may be, is in my opinion lacking in the faculty of reason. All of you have heard him tonight. I believe that the burdens of his work have been too heavy for him, that he needs our support."

There was the hum of low voices around the room. John sat in his chair looking pale and frightened.

Another voice began speaking, an elderly man sitting beside the first speaker. "I think we should come to the point," he began. "We're making our young brother very uncomfortable, and that certainly is not the purpose of this gathering. Mr. Vogel, the objective of this meeting tonight is twofold. We have heard that you are having difficulty, and we are concerned. This is the point we have made. The second is a little more pleasant. Our board of missions is willing to make you an offer. We will take the responsibility for the entire project, finance and operate it, and set you up in a position of leadership within the organization."

John's head went up as though he had been hit in the stomach. "What kind of plot is going on anyway?" he asked angrily. "First you try to prove that I'm crazy, and then you offer to relieve me of my life's work. Thank you very much, but I think I'll refuse! As long as I live I'll stay as I am, independent and free to operate by faith in God. He hasn't let us go hungry yet!"

"But Mr. Vogel," said the second man kindly, "can't you see that God is answering your prayers for now and the future by leading us to underwrite your work? These children will never lack for anything if we back you."

I was wide awake now. The idea of having all these grandfathers take care of us, of never having to worry about money coming in the mail or about God's anger sounded good to me. I was hoping against hope that John would listen to them, would accept their help. But there was a faraway look in his eyes as though he was remembering something from long ago.

He raised his head and looked around the room with a shy half-smile tipping up his mustache. "I must admit it strikes me rather strangely to have to justify to those who are the defenders of the faith the fact that too much belief in God has made me illogical."

he began. "As you all know. I was born and raised in your church, a Pharisee of the Pharisees, until God laid His hand on me. I attended your high school in Chicago, your college in Grand Rapids. At a certain point I had to drop out for lack of funds. I attended schools in Chicago, among them Moody Bible Institute, and there I received the vision of going to Kentucky.

"I went to my home church in Oak Lawn and asked them to support me as a worker in Kentucky. They gave me twenty dollars out of the poor fund and bade me Godspeed. As far as supporting me was concerned, they told me it was against church policy. Then we went to another of your churches, which my wife Anna attended, and they gave us ten dollars and God's blessing. With those thirty dollars and your blessings ringing in our ears, we went to Kentucky.

"And, now that we've established a work, the church wants to take it over. We built that place with sweat and tears, and we do not intend to sell out! We have something to prove, and will die proving it! We will not sell out to the world, the devil, or the organized church!"

There was a loud buzz of angry voices. Men rose to their feet. John came and took my hand. I was still watching to see if he would change his mind, but the men had turned their faces away from us, and I knew it was over.

"Let's go." John said. We put our coats on and walked out into the cold dark night.

When we came home, the hills and hollows were in full bloom with dogwood and redbud. The wind swept through the pines and over the ridges, and I breathed in the freshness, the sharpness, the sweetness and bitterness of home.

A few days after our return the Cox family arrived. They were the closest to perfect beauty I had ever seen. Every one of them, from Maxine, the eldest, to Winston, the youngest, was flawlessly beautiful. Maxine and Winston were green-eyed blonds, and Ernie and Julie were dark-eyed brunettes. Among our generally big-eared and knock-kneed bunch, they were almost too good to be true.

Winston was only eighteen months old, and he came to live in our cabin. Anna fixed a little bed, and I made the supreme sacrifice for him—the short pants off my big doll. It was the doll Gram had given me for Christmas, and the suit had come in a mission barrel.

The day Winston came, I knew I would finally have a brother. I had wanted one so badly, so long. In fact, it had been my need for a brother that had led me to an action that would have meant a whipping and bread and water for three days if it had been found out. The house John had originally built for a chicken coop had been cleared out, and the chickens had a new pen up behind the girls' dorm. The old chicken coop had been remodeled, and Anna had fixed it up as a playhouse for Christina and me.

I kept my doll in a bed in this playhouse. It had started out as a girl doll, but one day, eaten with the desire for a little brother, I had rolled a white handkerchief into a long tube and pinned it on the doll with a safety pin. This together with the boy-suit made him a brother. I lived in guilty fear of anyone finding out, and broke into a sweat when either John or Anna went into the playhouse. But once Winston arrived, I took the suit off the doll and frantically destroyed the damning evidence of my sin. No one ever found out.

The suit was put on Winston, and he toddled around, his golden ringlets bouncing and his green eyes sparkling. He was perfect, and I loved him.

Maxine was just a year younger than I, and we became special friends. She was sweet and beautiful and good, and I was feisty and gangly and full of fight. We made a perfect team. Everyone loved her, and I felt it was fair. John patted her head and gave her special favors, but she did not suck around after him as Carlita did. Maxine seemed to have a sense of human dignity and responsibility. I liked her so much that I forgot all about Homer and his runny nose, the imagined single flower that he never brought me anyway, and the false ecstasy, and began to build a friendship with a real person.

Before she had been with us two weeks, Maxine broke out in measles. Twenty people began sniffing and coughing and running fevers. Most of the girls were down sick, and the bedrooms at the dorm were full of feverish glassy-eyed patients. Next the boys began to sniff and cough and run high temperatures. Nobody seemed to have had measles, and all thirty-five children began coughing, vomiting, burning with fever. John, Anna, Nada, Clara, and Alice the laundress did twenty-four-hour duty as nurses. They moved among the burning vomiting children, trying to force down aspirin and soup.

At first, because of the shortage of help, I was in the dorm. Then Anna took me home and put me in her bed. My fever was 105, and for two days I was unconscious. A doctor came and forced a huge amount of medicine down me, and I wavered back to the land of the living. Anna and John were strangers bending over me, people I should recognize but didn't particularly care to. Anna cried and John prayed. Bit by bit hearing, seeing, and knowing began to come back.

"Where are all the other kids?" I asked, sitting up on the third day.

"They're okay!" Anna smiled, wiping my forehead. "You really have to do everything with a flourish, don't you?"

Soon I was well, except for a heart murmur that lasted all summer. But little Winston did not fare so well. On the tail of the severe measles came whooping cough, and his tiny body, fragile from days of fever, was now racked with long strangling coughing fits. I held and rocked him, aching inside each time he gasped for breath. His tiny ribs were sharp against me, and his eyes were glazed.

John took him to the doctor in Corbin. Maxine and I went along.

"Rent a room in Yeary's Motel down the street," the doctor ordered, "where I can keep an eye on him without having to drive over that god-awful road of yours. The kid's dehydrated, and he'll die if you don't get some liquid into his system."

I rocked and held him, trying to get him to take the bottle he had laid aside a few months ago. But he refused food or water, and every time the coughing began he emptied whatever was in his stomach. I was terrified.

"Please get well." I whispered in a kind of chant. "Please don't die . . ., please don't die . . ." On the second day in the motel I went out to the pop machine and got a bottle of Pepsi. When Winston saw the pop bottle, he reached for it. He tipped the bottle up and gulped the soda down in great thirsty gulps. Then he flopped on his stomach with his tail end up in the air and went to sleep.

The next day he started to eat.

"Well I'll be damned," said the doctor. "I never know what's going to happen with you people."

John and Anna were exhausted, frightened, and grateful to be alive.

For the first time in months they actually seemed to have something in common-gratitude that none of us had died. John was so weary after his round of the dorms at night that he stumbled home and fell asleep, often in Anna's bed.

There could not possibly have been a worse time for the letter to arrive from the church authorities in Grand Haven, informing John that it had come to their attention that he was engaged in practices inappropriate for a church member and there would soon be an investigation of his personal life as well as his financial records.

John, in a burst of anger, ordered Nada to type an immediate reply, daring them to do any such thing.

Back came a letter saying that their information had come from reliable sources close to the family and that the church would take action against John.

"This is the work of your meddling clan!" he accused Anna, and he wrote demanding that any papers linking him with the church establishment be removed, burned, and the ashes scattered to the winds.

The last letter from Michigan informed him that he had been excommunicated and was at the mercy of God.

John tore it up and laughed. Pieces of paper had never held any significance for him. He was free to do as he pleased.

He and his band of thirty-five children were at the mercy of God.

It was nearly Christmas again. December 1941. Nada's prompt
and gushing thank-you letters had won many friends for the home,
and John was jubilant. He prided himself on never asking anyone for
anything, and it seemed that a sincere thank-you letter brought more
repeat gifts than direct solicitation might. This year large boxes of
beautifully wrapped gifts had come to the post office, and the older
boys had to go with John to get them. They puffed and panted up
the hill, dragging the sagging cartons by their overtaxed strings.

On December 7, 1941 we were just building a fire in the fireplace
at our cabin. A light snow had fallen in the night, and the logs had to
be shaken dry before the fire would start. It was cold, and we shivered
as we dressed.

John rushed in from his room. The battery radio was turned up,
blaring above the static. Pearl Harbor had been bombed, and the
United States was at war.

We finished dressing quickly and ran to the dining hall, where
we clustered around Miss Smith's radio. The boys and Nada came
running up from their dorm, and we all stood stupefied, listening to
the news. We were at war. What did it mean?

"The Japanese dropped bombs on the American warships," Miss
Smith explained.

"What's bums?" Stumpy asked.

"Bums is what they're droppin' on the worn-torn countries," Hallie
explained.

"War-torn," Miss Smith corrected, "not worn-torn!"

I had always thought it was worn-torn too. War-torn didn't even
sound right. Were we going to be war-torn now? We sat around
shivering, eating hot musty-smelling oatmeal, and wondering what
would happen.

A draft board was set up in Corbin, and young men began pouring
out of the hills and hollows volunteering for service. The oldest male
in our ranks, aside from John, was sixteen, but when rumors began to

spread that John was going to be drafted he assembled a special meeting to pray that he would not be called. He said if he had to go it would be the end of the home.

I knelt at the prayer meeting a complete hypocrite. Aloud I had to pray that John would not be drafted, but in my secret heart his having to go loomed as an intriguing possibility. The idea of the home ending, of being free again, excited me as much as the war. I even wished a skyful of enemy planes would fly directly overhead and bomb the place. Or if John had to go to war, I could be proud of him, off somewhere fighting the enemy instead of hanging around the office. I would rather have the Japanese get him than Nada. So far, nothing too terrible had happened. Maybe the war would take him and rescue us all.

But the Corbin draft board deferred John because he was flat-footed and had thirty-five children. I was bitterly disappointed.

Miss Smith was a New England patriot at heart, and transplanting her to Kentucky soil had not dimmed her Pilgrim fire. Flag drills were carried out with new enthusiasm, and we learned "What though wars may come/with march of feet and beat-of-the-drum/for I have Christ in my heart." We planted victory gardens down by the sawdust pile and collected toothpaste tubes and rolled tinfoil balls. We read our *Weekly Readers* religiously, and now "Nip the Bar" was no longer our hero but was replaced by the young soldiers in uniform. We studied tanks and airplanes, and for Christmas I wanted a sailor suit from the Sears catalogue.

John, usually indulgent when he had money in his pocket, drew the line. "None of that," he said. "Next thing you know you'll be wanting to go into the service when you're eighteen. Do you know what those WACS and WAVES are? Just a glorified bunch of whores. Don't get any of those ideas!"

"But I wanted a boy's suit!" I begged. "One with pants!"

"No, no, no! I said no women in pants around here, and that means you. Women in pants are the most ungodly sight in the world! It's against nature."

"I'm only eight, and it's not against my nature."

"I said no women in pants!" he thundered, and I knew there was no way to win. Somewhere in the Bible it said that women shouldn't wear pants, and if the Bible said it, there was no arguing against it.

Miss Smith began to get letters from friends in China and the Philippines, classmates from Wheaton College who had become missionaries. They were in prison camps. One man had written under a postage stamp that his tongue had been cut out. We could not imagine what kind of people would cut out a man's tongue.

A hatred of the Japanese began to spread through the community. The postmaster. Mr. Decker, had a black mangy dog named Tojo, and everyone kicked him around and spat at him. Japs were added to the list of people to be hated, along with niggers, Jews, and Catholics. It was suspected that in some diabolical way they were all connected: they were all probably communists under the skin. It was the work of the devil, and the devil was trying to take over the world.

The round flowerbed in front of the dorm was edged with rocks and filled with petunias in the summer, but in the winter it was a brown muddy hole. Every day on the way to meals I tiptoed around it carefully, thinking there might be a bomb planted in it. You never knew.

But come what may, the saints need not worry. We were safe and needed only to wait for the coming of the Lord, which would surely happen any day, since the world was going to the devil and not fit for us. Yet, frankly, it was the "coming of the Lord" that worried me more than the war. I was sure I would be left behind to suffer the tribulation and the great white throne judgment. Thrown into this ratpack of adult contradictions, I had to lie and scheme in order to stay alive. I was afraid I was not one of the good ones and would surely be left. Sometimes I would come home after school and call for Anna, and if there was no answer I would panic.

They had all been taken to heaven, and I, grimy little sinner, had been left behind. I was in a state of terror until I found her.

There was sugar rationing and gasoline rationing, but the ration board was kind and gave us extra coupons. People still gave clothes. In fact, with more Americans having jobs in defense plants, the clothes they threw away were better. A slab shed was constructed down by the boys' dorm, and once a week Nada and Anna opened and sorted the boxes. It was the only thing they ever did together, and except for clothes days they seldom spoke to each other. After sorting for a morning, each went home with armfuls of loot, like dividers of the spoils.

More money came in as well. The war made for an economic boom, and the resultant prosperity sifted down to us. A new building for boys began to go up on the ridge beyond the girls' dorm. The barn behind our cabin was torn down, and a bigger one was built on the fields behind the neighbor's house. John bought the neighbor's property, and our territory began to expand. He dreamed of buying out all the neighbors up the road, of owning hundreds of acres of land that he could call his own. He wanted no interference.

The war brought long engagements, town jobs for country girls, floating wives, and for us a new crop of babies. Before, the children who had come to us had been toddlers at least, but now we began to get distress signals from young women needing to be relieved of their unplanned newborns.

A pink bundle appeared, here, a blue one there. No one was supposed to know who the babies were, and they all took the name of Vogel. Our cabin began to fill with cribs—Marcella, Beverly, Judy, Trudy, Phyllis, David . . . No one knew which baby belonged to the waitress in the City Cafe, or to the neighbor girl who had got a job in the munitions factory. It was all very secret and made for juicy gossip. No one was supposed to know that Jud Morgan had been engaged to Ellie down the road and had gone to war, and she had got a job and had an affair with her boss, and the baby was born. Jud said he'd forget it and take her back if she got rid of the baby, and that was one blue bundle. Anna went secretly and carried him home on the train. Nobody was supposed to know, but everybody did.

And what did it matter? We had all been born about the same way, no matter how it happened. One birth was as good as the next, and it was no place to flaunt a pedigree, if one had it. My birth seemed most banal of all, to married parents who barely tolerated each other. I would have settled for being an orphan or a bastard, or both.

I roamed the woods that summer full of the melancholy sweetness of war, plotting and planning with Maxine how we could discover some invention to help in the rubber shortage. We found some rubbery things, but Miss Smith only laughed and said they were edible mushrooms. She fried them in butter, and we ate them and forgot about the rubber shortage.

To vent our stirred-up aggressions, we played games of Indians, and Robin Hood, and we dramatized and staged in the woods every new story Miss Smith read to us. We dressed in leaves and made bows and arrows. I was Robin Hood and Maxine was Maid Marian and Carlita was the Sheriff of Nottingham, which worked until I shot an arrow that stuck in her butt and had to be pulled out, and the game itself was outlawed.

I turned nine, and winter came. It snowed, and John and O. B. made sleds so the kids could play on the pasture hill.

I watched the snow come down, pondering the floating flakes as they fell and melted, feeling an urge to capture them, to make them permanent. I no longer felt like a child. Life was passing by, and it must mean something before it melted back into the gound like these frozen stars.

I found some school colors, and made a simple painting of the picket fence, the snow, the oak trees clinging to their rusty brown leaves. There were no figures in the painting. People were too hard. People moved and changed. The painting was of earth and fence and sky, things that would stand still, things that could be captured.

I set the picture on the fireplace mantel and went out to play in the snow, satisfied.

In some ways war was a lovely thing. It was beautiful to have Hitler to hate instead of one another. In our dislike of the distant powers of evil, we were almost united. In our hatred of the Germans, the Japs, and the devil we almost grew kind to one another. Someday we would win. But there was that other war, the one being fought inside our little world, and its outcome was not so easy to predict.

Christina was six now-and had lost her baby cuteness. She was thin and scrawny, and her speech impediment was noticeable. For some reason, John could not stand her. In our crowd no one's ancestry was that glorious, yet he seemed to dwell on the fact that Christina was the product of sin. It was as though every time he looked at her he could practically see her teenage mother fornicating, and it made it easy for him to strike her or blame her in arguments between the kids when the fault was not hers. Even though Anna tried to be kind to her, Christina began to feel despised and unwanted.

One day I was given a glimpse into her mind that left me shaken. Christina had a cat named Bluie. The cat was pregnant and we all waited eagerly for the kittens to be born. One morning when we went into the barn, Bluie had had her kittens. They lay on the straw in a bloody heap, dead. The mother cat had bitten them all in the head and killed them.

"Why did she do that?" Christina wailed, picking up the dead creatures. "Why did she kill her own kitties, that bad cat!" She sat and rocked them in her skirt tail, as if to bring them back to life.

The next day Bluie was gone. She had crawled under the rafters in the hayloft and died. We found her body, stiff and cold.

Christina looked at the dead cat with wide eyes.

"Did Bluie know she was going to die?" she asked.

"Maybe," I said.

"And she killed her kitties so no one would be mean to them?"

"Maybe," I said, beginning to wonder what she was thinking.

She reached down and stroked the cat's blue-gray fur. "Good Bluie." she whispered softly. "You were a good Bluie."

I put my arms around her and hugged her. It was the first time I had done it in a long time. She squeezed me back so hard she nearly suffocated me.

We picked up the cat and went to bury her in the woods. We dug a hole in the ground, and Christina sang a little song to Bluie, the good mother cat who killed all her five baby kittens so no one could ever, ever hurt them or be mean to them.

And I cried, but not for Bluie.

CHAPTER FIVE

To most people, John was a charmer. Children piled on his lap and ran their fingers through his hair. They followed him from building to building as he went his daily rounds. At night he walked the circuit kissing them all good night—there were forty-five by now—trying not to miss a one. When he went to town, everyone wanted to go with him, and the selection process was difficult. He usually solved the problem by taking along whoever looked the best and would create the best impression.

The town of Corbin was beginning to take favorable notice of the development out on the Bee Creek road. They smiled and nodded at the shaggy-haired pied piper from the hills as he bought his groceries and building supplies. They treated the children to candy and soda pop and bought them toys. They handed John money, and felt richer.

With money in his pocket, John began to stop in the local restaurants to buy a meal or a hamburger for whoever was with him. The restaurant owners usually would not charge him, and most stores in town gave him a discount without his asking. On the edge of North Corbin, a man named Harlan Sanders owned a motel with a restaurant where we would sometimes go to eat, and the white-haired proprietor with the red face would come to our table and chat genially. He had a special affection for John and treated him like a son.

But John was restless. Things were getting too easy. Although he needed praise and approval, in some perverse way they made him guilty and embarrassed. His prayers for daily food and clothing had been answered, and for several years the home had ambled along peacefully, to all appearances, but had made no great progress.

John began to dream of bigger things, greater challenges to test his power with the heavens.

Just beyond our land, up the dirt road, the Hensley farm spread over the hills and valleys. In our early years in Kentucky, the Hensleys had been our nearest and closest neighbors. During the first winter, they had taken us in and let us sleep in their featherbeds when our cabin was freezing. I was dropped off at the Hensleys' every time John and Anna went to town. Mrs. Hensley's kitchen, with the aroma of boiled leather-jacket beans, fried apples, and cornbread, was an integral part of our early Kentucky experience— the rich smell of foamy buttermilk and raw onions, the slop pail for the hogs and the rich-pine kindling behind the stove. But now the Hensleys had served their purpose, and John wanted to buy them out.

Every time we drove past the Hensleys' farm John would say, "I'd like to have that place. We could dam up White Oak branch and make a good-sized reservoir. Someday when electricity gets back in here, we could have our own pump station and water supply. And anyhow, that Sary Jane Hensley is nothing but a big gossip. I'd like to get her out of the country."

When we would go for walks down toward the river on Friday night, to fish and fry fish on the riverbank, John would stand and gaze up at the trees.

"We're going to need more lumber again if we go on with the building," he would say. "We could use this piece of land. There are seventy five acres here and a hundred and fifty thousand feet of timber. Old Doc Sears owns it, and nobody's using it. I'd like to get hold of it."

When we drove past the Gibbs property up beyond the Hensley place, he would say, "I keep talking to old lady Gibbs about selling this farm. She's one of the people who objects to our buying the county school. If the Gibbs children moved out of here, and the Hensleys, there'd be no reason for the county to object to our buying the county school property."

"What are you trying to do?" Anna asked him. 'Why do we need all this land?"

"We have to plan for the future." John explained. "These farms will be more valuable before too many years. If a road comes in here, and electricity, these places will double in value. And besides. I'm fed up with these county school kids tramping through our property every day to go to school. That public school is a nuisance and an eyesore!"

I listened, knowing that these were not all the reasons. It was his dislike of near neighbors, his fear of gossip about the home, his apprehension that the county school kids would lean over the fence and talk to us that bothered John. He liked his world private, with no intruders. He wanted to buy a safety zone around his growing family of six women and forty-five children.

But while John thought of the future in terms of tighter security, Anna became more unsure. She sat and stared into space in the evenings after the lamps were lit, tapping her fingers on the table and thinking.

"I'll need some money," she told John one night. "I have to buy some new clothes. I'm going to my sisters' for a few weeks, and I'm taking Lenore with me. We'll need train fare for two—a fare and a half. This is the last time she can go for half fare."

John looked dumbstruck. He was not used to Anna asking for things or telling him what she was going to do. "Where am I going to get the money?" John asked, "I don't have a cent!"

"Then you'd better pray," Anna said evenly. "I'll need the cash in about a week."

Not knowing how to cope with this new attitude, John meekly handed over the money when it came in the mail.

We packed our bags and sent the other children in our cabin to the dorms. Then John drove us to Corbin. As we stood in the gray sooty station waiting for a train, I was aware of a struggle going on, silent this time, but strong. John had his future laid out; Anna was going to consult with her sisters—and I was caught in the middle. I walked off a few paces, not wanting to stand too near either of them, to take sides.

The train came, and John gave me that look—that you-won't-leave-me-too-will you look—and kissed me goodbye.

The streets of Corbin began to move slowly by, strange and misplaced when seen from this new angle. Going over the railway underpass instead of going under it, past the backside of the Wilbur hotel, the tankside of the Gulf Oil Company, past the alley behind Mr. Sanders' motel. Then the country, the clanging railroad crossings with patient muddy pickup trucks waiting, the pastures dotted with grazing animals. I leaned back thinking of the look John had given me, and wondered what Chicago would be like. Anna had fixed clothes for me out of the mission barrel, and I hoped I wouldn't run into anyone who had owned then previously. It began to be dark, with red crossing lights flashing past, and Anna asked me if I wanted to eat. I realized I was motion sick, and food sounded terrible.

We chugged on through the night, puffing and hooting, turning and swaying, with the clackety-clack of the wheels on the tracks winding something inside me tighter and tighter. My head ached and I kept walking to the bathroom.

Midnight. We grabbed our bags and began going down the long ramp, heading for the vaulted dome of the Cincinnati station. Inside it echoed with calls over loudspeakers, hundreds of feet rushing, going, coming.

"I . . . I'm thirsty!" I said to Anna suddenly.

"There's a water fountain." she said.

I stood over the fountain, a large marble basin with several drinking spouts. I opened my mouth, and all the green tightness rushed to my head. I leaned over the fountain and vomited.

I looked up and saw a face, only inches from mine, the shiny black face of someone about my age. He was doing the same thing. He looked at me and grinned. "Hey." he said, "you sick too, huh?"

I nodded and smiled. He was the first black child I had ever seen.

It was seven o'clock the next morning when we reached

Chicago, wrinkled and night-worn. Anna knew the way from the train station through the maze of streets to find the right streetcar, and before long we were walking down the sidewalk to Perry Avenue.

Aunt Della's house, the house where I was born. Aunt Della rushed out with arms spread, and smothered us both in her motherly embrace. She was the elder sister, and Anna was almost like her child. Her house was warm and breakfasty, with cousins crowding around us to see this curious aunt and cousin from Kentucky.

Aunt Della put her arm around my shoulders. "What would you like to do first" she asked indulgently.

"Take a bath in your big white tub," I said, and everyone laughed. A strange treat to choose.

But I luxuriated in the white tub of water. Then I rushed out to roller-skate on the street and ride my cousin's bicycle. Last but not least, I borrowed a huge stack of Batman comic books, which were forbidden at home. Uncle Henry gave me a nickel and I bought a pack of gum, also forbidden, and I was all set to enjoy being a Chicago sinner for two whole weeks.

But it seemed strange. The Chicago cousins, for all their gum and Batman comics, had a dimension of reverence in their lives that had been missing in Kentucky. On Sunday morning Aunt Della, Uncle Henry, and all four cousins put on their Sunday best and walked down the street to the stately Dutch church on the corner. Inside, scrubbed people exchanged quiet greetings, then sat in solid rows of families, quietly listening to the solemn music from the majestic organ. The strict reading of the law was tempered by the spicy tang of peppermints being passed along the row. There were sternness and order, but there were also firmness and solid strength. When Dominie Hoekstra stood behind the lectern and read, there was as much humility as power in his voice. I looked around the hushed church, sensing the solidarity of tradition being handed on to the smallest peppermint eater.

How different from our Sundays in Kentucky! We met in the school, smelling of chalk and textbooks, and ground out our tunes on a pump organ. John preached to us, but the measured air of disciplined humility was absent. In many ways we seemed to make up our religion as we went along, bending it to mean what John said it meant. There was none of this feeling of solemnity and weight. And there were no peppermints.

During those days, Anna and her sisters talked seriously. Della sipped her coffee and shook her head. "Hah," she sighed. "The only sister to marry a man who says he's a minister, and the only one to be thinking of a divorce. Too bad."

"I'd have to sue him for adultery," Anna said slowly. "And what would that do to the home?"

"Are you still defending him? Hasn't he caused you enough grief?"

"No. I'm not defending him, but there are forty-five children there now—kids I've taken care of since they were newborn—and I feel a very strong attachment to them, kids like Winston and Phyllis and David. They would have nowhere to go if we didn't take care of them. If I sued him for adultery . . ."

"Let him sit with that! You might have to do it to save your sanity, you know. How old are you now?"

"Twenty-nine. I'll be thirty in June.'

"Oh, Anna! Your life is just beginning! Don't let him wreck the rest of it! You can't help him."

"But what would I do? I gave up going to college to marry him, and now I'm not qualified to do any kind of work."

"Anna, wake up. You were the bright one in the family. There are years ahead of you. You could go back to school."

Anna was crying quietly. "But what would it mean now? So I divorce John and come back here and try to start again. It wouldn't be the same. I couldn't fit in this community anymore. This is the community of people who have done things right. The church-the church your whole life centers on-what would *they* say? You know the feeling about divorce. At thirty I would be a divorcee, a social leper. If I stayed single I'd be shied away from, and if I remarried I'd commit a sin. The church protects the family, but it hasn't much to say when a person's life has fallen apart."

They were quiet, sipping the hot bitter coffee.

"What would happen to Lenore?" Della asked.

"I'd lose her. Her father has a terrible power over her, just as he has over everyone else. She'd leave me. What would my life mean?"

Della reached out a hand and stroked her sister's arm gently. "Take her, and come to live with us." she said finally.

"I can't."

When we visited Aunt Renzina, she was kind but curt.

"Well, you'll have to make up your own mind." she said, pouring coffee. "I told you not to marry that nut, and in my opinion that's exactly what he is, paranoid and schizophrenic with delusions of grandeur. But marry him you would, and you did. Now you've made your bed, and you'll have to sleep in it or get out in the cold."

Aunt Renzina was the second-oldest sister in the Klugman clan. She was a good sort, fortyish, and helpful to a fault. Whenever we were due at her house, she began calling up all the friends and relatives, arranging a tight schedule of visits from morning until night. I was dragged from the Boenders' to Cousin Cora's to the second-furthest relative on Uncle Peter's side of the family until I was stuffed and exhausted.

"Good grief!" I wailed to Anna. "Why can't we just come and see her?" Why do we have to go see all these other people I don't even know?"

"You have to take Aunt Ren as she comes," soothed Anna. "She's really a very kind person, under her frankness. She'd give me the shirt off her back."

I could believe it. Aunt Renzina had never forgotten to send me a birthday present or a Christmas gift. She had no children of her own and had taken on as her responsibility the less affluent of the nieces and nephews. Her responsibility to me, as she saw it, was to make sure I read every children's classic in print: *Little Women, Treasure Island, Uncle Tom's Cabin. The Swiss Family Robinson.* These and more stood on my bookshelf, presents from

Aunt Ren. Thanks to her I sobbed through *Beautiful Joe* and *Black Beauty*, explored with Robinson Crusoe, and sailed the skies with Mary Poppins. However matter-of-fact she might be, she provided my escape to fantasy.

Aunt Alice wore bright red lipstick which she got all over my face. Uncle Henry came home at noon and slept on the couch with a pillow over his ear. Uncle Rich sat in a leather chair, his eyes red from too much beer, talking to his repulsive little pug dog Toots. He called me Toots, and he called his daughter who was my age Toots. There seemed to be myriads of relatives. They gathered at Aunt Della's house, hordes of uncles enveloped in clouds of smoke, droves of aunts eating and weighing and laughing and chatting. The uncles spoke in low undertones, laughing conspiratorially, the aunts compared their weights and fashions and pregnancies. The cousins ate and skated and rode bikes and read comics and traded Cracker-Jack prizes and fought. I felt as if I were in another orphanage, only this time I was related to everyone. I belonged, just because I had been born.

One morning when we were at Aunt Ren's, I was skating past the garage looking at Uncle Peter's pickle barrels, and I flew off a drop in the sidewalk with my right arm bent under me. It hurt, but I didn't want to tell Anna, because I wanted to go bike riding that afternoon.

After lunch I put on a jacket to hide the swelling and got on a bicycle. Crazily. I lurched out into a busy street. A car honked and its brakes screeched. I dropped the bike. The handlebar came down on my sore arm. I groaned. Now there was no way to hide what had happened.

Anna gasped when she saw me. "Good Lord, what will your father say? And your right arm too!"

I was so absorbed in what everyone else was saying, for once I didn't worry about what John would say. Aunt Renzina was running around in her ankle socks and high heels, putting ice packs on my arm. Then she drove us to Cousin Cora's to put a sun lamp on it. Everyone had an opinion as to what should be done, and by the time they finally took me to the doctor the arm was so swollen the jacket had to be cut off. I had a compound fracture.

But I was rather proud of having a broken bone, or rather a bone broken roller-skating in Chicago. It smacked of comic books and chewing gum, with just a touch of peppermint. I could hardly wait to get back to Kentucky to show off my cast. The only thing that dampened my enthusiasm was a vision of Miss Smith looking over the classroom as if there were solid rows of casts and saying in her best New England voice, "There will be no allowances made for those of us who have been rash enough to acquire broken bones. The math assignment is . . ."

When we returned, Anna was quiet and reserved. She collected the five small children who had become her charges and settled into life in the cabin, for better or worse. As she usually did to mark a new period in her life, she ordered new white curtains from the catalogue, and hung them clean and fresh in every window. She also hung up a plaque that one of the aunts had given her. It was made of brown colored plaster framed with blue morning glories, and it said: IN QUIETNESS AND CONFIDENCE SHALL BE YOUR STRENGTH.

Personally, I had never believed in quietness as a way of getting things done, but when I looked at Anna and at the plaque, it seemed she was waiting, knowing, depending on something I did not quite understand.

"You don't have to shout the truth." I had heard her say to her sisters. "It will speak for itself, sooner or later."

While Anna was away, John had been planning his kingdom. He had talked to Snow Hensley about his farm, but Snow refused to move. Then John had Nada type a letter asking about the river land, but old Doc Sears wrote back and said the timber rights had been sold and the land was not for sale. When he learned that the Gibbs family had sold their land to Mrs. Gibb's brother-in-law, who owned Tripplet's store in Corbin, he went to Fessor Tripplet and asked what he would take for it.

"Well." said Fessor, shuffling his big unbuckled boots, "I reckon I might take fifteen hundred for it."

"I'll give you a thousand," John said, who as usual didn't have a dime. But the price didn't sound right to Fessor, and the matter was dropped.

The next time John went in to buy groceries, Fessor brought up the subject. "Ought to buy that farm of mine," he said while packing up the groceries.

"What's your best price?" John bartered.

"Well, me and the old lady was talkin', and seein' as you're doin' a pretty good thing out there, maybe we'll sell for a thousand."

John stood and blinked, unable to believe it. "I'll take it," he said. "What shall I put down?"

Fessor waved his big hand. "Aw, your credit's good." He grinned offhandedly.

That week John paid one hundred dollars. A few days later the mail brought the news that a friend of Nada's father had died and left the home exactly one thousand dollars.

John was jubilant. He walked the hills and hollows of the home with a defiant new fire in his eyes. His prayers had been heard. God approved of him. Who then could disapprove?

He laid out his moves, one by one. The Sears land, in his mind, was the next conquest.

That summer Miss Smith went back to Massachusetts for a vacation. There had been a running argument between her and John about training the children's voices for a choir. John insisted that the folding organ, which to the ears of the mountain people gave the music a wailing quality, should be abandoned in favor of a cappella singing.

Miss Smith insisted it could not be done, that the children would go flat without any instrumental accompaniment, and the result would be a disaster.

So that summer while she was gone he collected two dozen of us and went up to the ridge beyond the dorm where the land was staked out for a new building.

"There's going to be a church here someday." He told us. "And you're going to be the choir. We're going to have two choir lofts facing each other, and you're going to sing in antiphonal style."

We looked at one another, wondering what in the world that was. None of us knew, but if John said we were going to sing in antiphonal style, we believed it.

He worked with us all summer, sorting us into parts, shouting, smiling, cajoling, sweating, charming, and getting angry by turns, until, building on the group's natural ability and Miss Smith's patient training around the organ, he hammered out an a cappella choir. When she returned, he lined us up in the main room of the dorm and had us perform.

She nodded and smiled and brought out a pitch pipe and sounded a mellow tone. "Hmmmmmm. Only half a step flat," she said. We crowded around her to get a look at the small silver instrument she had brought back, and she was again the center of our musical life.

I looked at her, admiring her ability to handle a man like John. She gave him the impression that she did not care two cents for him personally, but she was half a step ahead of him in implementing his ideas. Some women had a knack.

She also had a very flat chest.

It was a preoccupation of ours, as we grew, to examine the underwear of the various adults as it dried on the clothesline. We never did this openly, but covertly, in passing, and we talked about it in secret. It was the consensus that Nada was overpowering, Clara about right, and Miss Smith small and compact. Strangely enough, their placement in the power structure seemed to bear some relation to their bust measurements. It wasn't hard to figure out. Alice the laundress (whose blouse bagged) had left, and a new worker named Molly came. She was a teacher for the children in the lowest grades and hung out tiny bras. It figured. We all concluded that big boobs meant power, and determined to grow as big as we could.

In the meanwhile, a secondhand piano was moved into the main room at the girls dorm, and Miss Smith began to give piano lessons on Saturday. Being the best in music could confer a kind of power too, and Carlita. Maxine, Pearl, and I practiced hard, half out of love for music and half out of fierce competition. In the spring Miss Smith held a music recital, with all the pomp and ceremony associated with such occasions. The main room was festooned with peach blossoms, and the boys, clean and miserable, had to sit yawning and scratching through the whole thing. They never forgave us, and died of relief when they smelled a skunk outside and had a legitimate reason for laughing. It was decided that Carlita and I both had definite musical promise. As a result, I couldn't decide whether to be an artist or a musician, in view of my secret promise to the Legendary Grandfather. But he sang as well as painted, and I felt that following either path would be loyal to him, would carry out that search for beauty which would save me from being sucked into nothingness.

Gram had given me a set of beginner's oils for Christmas, and it was like a secret signal between us. In the evenings when the grounds were quiet. I began to gravitate to the room in the laundry where Aunt Molly now lived. She was a kind woman with a worried face and terribly thick glasses. At night she was totally blind, and had to be led around by the hand between dorms, but during the day or by the light of the lamps she could see quite well. She would trace and cut out handwork for her kindergartners for the next day, and I would copy a picture off a carton or apple crate using my new box of paints. It seemed a far cry from being a portrait painter, but at least it was a start.

"Do you think I could teach myself to paint?" I asked her.

"I believe you could do anything you really tried to do," she said, cutting out construction-paper rabbits.

"Well. I feel this way about it," I confided to her. "Nowadays people have teachers to teach them everything, but there must have been a time way back in the beginning when the first teacher was born. I mean, he wasn't born a teacher, but he had an idea, and he picked up a brush or a stick and he made something. Somebody had to be the starter. And after that, people taught each other. So there had to be *ideas* before there were *teachers.*"

"You'll be some kind of an artist all right," she said. "And when you're grown and rich and famous . . ."

She went on, and I felt like kissing her out of pure gratitude, but I only stared at the burnt sienna mess I was making and felt a warm glow.

All this time, John was busy trying to get Snow Hensley to swap for the farm we had just bought from Fessor Tripplet. Snow wanted to, but his wife, Sary Jane, refused, sensing it was her presence John wanted to be rid of. So every Sunday afternoon John took us for walks on the land by the river. The countryside was beautiful, rolling hills with lush timber, cool rushing streams bounding toward the lazy brown waters of the Laurel, and large mysterious caves. One cave in particular was a source of fascination. It was at least a hundred feet high at the entrance and curved like a huge bandshell. A creek fell over it near the center, making a splashing waterfall that ended in a crystal pool. The floor was soft and powdery and strewn with rocks that smelled like gunpowder when we rubbed them together. We loved to take picnics and eat in the cave, shedding our shoes and running through the cool water afterward. The water was clear, and clean enough to drink when we caught it in our mouths.

John would collect us around him in the cave when we were tired. "Would you like to own this?" he asked.

"Yes!" we all shouted, and the cave rang with the echo of our voices: *Yes, yes, yes!*

"Then pray!" he said. "Pray that God will give us this land. Believe that He will do it, and the land will be ours!"

We prayed.

The choir was becoming well known. Every local "all day singin'" and "graveyard decoratin'" featured the voices of the Galilean Home. Word spread to Corbin that the orphans on the Bee Creek could sing like angels. The First Christian Church invited us to sing for them, and we piled into the Dodge farm truck that was our new acquisition and arranged ourselves on the rows of benches. At the First Christian Church, with its Ionic pillars, we climbed out of the truck, marched into the church, and sang. Soon after, a church in Covington, Kentucky, invited us to come for a weekend and sing in a series of special meetings. The church people would feed us and put us up.

It was our first long-distance public appearance, and we were terribly excited. Nada pressed all the boys "singin' britches" and carefully matched their shirts and suspenders. The girls' dresses were starched and ironed, and the polished shoes stood in long rows. Miss Smith rehearsed us until we were hoarse and the boys started going flat. Anna made dozens of chocolate cupcakes and a huge dishpan of potato salad. Then, with the blue farm truck washed and waxed, we climbed aboard and headed for the big city.

It began to rain, and we had to stop and tie the tarpaulin on the truck. Only the lucky ones on the sides could look out between the cracks of the truckbed and see the sights. We sang until we were sleepy, and then took turns pressing our noses against the cracks to see. Just under the tarpaulin was another crack, and we formed a second waiting line. When it was my turn, I stared out at the miles of gray wet pavement sliding under the truck. It was as though we were standing still and the road was sliding backward under us. It made me dizzy, and I gave my place to the next person.

"All those miles of roads," I said to Miss Smith. "Don't you ever wonder where they go, and who goes on them, and why? I mean, where is everybody going, and what will they do when they get there?"

She looked at me strangely. I don't think she knew what I meant.

"You should study the map of northern Kentucky more closely," she said. "There's one in the back of the school."

It was dark when we stopped for gas. The back of the truck was still covered, and the rain pelted down on the tarpaulin. Most of us were asleep, but there was still a muttering and a chatter of voices.

The truck door slammed, and John got out. A man came from the station and began to fill the gas tank. "What you got in there, a load of chickens?" he asked in a friendly voice.

"No, that's my family," said John.

"Your family?" the attendant said. "What the hell you mean by that?"

"I have fifty children." John explained. "I'm a preacher from . . ."

The conversation floated in broken bits. The hose clicked back in its place near the rear of the truck, and we heard the station attendant mutter, "Fifty kids! My Lord. I always did think these mountain preachers was a screwed-up bunch, but that beats all hell."

The trip to Covington was a musical success, but it embarrassed John. The truck was good enough for the farm, but he could see that for transporting his family it was hardly appropriate. He began to dream of something better, and one day he stopped at the Dodge garage in Corbin to get information on a school bus. The one he picked out cost four thousand dollars. He brought home a picture of the yellow bus, and had me cut it out and paste it on a sheet of blue construction paper. Underneath it I was instructed to cut out four letters in yellow that spelled PRAY. John hung it in the dining room by his reading post.

This time Nada jumped him. I don't know whether she had her nose out of joint because the picture had been put up without her consent, or whether we really were in debt, but she turned on John.

"You know we can't afford that!" she said, pulling the thumbtacks out of the picture. We all gasped. Nada never crossed him.

"We'll have to," he said stubbornly. "I've already placed the order."

"Well you'd better cancel it, or get someone else to keep the books!" She flounced across the dining-room floor, shaking everything north of her belt with enormous emphasis.

John trotted after her, and they went down the hill, leaving the bus picture swinging by one tack. They were arguing loudly. We were aghast. The two top powers were at war. They kept it up for a few weeks, and finally Nada talked him into canceling the order.

But when he went back to the garage to cancel it, the dealer shook his head. "Can't do it now. Preacher." he said. "The chassis has been delivered to the body works. Can't be canceled now without a lot of trouble."

"Okay, let 'er go." John said.

It was the first time he had risked Nada's disapproval.

Rumors were going around about John and Nada. We all knew that she influenced him more than anyone else at the home did, but kids began to see things.

Stumpy had already turned thirteen and was as short as ever. I had never heard him mention either of his parents again after the day he came, or talk about what had happened to his father, but one day when we were coming out of school he stopped me. "Can I see you a minute?" he asked, his face white under the freckles.

I looked around a bit nervously. Boys were not supposed to talk to girls privately, and Miss Smith had orders to enforce this law. I stepped around the corner of the schoolhouse. "What is it?" I whispered.

"You know, it wasn't really the saddle they was fightin' over, my daddy and my uncle, it was my mother. It don't look so good, you know, to see somebody's brains busted out."

"Stump, what are you talking about?"

"I seen somethin' down at the dorm between Daddy and Mamma Nada. She ain't his woman and he oughtn't to do that. It ain't right what he's doin', and somebody's goin' to get hurt!"

Stumpy was sweating, and he looked sick. I wanted to put my arm around him and tell him it was okay, but I was scared someone would see me.

I thought about it all afternoon, and the more I thought the better it seemed to go directly to John. He was beginning to trust me, to rely on my help. The least I could do was to tell him if people were talking about him. I had wanted an excuse to say something to him about Nada for a long time, and now I could just say that other people were raising questions.

I walked into his room boldly and told him that people were talking about him and Nada, and that if he expected the kids to respect him, he ought to be careful.

His face colored a deep red. "Exactly who is talking?" he asked. "And what are they saying"

I hadn't figured on this. I couldn't tell on Stumpy. He would be in trouble, maybe even be sent away.

"Oh, everyone." I laughed. "It's just . . . talk!"

"I'll get to the bottom of this," he said angrily. "I see there's been more of this jealousy and plotting against me!"

A shot of panic ran through me. It had been a long time since the last gang whipping, but none of us had forgotten. "Don't make any trouble!" I begged. "Just be careful."

But John called a meeting at the dining hall.

"I hear that there has been gossip about me and a certain worker," he said threateningly. "Does anyone have anything to say?"

We all looked at one another and looked away. Who would be foolish enough to speak up? What could we prove? It was absolutely quiet. Nobody said a word.

I wanted to crawl under the table. I resolved that in the future I would not be my father's keeper.

John roamed the woods that fall like a lost soul. Often he stayed out all night, and we never knew if he was at Nada's or out in the forest praying for the river land and money for the bus.

Just before Christmas news came from a lawyer in Williamsburg that old Doc Sears had died and had remembered the home in his will. He left us all the river land, and eight thousand dollars. John's face shone like an angel's . He had his land, could pay cash for the bus, and start building again with what was left over. Strengthened by his new sureness, he even talked the Hensleys into swapping for the Gibbs farm and was rid of Sary Jane.

Now his authority was solid and unchallenged for miles around. He had over five hundred acres of land, four thousand dollars, fifty children, three vehicles, three houses, two women, and the favor of God. His power was becoming absolute.

He had even humbled Nada.

A new building appeared next to our cabin, called the study. It was John's private dwelling, his castle. It contained one room with a desk and a bed, one reception room, and a washroom. Hallie had grown into a buxom teenager, and she was the first to have the job of cleaning the study. John said he had moved out there because our cabin was full and spilling over. He joked about having to move into the doghouse, but we could see he was not suffering. There was a new twinkle in his eye, a new confidence in his step. He did what he did for his own reasons. And because he clearly had some mystic authority on his side, no one dared question him.

The war ended that year, and Army surplus goods became

available. John bought a set of Army field phones, and a young man from Chicago named Hank came to install them for us. He tramped the woods, first with John and then by himself, installing the phones in the dorms, the cabin, and the study. He was a tall good-looking Dutchman with a shock of blond hair falling over his eyes, gentle and goodnatured, quiet and kind, masculine and rugged, and every girl over six adored him.

Aunt Clara, of the apple-slices fame, particularly adored him. In the building spurt a house had been erected on the next ridge over from the girls dorm and Aunt Clara had been put there with the smaller boys. It was a long way from the central dining room, and sometimes she did not want to make the trek twice a day with the little ones. One baby named Danny was quite badly retarded, and she had formed the habit of staying away from the dining room at noon rather than carry him all the way there.

But when Hank came, Clara's interest in mealtimes was renewed. She asked if any of the older girls would take her place with Danny at lunch. Since being twelve classified me as "older," I magnanimously volunteered for the job, bowling her over with my willingness. My first ulterior motive was to see if Clara really would fall in love with Hank and what John would do about it, but the second, and perhaps the stronger, was my curiosity about Aunt Clara's books. She had the only uncensored library on the grounds, and I had seen it. There were real love stories in it. The first time I babysat for her, I quickly took care of Danny, put him to bed for his nap, and selected a book. Time was short, so I flipped through it until I found an exciting passage, then read it over and over, my juices flowing. Every such passage had been removed from the books at school, even the classics. Stories ended abruptly, pictures were missing, paragraphs were blocked out in black. But here, when it came to the proper place, the hero and Heroine kissed, or he touched her hand, or even sometimes the small of her back. That one really got me. *He touched the small of her back.* I shivered from head to toe.

The romance between Hank and Clara blossomed, and the field phones were finished. We could crank a handle at the girls' dorm and call the Vogel house, the study, the boys' dorm, or the new dorm. There was no need for the time-honored practice of calling from hill to hill. His work finished, Hank reluctantly left. But he wrote, and John handed the letters to Clara stormily, letting her know he did not approve. Then one day John called Clara on the new phone and said he was coming to talk to her. He arrived at the new dorm and laid down an ultimatum. Either she stopped this nonsense with Hank, which was having bad effect on everyone, or she would leave.

She left, quite happily.

Afterward John called all of us together and lectured us on the choices one had in life. Either one could choose to follow God and give oneself in service, as Nada and the others had, or one could be tempted by the lusts of the flesh and follow the devil. Clearly Aunt Clara had forsaken God and His calling and had given in to the "lust of the flesh, the lust of the eyes, and the pride of life." Aunt Clara would be judged.

When Clara and Hanks' wedding picture came, it was considered contraband and we were not allowed to see it.

Out of the distant mists of Chicago came a letter from Gram. She and Grandpa Will had raised their joint son, Peter, and now were ready to do something different with their lives. They offered to sell their home by the railroad tracks, bring the money, and join our Kentucky group. We were delighted. Having grandparents around made everything seem a bit safer. Christina thought it would be heaven on earth because Gram and Grandpa Will loved her in a special way ever since they had cared for her as a baby. To John, Christina was an object of historical interest, the "thing" that had started the home. To Grandpa Will she was "mine old girl."

Gram's coming caused a general shake-up. The boys in the newest dorm were moved to the county school building, and the grandparents moved to the new dorm. It became known as Gram and Gramp's, and as a haven from the troubles of a puzzling world.

The swirl of adults and children continued. A few, like Aunt Clara, chose the world, the flesh, and the devil; but more sprang up in their tracks. There were two new dorm mothers for the girls, one who fell asleep at prayers every night, and one who was always ironing. There were more aunts than an antheap, and we accepted each of them with a nod of the head and a quick appraisal. Were they strict? Did they have false teeth? Did they wear a girdle? Some were good, some dull, some cross, some social rejects who could hardly have survived in the outside world. One was very short and fat, one always had diarrhea, one had repetitive speech patterns and hitched up her glasses whenever she talked. There were all kinds. The only men who came to work were married, and they were considered safe.

Then Aunt Kay came . . .

Front the beginning we knew she was different. She came from Washington. D.C., one summer to help out with the vacation activities, and we begged her to stay forever. There was a gentleness about her, a playfulness in the way she wrinkled her nose when she laughed. She was a hugger, with an indefinable charisma.

After her first summer she decided to stay, and she became the teacher for the upper grades. I was a lucky seventh grader.

A huge new dining hall was being built. One of the rooms on the second floor was finished as a classroom, and this was designated as Aunt Kay's room. It became the center of meaning for many of us.

I was in the throes of growing up. Maturing anywhere is a

trauma, but trying to grow up in the atmosphere which surrounded us was disastrous. The day John decided I needed a bra I almost died.

I was wearing a silk dress, and John thought I looked indecent in it because of my budding bosom. He told Anna to take me to town and buy me some proper undergarments. She took me to the dime store, and I slid along behind her in hot embarrassment while she purchased a 30-A. When we got home I hid in the closet, feverishly trying to get it on with all the clothes hanging in my face. It was too big. It hung there making wrinkles under my clothes. I was mortified. I would be the only woman in history who wore a quadruple-A bra.

I went to dinner with my shoulders hunched, afraid someone would know I had the thing on. If anyone ever saw it hanging on the line, I knew I'd die. It classified me as completely powerless.

We were all growing taller except for Maxine, who still looked like an angelic child. On the cow-feed scales at the barn I weighed almost a hundred pounds. Everyone said I was tall. Homer was the only boy in school taller than I, and we started being friendly again. It was dangerous, but I began giving him sly glances when Aunt Kay wasn't looking. Then I discovered we didn't have to be sly. In her classes romances were not forbidden. No one said anything, we just knew. Homer was physically large for his age. His voice had deepened, and he still had those wonderfully wicked eves.

Everything in Aunt Kay's class had an edge of excitement. Math, which I detested, suddenly became a challenge and I started getting A's. English was fun, but she was even worse than Miss Smith about not tolerating improper grammar. We had long hot arguments about the use of I and me, but Aunt Kay never got angry or put us down. She would say I was a stubborn hot-headed rascal, but then she would laugh and wrinkle her nose and I knew I was okay in spite of it.

By eighth grade I would have walked the plank for her. She

was such a good teacher she even made Bible study interesting, thanks to her rare blend of personal religion, scientific savvy, and common sense. I could hardly believe any one person would have them all.

Betsy had grown up too. A decree had gone out from the office that all girls were to have the tips of their bras sewed down flat, but Betsy was only twelve and didn't wear a bra although she was quite developed for her age and wore tight sweaters. She let her perky nipples poke against her sweater and enjoyed the boys' fascinated stares.

One day we were kneeling by our desks after a very inspiring lesson. The kerosene stove was glowing warmly and the room was cozy. A movement next to me caught my attention and I opened my eyes. I saw Homer punch Betsy. The next thing I knew, his pants were open and he was exposing himself. Then he saw me and pulled his sweater down.

I was incensed. Homer was mine. If he was going to expose himself, he could at least show me, not Betsy. Of course I would have refused him, but he could at least have given me first rights of refusal.

At supper that night the news was out. Homer had met Betsy under the dining hall and done it to her. Someone had seen them. Homer was packed up and banished to his sister's house in town the next morning, and Aunt Kay was accused of promoting loose behavior. It seemed a sad end to a beautiful relationship, I thought, but then, what did one expect of men?

I decided to give them up and devote myself to the cultivation of my mind.

Only Janey and I were left in the eighth grade, and since we were the only ones graduating I became the valedictorian and she the salutatorian. I chose as the subject of my speech "The Alimentary Canal."

When I brought the title to Aunt Kay for her approval, she struggled to look grave. "I know you've enjoyed studying this subject," she said carefully, "but do you think you could give it another title?"

"How about 'I Am Fearfully and Wonderfully Made?'" I suggested, "in the psalms-"

"But this is a speech, not a sermon," she objected. "You don't have to have a scripture text to back it up."

"Don't you?" I said. It had never occurred to me that I could say something in public without the Bible to make it valid. John never did.

Aunt Kay worked on the speech with me. I wrote it up to the point where the food got to the lower intestine, and then I didn't know what to do with it. I couldn't stand up in front of everyone with my corsage pinned on and tell about the next stage.

Puzzled, I stopped reading the paper and looked at Aunt Kay.

"Where do I take it from here?" I asked seriously.

It was more than she could control. Suddenly her grave sympathetic mask broke and she was convulsed with laughter. I began to laugh too, and the two of us laughed until our bellies ached.

Nonetheless, the graduation was conducted with due solemnity. Janey and I stood up in our new pink dresses, $5.95 from J. C. Penney's, and received our honors. I took the alimentary canal as far as I could and ended in the psalms. Everyone thought it was wonderful.

Then came the matter of high school. Janey began working at the office, taking typing, shorthand, and filing, but I became a problem. A county school bus came down the Bee Creek road to pick up high school students and transport them to town, but John would not hear of my taking it.

"We've protected these children from evil all these years, and now I'm not going to throw them into a public high school!" he declared. "It's like throwing them body and soul into the pit of hell!"

I was getting old enough to talk back. "How do you know so much about it?" I asked. "Did you spend a wild wicked youth in some sinful high school?"

"Not me." he said. "I was always the loner. I even got into trouble because I wouldn't undress in front of the other boys in gym class. I was always out of it."

"Well, I don't want to be out of it." I said. "I want to be in it!"

"You don't know what you're talking about," he said darkly.

"Then what am I going to do?" I said, near tears. "Where am I going to go to school?"

Anna came out of her blanket of quiet and tried. "John, I think this is an important step in Lenore's life. Why don't we let her go to Chicago and stay with my sister Della? Della has offered, and Lenore could go to the parochial school in Chicago with Della's kids."

"I see this has all been discussed behind my back," John said hotly. Why don't you take her and go? If she goes, you go with her, and neither of you ever need come back. What would she be like after four years of exposure to the world? She'd never fit in here again!"

"But John, how can you sacrifice the child's future?"

"I said, Take her and go!" he replied. "Or let it be up to her. Why don't you ask her what she wants to do-go with you or stay with me?"

They put the question to me. I was frightened. An education, which I had always considered my natural right, had suddenly become invested with the responsibility for my parents marriage. I knew I was important to Anna, to her sense of herself. I also was deeply under John's influence, and I sensed that for the present it would be best to keep his approval. This, along with a genuine if confused affection for him, blurred my thinking.

"I'll stay." I said. "if it's going to cause all that trouble. But what am I going to do for school?"

John got Nada to make inquiries, and it was decided to enroll me in the Calvert School in Chicago, a correspondence school used by young people in isolated places to get a high school education. I also strongly suspected it was used by hunchbacks and forty-five year-old people with pink and purple striped faces. At fourteen I began to feel like a social misfit.

I walked the woods kicking the trees with desperate helpless anger. I wondered why there was no one to help me, no one stronger than I to say what was right. Why, for once, would Anna not stand up to John? Why would she not fight for me? Was there not some impartial power, were there no laws to prevent this kind of thing? Anna had too much at stake personally to take my part against John, and that was the problem. She must have known that if I were publicly asked to choose, I would betray her, would choose John, for some reason more complex than I understood. She did not dare stand up for me, because I would leave her too, and she would be alone.

Grandpa Will began to take over the care of the gardens and flowers. Under his skilled hands the blossoms began to flourish. Up and down the road and along the pasture fence, zinnias and petunias, larkspur and begonias flashed their colors. He came and hoed every day, wearing his little Dutchman's hat and carrying a pocketful of peppermints. I grew fond of him, not in place of the Legendary Grandfather but as a person on his own. He and Gram were both tiny people, barely five feet tall. At fourteen I was five inches taller than either of them, and I began to feel like a great stupid giant, far above my feet, looking down on the ground, which grew farther and farther away from me. I was terrified of my body and was ashamed of my inquiring mind, which John declared was the enemy of faith.

The first lessons came in a brown paper envelope. Books came, and I began to study, sprawled on a blanket out in the woods under the Indian summer sky. American literature with its singing lines fascinated me, and I read the whole book through in one gulp. I was obstinately searching for knowledge, the magic key to freedom. The miracles of biology thrilled me like a love story, and I read. The world was a marvelous beautiful place after all, and I was beginning to understand it. No one could stop me now. No one could make me ashamed or imprison my mind. It was the part of me that would be free.

Yet sometimes I lay on the blanket and cried in anger, stung with a longing I could only define with some subconscious part of me, the longing to be in touch with wholeness, with integrity.

We went to town to buy supplies, and I saw them, the typical high school students, hanging around the drugstore, beautiful and profane. I saw them sipping Cokes at the soda fountain, or crowded into a booth laughing and carelessly wearing their school sweaters with the big C. I saw their faces bright with lipstick and mascara, and then I caught a glimpse of my face, withdrawn and lifeless, pale and frightened—no makeup allowed—and I felt older than the mountains. I would be allowed no youth, no foolishness, no chance to be evil. I was a prisoner of good.

I went home and looked in the mirror again. Since I had no makeup I pinched chimney soot out of the fireplace and tried to darken my blond brows and lashes. I bit my lips and slapped my cheeks, trying to force color into them. I peered sideways into the mirror, imagining myself crowded into a drugstore booth with laughing boys and girls my age. The pain was too intense, and I scrubbed the whole sooty business off and went back to the books. If anything ever got me out of this complex tangle, it would be the ability to understand myself, my world, and the people around me. Chimney soot or any other makebelieve would only cover up the real problem.

CHAPTER SIX

People were becoming curious about these orphans who lived by faith and sang like angels, and about the shy wonderful man who was Daddy to them all. Sunday afternoons we could no longer go on walks to the river or run through the caves. Visitors came, and we had to be on display.

As in any zoo, it was a two-way stare. They observed us, and we eyed them. When the reporter from the Knoxville newspaper arrived, I gazed at his wise face with its small black mustache, wondering what it would be like to have a face that exciting and free.

"He's probably very ungodly," I said to Maxine with a twinge of envy.

"Probably," she agreed. Maxine seldom disagreed with anything I said.

It had all started when we took in Barbara Hatfield. One day a woman from Barbourville asked to talk to John. She told him a sordid story of a young child, not more than seven, who had been born in the shanty section of town and for the last few years allowed to run wild. Several people had caught glimpses of this long-haired wildeyed creature, but no one had been able to get close enough to see if it was male or female, human or animal.

One day when this woman was pouring slop into her pig trough, she saw the child dart out from the barn fence and fight the pigs for choice scraps from the slop. She and a neighbor cornered it and called the country authorities. They in turn suggested our home as a place for her.

Barbara was more animal than human when she arrived. She walked in a half-crouch, as though she were accustomed to running along the ground on all fours. Her bottom lip drooped, her eyebrows were bushy, and her glance was half afraid, half insolent. Her hands hung down loosely at her sides, and her hair stuck out in bristles. She was the closest to a wild thing one could imagine.

"Who's going to take care of her?" we asked one another.

Even our social system seemed inadequate for such a child, although we were well organized now, with every teenaged girl responsible for three or four little ones. Every morning the older girls laid out clean clothes for their young charges, helped them dress, took them to breakfast, and saw that they ate properly. In the evening each of us was responsible for bathing our own little ones, washing their socks, and making them feel loved and protected. It was a good system and provided individual care for the younger children. But no one dared to be Barbara's "big girl." and it was decided that an adult had to be directly responsible for her.

We tried to talk to Barbara, but for the first few days she seemed to understand little and would only reply with a grunted "uh" or "uh-uh." The dorm mother tried to bathe her, but she fought like a frightened cat being drowned. When some of the girls tried to wash and curl her hair, she pulled all the curlers out and threw them away, tearing out handfuls of hair in the process. She grabbed food and ate with her hands. For weeks we were afraid of her. She would bite viciously when she was angry or felt threatened, and her nails had to be cut very short because she clawed like a cat. But bit by bit she began to calm down. She began to talk in short sentences as though she were recalling a language she once knew, and one day she smiled and offered a piece of bread to the child next to her. She was beginning to be human.

Barbara was one of the survivors of the famous Hatfield clan of the Hatfield-McCoy feud, and it was because of her that Burt Vincent, the newspaper reporter, came to the home. He sat in the study and talked to John, was taken for a tour of the buildings, heard the stories of the miraculous gifts of money and land, saw the neatly creosoted buildings and the well-hoed flowers. He saw the small children flocking around Daddy Vogel, the beautiful faces of Winston and Phyllis, and John's gentle treatment of them.

He heard the children sing, and he was genuinely moved. When he returned to Knoxville he wrote two articles about the home in his column.

Through the mysterious channels of mass communications, the article was picked up by a radio program in New York City called *We The People*, which was sponsored by the Gulf Oil Company. They could not reach us by telephone, but they sent word out from Corbin that John was to call them about appearing on their program. When he returned from phoning, he told us that he and Anna, Barbara and Phyllis were to go to New York. Everyone was excited.

The Corbin Times-Tribune, catching the excitement, published the following story:

> Mr, and Mrs. John Vogel, of the Galilean Children's Home, will leave Thursday for New York City where they will appear on the *We the People program*. CBS. 9 PM, next Thursday. Accompanying the Vogels is their daughter Lenore, little Phyllis of the home, and a seven year-old of special interest. This is the girl who wandered homeless for over a year and became animal-like. Mr. Vogel gives credit for the invitation to Burt Vincent. *Knoxville News-Sentinel*, who recently devoted two of his columns to a description of the home.

> To demonstrate Corbin's support of a worthy cause and the big heartedness of its people, a group of local merchants has decided to outfit both Mr. and Mrs. Vogel from head to foot. From a previous item in this paper, it was learned that the invitation did not include expenses for the Vogels' daughter, Lenore. The employees of the L&N Railroad shops decided that her expenses will be paid by them. The employees of the *Times-Tribune* asked to join in the fund-raising when word came that C. A. Black, local distributor for Gulf, had offered to pay her way and is doing so with a sizable check.

All this is a splendid tribute to the Vogels for the fine manner in which they and their workers have conducted the home. The value of this home to Corbin cannot be estimated. Many children, at present more than sixty, have been provided with wholesome food, adequate clothing, good shelter, and a Christian training. Otherwise many of them would have become public charges or menaces to society.

The appearance on *We the People* will no doubt be of great value to the home, and reflect credit on Corbin and vicinity. Everything considered, this trip is a prize indeed, and We the People of Corbin rejoice with them.

It was February 1948 when the five of us boarded the train in Corbin. We were an oddly matched group, ill at ease with one another. John and Anna behaved with the politeness of strangers. There was tension between John and me over the school situation and between Anna and me because she hadn't the courage to stand up for her rights or mine. The two girls barely knew each other and could hardly have been more of a contrast: Phyllis, a beautiful brown-eyed child who had been one of the war babies and had grown into a quick-witted five-year-old, and Barbara the flatfooted seven-year-old semi-human. Both were nicely dressed, but no matter what Anna put on Barbara it seemed to come unfastened, and she looked like a chimp in a costume. Her belts hung, her shoes were unlaced, her hair refused to behave. She turned on the water faucet in the train washroom and didn't know how to turn if off, so stuck her finger in it, thoroughly dousing everyone. In the train she licked the window clean so she could see out. Phyllis was alternately amused and terrified by her actions. But no matter what Barbara did, I was glad to be assigned to baby-sitting in order to avoid empty conversation with my parents.

New York, and the Plaza Hotel. It was such a contrast to the hills of Kentucky. I was struck dumb. The public relations people, the taxicabs, the guided tours, the stage, the smooth-spoken announcer, devilishly handsome. The script. Fortunately I had not been expected and had no part in the performance. Everyone called me a pretty girl, and I was in a state of trauma. The breathtakingly handsome announcer told me my slip was showing and I rushed out a stage door hoping never to see anyone I knew again.

I perspired profusely. John gave me money to buy deodorant, which embarrassed me more. My face was constantly red.

We got through the program, Phyllis charming everyone and Barbara performing like a curiosity. I was amazed to see that the people in the studio audience were told when and how much to applaud. When it was all over, Lauritz Melchior, who had been on the program as well, sat on stage with Phyllis on his lap.

Anna brought a tall sophisticated woman over to where I stood and introduced me to her. I simply stared, thoroughly confused.

The woman nodded sympathetically at Anna. "Oh, I'm sorry, my dear. Doesn't your daughter speak?"

The sudden rush of anger I felt was the only thing that could have cleared my head. "Yes, ma'am I do speak," I said loudly. "But what in the world is a person to say, with all this going on?"

We went through Chinatown and saw Oriental faces. I had never seen an Asian. They looked wicked and beautiful. John said they worshiped idols and were under the power of the devil. I felt relieved, and justified in being afraid of them. Then, just before we left New York, Anna and I had a few hours to shop. Mr. Black of Gulf Oil in Corbin had given me some spending money, and I bought a turquoise gabardine dress with a nail-studded belt. For the first time since I was a child, I actually had a piece of clothing I was proud of.

But it was good to get home a few days later. The white dogwood and the yellow-green of the weeping willows along the creek were beginning to crack through the brownness of winter, and the hills had never looked so beautiful. I breathed in the peace of the mountains. In contrast to the city with its traffic jams and its tense people, Kentucky seemed like heaven. For months after coming back I felt nothing but relief to be hidden again. Here at home there was agony and quiet suffering, but out there in the vast wasteland of the world, the flesh, and the devil, who knew what evil went on? Any known misery was better that the threatening unknown.

The publicity created by the broadcast caused varying reactions. One was a visit from the state authorities, which first frightened John and then affirmed him. Thanks to Nada, he had had his own legal guardianship system set up. The papers for each child were signed by the parents and notarized in the county courthouse at Williamsburg. But the welfare department in Frankfort, the state capital, had been unaware of our existence. When the inspector came, John was nervous. He took great pains to show the man every nook and cranny of the home. As they walked through the wooded trails he spun tales of his answered prayers. He let the inspector meet the rollicking younger children. The inspector ate with us, and we sang for him.

A few weeks later, his report came. He had visited settlement schools all over Kentucky, and he wrote:

> The most beautiful, and perhaps the least scientific, of these schools is run by a man who is a religious fanatic. These people do a wonderful job with little money and poor materials, yet it is easy to see that the children are well fed, happy, and healthy. They are, in fact, the happiest children I have ever seen. The place needs to be put on a businesslike basis, to have a budget and a better system of bookkeeping. The organization could be very well managed, but it does not seem to take into account any planning from day to day. So far they have prospered, for they have over four hundred

acres of land and thousands of dollars worth of buildings
and equipment. The director started with one dollar down.

In regard, to Child Welfare, as I have said, the director is a
religious fanatic, but he is doing a tremendous job and is a
very kindly man. I think we should try to find a way to help
him improve the efficiency of his institution. The home is
only eight years old.

The report both pleased and annoyed John. He laughed at
being called a religious fanatic and said it had nothing to do with
the children's welfare. Having a budget, he said, would interfere
with his religious convictions, since his main objective was to prove
that God would provide from day to day. For this reason, he refused
two thousand dollars a month from the state, but the real reason
was his fear that his activities would come under stricter state
supervision.

Once the publicity ball started rolling, there was no way to
stop it. The townspeople of Corbin, regarding the home as an
asset to the community, began to campaign for a better road
through the flatwoods in the hope that the home would become a
genuine tourist attraction and a boon to the surrounding
tradespeople. A few powerful people in Corbin took up the cause.
Mr. Sanders, in his white suit and black bowtie, began to make
the perilous trip out over the rocky road in his Cadillac. When he
arrived, word would spread quickly from ridge to ridge, and we
would come flying from every corner of the grounds, eager to see
him. The greatest reason for our eagerness was contained in the
trunk of his car. He usually brought a hand-turned freezer and
made homemade ice cream for everyone. Then, after alternately
blessing our hearts and cursing the horrible road, he would feed us
ice cream and return to Corbin, vowing to prod the governor of
Kentucky into action and get us a road.

John, amused at his familiarity with the state authorities, asked
Sanders how he dared to go to the governor with such a request.

"Shaw, why not?" said Sanders. "Who is he? He gets into his pants the same way I do every morning!"

The other pusher for the road was Mrs. Nevils. She was a high-powered thin woman who was terribly perceptive. Whether she wanted the road so that the world could see John's establishment or to open up the world for the rest of us to see was debatable. She singled me out, looked at the poems and paintings I had done, and asked me where I was going to school. Filled with shame, I told her. She nodded and looked at me keenly. At Christmas she presented me with a beautifully illustrated history of world art. I treasured it and memorized each page, the paintings, the schools (especially the Dutch ones), the styles, the artists' names. It became my private artist's bible.

But whether the road was to be a way in or a way out, a date was set, and a huge work force of business and professional men came out to labor with axes and saws to clear the right-of-way. The Women's Club in Corbin provided a giant picnic in the forest, and in two days they had cleared the five-mile strip inside the strings stretched for the new road. Furthermore, Mrs. Nevils was a friend of the state road commissioner, and before long we were informed by telegram that a contract had been authorized for the grading and graveling of the road from the highway to the log cabin. All summer the grading and blasting continued, and by fall a sleek new road turned gracefully through the forest to our home.

We were in touch with the world outside.

Then Mrs. Nevils arranged for us to go and thank the governor personally. We were rehearsed and dressed and scrubbed to a shine, loaded into the school bus, and driven off to Frankfort. Stumbling and fumbling, children who were more at home in cliffs and hollows, we were taken into the governor's mansion. The high ceilings and carpeted floors filled us with a terrible feeling or our own poverty, and we stood there out of our depth and overawed. Then we were lined up and asked to sing. Most of our knees were shaking so hard we could hardly get out a squawk, but the governor and his wife were gracious and complimentary and shook hands with each of us. After the formalities and refreshments, we were shown the ballroom.

Stumpy, who looked as if he'd much rather be in the barn, whispered to me behind his hand. "Goodness," he said, "sure is some fancy place to play ball!"

Behind the shiny promotional facade, the struggles in the inner circle were beginning to take on a new fierceness. John was spending more and more time in the study and less time at the office, and this set Nada on the warpath. Hallie, who had been assigned to clean the study and iron John's shirts, was beginning to develop a strange personality. She had grown grossly obese. What had once been a buxom figure developing on a large frame had turned into a solid bulk, yet she was extremely conscious of her appearance and powdered her face white, licking her lips to make them red by contrast. She began to hang around the study constantly.

Anna was suspicious of Hallie's complete deference to John and her fawning attitude toward me.

"Stay away from that big hulk." Anna warned me. "She's a dirty sneak."

But I could see nothing wrong with Hallie. She was a big fat slob, but she was nice to me and I needed all the friends I could get.

I was growing, growing in power and importance to John. He consulted me about building designs, color schemes, and the brochures he was beginning to mail out. He encouraged me to paint and bought me oils and canvas. When I finished a painting, he was my chief critic and source of encouragement.

The study became a kind of cultural center, the place where paintings were hung, the plans for buildings were drawn, and the musical instruments were kept. But it became a place of mystery as well. Strange things happened in there. Often I would come to the door and knock, and the door would be locked. I would wait impatiently for someone to come. Inside, there would be quick footsteps, and finally Hallie would glide to the door, her face powdered like a ghost. Something about it made me shudder.

I would storm in, full of ignorance and bravado.

"Good grief, it stinks in here!" I said one day.

John looked alarmed. "Like what?" he asked.

"I don't know. Its a funny smell, like bleach or something."

"It's probably the scouring powder," John said. "Hallie was just cleaning the bathroom, weren't you, Hallie?"

There were over sixty children now, four dormitories, a school, a dining hall, all operated by a staff of twenty. We had no electricity aside from an Army surplus generator that was forever breaking down, no running water, no central heating. A road had opened us up to the public, and now an electric power line was coming across the hills. If we had $25,000 we could electrify our buildings, put in running water, and install central heating. But $25,000 was more money than any of us had ever dreamed of. Night and day John drummed that $25,000 into our heads. It was mentioned every morning with the Bible reading after breakfast, every noon, every dinner at prayers, every night at bedtime devotions. Praying for $25,000 became the fill-in phrase in prayers, like praying for the worn-torn countries in Europe when we were younger.

Then one day, as naturally as if he had been sent from heaven, John Maloney appeared, sent by the *Saturday Evening Post* to do a story on the Galilean Home.

News spread over the ridges like wildfire.

"You know the *Saturday Evening Post*?"

"Shore, there's a stack of them in Daddy's study."

"Yeah, but what about it?"

"There's a man here, a short little man with gray hair, and he aims to write a story about us to put in that magazine!"

"Us? Why us?"

"Us? Good grief!"

"Hey, yoo-hoo!"

From all corners of the grounds we came running to stare at the stranger. He was standing out in the newly graded parking lot that the road contractor had included as a bonus, a short stocky man with the air of command I had begun to associate with writers and journalists ever since Bert Vincent's visit. Sent from heaven or not, Maloney had the look of the gods.

He glanced up at the crowd surrounding him. "These all your kids?" he asked John.

"No, there's a couple dozen more hiding somewhere," John grinned.

They were going to get along famously.

They talked all that night. Maloney had been shown every building, every tract of land, every path, and had heard every story. He heard about the dollar down, the miracle hundred that came just in time. He heard about the wills, and the feeding from day to day. Being a writer, and therefore a skeptic, he tried to sort the fact from the fantasy. But the next day John turned him loose with the boys. A great transformation had taken place in the male group since the early days of the home. The first gang of toughs had mostly gone away, either to the Army or in moral disgrace, and the upcoming group had all been taken in as small children. Day after day they had been told Bible stories, had heard nothing but hymns and prayers. They were innocent boys, thoroughly indoctrinated in the beliefs John taught.

Maloney was impressed. That night he talked to John again. "My God," he said, "how do you get kids to talk about religion like this? I've never seen anything like it! These kids really believe!"

John smiled and looked modestly at the ground. "It's the work of God," he said.

For several days the study was off-limits. Maloney's tape recorder whirred on, and we listened at the cracks and around the windows, catching what we could, bringing coffee when it was needed. Magic was happening, and we wanted to touch it.

Then John Maloney was gone. I was genuinely sorry when his car disappeared for the last time. I had fallen in love, this time not so much with a person as with the magic he represented—the excitement of being a writer.

Sal Pinto came next. He was an artsy-type cameraman, loaded with equipment and ready to take hundreds of pictures. We were placed in dozens of poses, doing everything from sawing wood to peeling potatoes. Our mill-shed school was photographed; so were Nada and Anna, opening the boxes of clothing; so were the dorms with piles of children tumbling in the grass. On Sunday we were loaded into the school bus and taken to a local church to sing, and Pinto rode along taking shots of us drinking pop at the country store afterward. Like Maloney, we idolized him. He was an artist, fresh from the real world with the smell of sin and cigarettes on him. We loved him and Sal felt our love. Through his eyes we saw ourselves as innocent and beautiful, with a primitive kind of goodness. He made us like ourselves.

When Maloney's and Sal's article appeared, the first copies that came in the mall were rushed to the dining hall, where we spread them out and searched for our own pictures. John was featured as the "Kentucky Samaritan," and the full-color spreads made our simple home look like paradise. Grandpa Will's gardens were bright and colorful, and the cute faces of charming children grinned from the pages.

We were famous.

Almost before we could handle it, the avalanche of mail began to come. Nada, John, and Janey worked long hours at the office opening and recording gifts. For the first time in our lives people were sending us hundreds of dollars instead of tens. Every state in the nation responded; so did twenty-four foreign countries. There was even a thousand-dollar check from someone in Shanghai, China, an ambassador's wife.

The day soon came when John stood in the new dining hall between the girls' dining room and the boys'. He bowed his head for a moment, and the chattering of voices and the clink of plates quieted. Then he said gently. "Children and co-workers, I want to tell you what has happened. As of this morning, our prayer has been answered. To date, we have received as a result of the Post article, twenty-five thousand dollars."

There was a whoop and shouting and a great clapping of hands. Without anyone to start it, we began to sing "Praise God from Whom All Blessings Flow" and to hug one another. It was as though a fire had been kindled and each of us felt encircled with the warmth of a great glow.

In such moments I was able to forget my doubts and misgivings and to vow secretly to give my life to this place.

With the new money in his pocket, John wasted no time. The REA electric line was coming in across the hills, but before putting in wiring he wanted to remodel and enlarge several of the buildings. We were far too crowded. He installed a drawing board along a wall in the study and began to lay out designs for the new and remodeled structures. One of the first to be tackled was our cabin, still only a four-room structure and now bulging with twelve girls. We were so crowded that bunk beds were shoved together to make one giant bunk. It was like sleeping in a flophouse. None of us minded being crowded, but John was getting upset about people sleeping together. He seemed particularly upset about Maxine and me sharing a bed. One night he voiced his disgust that she and I were snuggled together under the same blanket. We were best friends, innocent as newborns, and couldn't see what was so evil about touching each other.

I had a knack for sounding like a know-it-all when I actually knew nothing.

"What's the matter with that?" I asked.

"I just don't like it," he said darkly.

I had the leap of imagination that comes to poets when they write what they do not understand.

"Well, if anything happens, we'll name it after you!" I said, trying to be funny. He didn't think it was funny.

Soon a log cabin was put up by a new work crew, to be used eventually for the high school, and the day it was finished all of us from our old cabin moved in. It was soggy wet weather, with snow melting in gray puddles. We carried in the bunks from our house, and then we hauled all our clothes and belongings over and stacked them on and under the beds. A stove was connected to keep us warm, and we set up our winter headquarters, waiting for our own house to be redone. Anna lived with us, and John lived in the study. The old original cabin was gutted to the walls, and a huge new section added, taking in the whole back yard. It was a long horrible winter even though people who had read the article kept turning up, and a car dealer from Illinois drove down with a red jeep equipped as a fire fighter, and made us a present of it. With our backward plumbing system there was no possible way to hook it up to water, but it became our favorite form of transportation on the sprawling grounds. Each day at meals, instead of walking across the pasture, a mob of children piled onto the jeep and John drove across the open field to the dining hall, the children laughing and hanging on like some sort of circus act. John roared and jerked and honked the horn, giving it the full effect, laughing along with them.

My studies were getting harder. Often I'd find an encouraging comment written on my paper by some distant teacher in Chicago, but I felt terribly at sea. There was no one to help me, no one to ask. Anna knew a great deal, but she was hesitant to advise me at the high school level. She had always had an extensive vocabulary, and knew reams of facts by memory, as well as poetry from Shakespeare to Longfellow ("Be a hero in the strife . . ."), but she seemed to have little confidence in herself anymore. She ironed quietly and sewed adorable outfits for the little children and kept herself out of trouble as much as possible.

Among my courses of study introductory psychology both fascinated and troubled me. I soaked it up, reading far ahead of the assignments. In the back of my mind I remembered Aunt Ren's flippant diagnosis of John as "paranoid, schizophrenic, and suffering from delusions of grandeur." I looked up these terms with a growing suspicion in my mind that she might not be far from right—and then I tossed out the whole idea as dangerous, presumptuous, and something I knew nothing about.

John had told Hallie she was no longer needed to perform her duties in the study, and had asked Carlita to take over the job. Hallie felt it was her place, and fought with Carlita. Carlita, sweet and vacant-eyed as ever, appealed to John. One morning we heard shouting and screaming, and John came out of the study slamming the door behind him. The dinner bell rang, and John got into the jeep, loaded on a bunch of children, and roared off to the dining hall. While we were eating, Anna came in. She told John she was worried by the screams still coming from the study.

John shot out of the door, and several of us followed him. He swung into the jeep and roared across the pasture.

Hallie was screaming like a hog being butchered. Her words were strangled, but we could make them out: "I'll kill . . . kill myself . . . kill myself."

By the time we reached the study and dashed in, Hallie was unconscious on the floor. She had done the very obvious thing of taking sleeping pills from the medicine cabinet, and now she lay on the bathroom tiles like a beached whale. Saliva trickled out of her mouth. She was a horrible sight, more bluish than ever under her white face powder.

John called two workmen. They picked her up and flopped her in the back seat of the car, her fat arms and legs stuffed in at odd angles.

At the hospital in Corbin they pumped out her stomach. She lived, but all of us understood she was somehow on the accursed list. When she regained consciousness she was sent to the psychiatric ward of a Lexington hospital.

"It's clear she's off mentally." John said in a professional tone.

"There's a history of insanity in her family, and I would guess that this breakdown was caused by excessive self-abuse. You have no idea what that girl was capable of—what filth!"

Anna went with him to Lexington, and John ordered her to sign the commitment papers. She returned pale and shaken.

"That girl was only seventeen." she said, "I wish I hadn't been asked to do that. I had no idea how easy it is to commit someone to a psychiatric ward. It's absolutely frightening!"

The next day Carlita took up her duties in the study.

"You should get to know Carlita better," John pressed me. "You and Maxine always hang around together, and Carlita feels left out. You're not very nice to her."

"I don't like her," I said bluntly. "Carlita is dumb."

"I wouldn't be so quick to say that," he countered. "She's very talented musically. Miss Smith says she's the best music student of all."

He stopped mid-sentence, sensing he was treading on dangerous ground. When it came to music, Carlita and I were bitter competitors.

"If you can't choose your relatives you should at least be able to choose your friends," I said hastily, and then broke off, frightened by what I was saying. Sometimes words came out before there was a chance to censor them, and I got myself in trouble.

To my surprise. John laughed. "You've got a big mouth," he said. Then in a more sober tone he added, "But you really should get to know Carlita. She has a deeply spiritual quality about her."

I nearly puked.

Carlita and Pearl's father, Mr. Powers, had always had special visiting privileges and had been unusually faithful in visiting his children. He always came on Sundays, and the three of them had been allowed to spend time by themselves, walking the paths or talking at the dorm. Now his daughters were asked to visit with him in the study while John hovered about them like a worried mother hen.

Meanwhile, Nada began to view all of this with a jaundiced eye. Sometimes when John went to the office he would invite Maxine, Carlita and me to go with him. Nada, no longer alone with him in the cozy office, eyed us with ill-concealed malice.

"My my, Johnan, look at the bevy of beauties you have in tow these days. Why it must do your heart good! Don't they keep you young?"

And John, who was nearing thirty-eight, blushed. "They're our hope for the future, Nada," he said, patting her fanny absentmindedly. "Our only hope for the future. These are minds we have formed, the only minds that can carry on when you and I are old."

Nada, who was getting close to forty herself, ogled us from head to toe. Clearly it was not our minds that she was concerned about.

"My, but you're getting tall," she said to me. "And not such a skinny little thing as you used to be either. Why, turn around. I do believe you're putting on weight in the behind. Why look, Johnan, she's going to be a big woman like her mother!"

I wanted to strangle her. I rushed back to the makeshift cabin and dug Anna's scale out from under the bed. I weighted 125 pounds. Suddenly I felt gross and repulsive. I skipped dinner.

Now Carlita reigned supreme in the study, the inner sanctum where my father retreated. The door was always locked, and I knew she delighted in making me stand outside as long as possible, even if she was only polishing John's shoes. She was inside the locked door and I was outside. She was in control, and flaunted it.

My resentment of her affected airs, the whole mystery of the study, our mixed-up makeshift housing, and the worry about my schooling, present and future, began to work on my mind. I stared at my books listlessly. Who really cared if I had an education or not? John laughed at learning and constantly spoke of reason as the enemy of faith. He was always quoting Thomas Paine or some other poor unfortunate who had raised his fists to heaven and yelled, "Oh that the age of reason had never been born!"

I began to wish I had never been born. A great wall of despair began to close around me. I would be forever locked in this crazy-world, this madhouse of the faithful. Worst of all, this place that seemed so upside down to me, so lopsided in its thinking, was growing so popular with the public that visitors almost fell at John's feet. They gave him gifts, they praised him; they came to look at the home and left in tears. Yet I too knew it was a wonderful place in some ways and that John had chosen some of us to be its future leaders. And I . . . I was caught. If I stood up and walked away, who would be considered the mad rebel? Who would be branded as ungrateful and ungodly? There were no windows in the dark wall that surrounded me. There was no way to escape. I could not discuss it even with Maxine or Aunt Kay.

One day soon after my fifteenth birthday I decided I wanted to die. I lay down on the tumbled mass of clothing and bedding in the shack and fell asleep. I slept for three days and nights, refusing food. By the fourth day, a glorious calm came over me. I could hear music, wonderful music, roaring up and down in my mind.

For a week I ate nothing, lying on the twisted humps of the bed. John came and asked me what was wrong. Anna tried to spoon feed me, but I turned my face and said nothing. I would waste no more words. Maxine brought a bottle of Pepsi-Cola, and sips of that kept me alive.

Dreams, clear dreams, wove in and out of the music in my head. An old man appeared in the dream, and at first I thought he was the Legendary Grandfather, and then I recognized the face of Uncle Jim, the old man who used to live by the river long before all the other children came.

One afternoon I had been at his cabin and it was getting dark. I had a long walk back through the woods and I was afraid of going it alone. But he took me by the hand and said, "Listen, little buddy, there ain't no need of you bein' scared of the boogerman. When you walk through them woods, and it's gettin' dark, you just open your mouth and sing as loud as you can. And I'll guarantee you as long as you keep singin', the boogerman can't get you!"

And I had scampered home through the woods with his words in my ears: "As long as you keep singin' the boogerman can't get you."

Suddenly, lying there in a heap, I had an idea.

A few months before, we had heard the Wings over Jordan choir in Corbin. It was their songs I had heard roaring in my head as I lay in bed ready to give up. I could hear the sopranos soaring high, the altos rich and mellow, the clear tenors and rumbling basses. I wanted to be a part of music like that.

> God's children down in Egypt land, let my people go
> Oppressed so hard they could not stand, let my people go!

I would sing! I would sing my way to freedom, whatever or wherever that was. Perhaps, for now, freedom was simply not dying, not giving up.

I jumped up, forgetting my wobbly knees. My body felt thin and my spirit light and clean. Let Nada laugh now, the old fat French whore. I would organize the girls my age. We would sing. We would all sing our way out of the woods.

The girls thought it was a great idea. We practiced in the study at night when the dishes were done and the little ones had been put to bed. There were thirteen of us, teenaged or near teenaged. Everyone was excited about the idea of singing spirituals and mountain songs with hand clapping and a strong beat. In our subdued way we were a group, the new blood.

We divided naturally into sections. Miss Smith had trained us in the large choir as sopranos, altos, and high tenors, and now we added a new sound, bass. A ninety-pound girl named Zula had developed an astonishingly low voice and could go below low C with no sound distortion.

The first night we practiced we formed a half-circle. I stood in the center, head bent, listening for the right blend of sound. We tried "Let My People Go" and "Rock a My Soul" and were delighted.

John came in from the other room and clapped enthusiastically. "Hey !" he said, "get up ten like that, and you're on tour!"

He was as good as his word and a trip was planned for the Galilean Girls, as we began to be called. At fifteen, I was responsible for selecting and arranging our music, getting the girls together to rehearse, and choosing the pieces we would perform in each place. I was in a state of nervous excitement.

Nada eyed me, this time in a new light. I was money in the till.

"My gracious, child, you're getting so thin. You should eat more, or all that talent will go to waste. You don't want to get ill again."

I looked at her, thinking. If you want me to live, stay out of my sight, you old pig. If anyone would make a kid want to lie down and die from sheer disgust it would be you.

That first trip was innocent. A whole busload of us went, adults and children. We chugged along for miles in the yellow school bus with our luggage under the black tarpaulin on top, singing our favorite songs and excited about performing for new audiences. Anna and Nada went, and Aunt Kay and Miss Smith. Boyd Littrel, one of the workmen, had become our bus driver, and his droll humor added a new note. We bunked in church basements and people's homes, and our meals were provided by the groups for whom we sang. We traveled through Illinois and Michigan and over to Washington, D.C. where we stayed at a campground on Chesapeake Bay. We filled the place.

All our singing was a cappella, and halfway through a meal I would begin to be afraid I would not strike the right pitch for us to start, and the tenors would be shrieking or the altos would be scraping. My stomach would suddenly seem full, and my hands would shake. But the thrill of belting out music, of singing "Let My People Go" under John's nose, of lights and crowds and applause, of people talking to us afterward as if we were stars . . . Who needed food?

People everywhere had read the *Saturday Evening Post* article, and we were fussed over and praised. Sometimes at night when I looked at my father shaking hands and receiving all the acclaim, I felt dark thoughts popping up in my mind, but I shoved them down and smiled and sang. After all, he was doing a good thing. Who was I to be the judge?

Young people crowded up after the service. When they asked me where I went to school, I let them think I had a heavy performance schedule and had to be tutored at home, like a star. They went away envying me, and I suppressed the feeling that I had lied. Everyone had to lie a little to survive.

Back to Kentucky we went, excited to see what miracles the workmen had wrought while we were gone. Our cabin, no longer a simple structure but the shell of a huge two-story house, was nearly completed. The room that had been the original cabin was preserved outside for old times' sake and the inside had been turned into one large cathedral-ceilinged living room, paneled with pine. Behind it was a spacious family room, a room for a bath, a nearly finished dorm kitchen, another bedroom, adjoining rooms for John and Anna, and a walk-in closet and ironing room. In the huge addition in back there were to be a library, a music room, an art studio, and a sundeck upstairs and three gigantic bedrooms, two tiled showers and a prayer chamber downstairs. It was like moving from the slums into a mansion. When it was finished we would have lights, refrigeration, plumbing, and central heating.

Anna would even have a bathtub.

It took some doing. Every day after our return, the finishing work went on at a furious rate. Electricians crawled in and out wiring the rooms, and plumbing fixtures were brought in from town on the truck. Anna, not usually bothering to get involved, decided she wanted a bathtub.

"Showers are better," John said. "Who needs a bathtub?"

"I do," Anna said firmly. "I've missed having a hot bath for thirteen years. You can say how the rest of the money is spent, but that's one thing I want."

The argument went on for days. One afternoon when it was the subject of discussion, Mr. Sanders was watching the building process. "What's this, brother John?" he asked. "Does Sister Vogel want a bathtub? Why, a lady's entitled to a bathtub. A bathtub she shall have!"

The next day a truck came from a plumbing company in Corbin. Anna ended up not only having a bathtub but a pale green one.

I hardly felt at home in all the grand new surroundings. A special room was decorated for Maxine, Carlita, Janey, and me, but when I first saw its motel-like elegance, I had no idea what a prison it was to become.

John was drunk with power. He bought a new wide-brimmed Stetson and began having his white shirts done at the laundry in town. He roamed his kingdom day and night, planning still more buildings and reservoirs, systems and programs. His light burned in the study until two o'clock every morning. More and more he pulled me into his plans.

"Look," he would say, shoving a rough sketch at me, "would you do up this design for me so the workmen can understand it? This is vertical pine, this is fieldstone, all of this is plate glass."

I drew them for him. I was becoming one of the study gang. We ate candy bars and drank soda pop and skipped meals.

There were endless plans to draw. The girls' dorm needed a facelift. The new office addition to the boys' dorm was nearly finished, and John had it decorated in bright modern swirls of color. I was surprised, because he was outspoken about the

ungodliness of modern art; and the swirling designs, with Nada
perched in the middle of them, surely did look ungodly. But it
wasn't my design, so I didn't worry.

We needed a school, both a grade school and high school. A
new crop of kids would graduate in the spring, and the high school
situation was becoming desperate. Maxine and Stumpy, Betsy and
Jessie's sister Arlene, Carlita and Eugene, and a boy named Bobby
were all in the new graduating class. John had to provide something
for them or send them to town.

A new grade school building was begun where the neighbors'
house had been, and the shack-cabin where we had wintered was
renovated for use as a high school. Bobby and Eugene were sent to
a boarding school in Canada, and Stumpy quit. He was sixteen
and not interested in school. He began to help Grandpa Will on
the farm.

The night the kids in Maxine's class graduated, I felt strange.
Little did they know what lay ahead of them. There was a big
dinner, but I couldn't eat. It all seemed like such a farce, making
such a God-Bless-America thing out of an eighth-grade graduation,
when for the next four years, or however many more, John would
be telling them their minds were a curse.

I walked through the dining hall, flaunting my non-presence,
and went up to Grams house. She wasn't there, but it didn't matter.
Gram's was getting to be the only place on the grounds where
there was any feeling of sanity.

I opened the refrigerator door, and took out a bottle of Pepsi.

I was only fifteen, and if I was careful, they wouldn't catch me,
wouldn't kill me. Deep inside somewhere, watered by tears and
Pepsi-Cola, there was a tiny seed, a tiny sense of Being handed
down to me by a man dead and gone, a man who believed that life
was art.

CHAPTER SEVEN

The Vogel house, our old cabin, was now splendid with brown stain, white trim and fieldstone. In the bedroom that Carlita, Maxine, Janey and I shared, a large plateglass window looked out over the central area brilliant with Grandpa Will's flowers. An American flag waved from a high flagpole, fluttering against the pines and mountains with a beauty that would have melted the most unpatriotic heart.

Altogether, a mob of twenty-two girls now lived at our house. The two big bedrooms in the new wing were divided between the middlesized girls Christina's age and the little girls Phyllis' age, among them Maxine's little sister, Julie. It became a kind of status symbol to live at the Vogel house, a sign that one was among the elite.

Julie had moved in under special circumstances. When she came to the home, she was an adorable little child, chubby and black-eyed, quick and laughing. But one summer she fell ill. She was listless and refused to eat. When she was given nourishing food, she vomited. She grew light and thin. John, worried about her, took her to the doctor in Corbin. After a thorough checkup he announced that she was diabetic.

A special routine was prepared for her. She was given a bed next to Phyllis; and Anna, who was a healer at heart, was put in charge. Every morning Julie had to be tested. If her urine turned bright orange when the little pill was dropped in the vial, she needed more insulin. If it was blue, she was okay and could eat a good breakfast. Mornings we would all stand around in a state of nervous tension while Anna dropped in the pill. If Julie got too much insulin, she went into shock. Too little put her in a coma.

For months Anna worked under the doctor's guidance, and finally Julie was stabilized. She began to eat the right foods, to glow with health again, and to run and play with the rest. To all appearances, she was a normal seven-year-old.

Then Dr. Forner came.

It probably happens everywhere when people acquire a bit of notoriety, or fame or whatever. We attracted a host of hangers-on. Some of these were religious groupies, eager for any new experience of a mystical nature, some were out-and-out freaks, and some became good and valuable friends. Dr. Forner was one of the hangers-on, and one of those men whom children instinctively dislike. Even the dogs growled at him. He was tall and skinny, with a scraggy goatee, a leathery face, and strange light eyes. We called him the Goat behind his back.

The Goat was quite a talker. He came one day in a rattletrap car, with two women who he said were his wife and daughter. They looked exactly the same age, in the same state of dilapidation, the same degree of subjugation. They were gray and goaty like the doctor. They all smelled strange.

The Goat was a specialist on many subjects. He sat in the study spellbinding John with his ideas on nutrition, magical herbs, and faith healing. If he had been a straight faith healer, John would not have listened to him, but there was a grain of half-truth in his arguments that caught John's attention.

The Goat claimed to have discovered the cures to many diseases through a combination of right thinking, right eating, fasting, and prayer, laced with doses of alfalfa. He boasted that with this method he had cured everything from cancer to insomnia. The medical profession, he said, was run by a clique of racketeers and charlatans who would not listen to his ideas because they were too simple, too pure, and too inexpensive.

For days, then weeks, the Forners stayed, all three crowded into one room of the study. We began strongly to suspect that both the women were his wives, but no one dared say anything.

One day John was at his desk, and the Goat was discoursing on the effects of natural foods on disease. Julie walked into the study, and John mentioned that she was diabetic.

The Goat's eyes lit up and his head snapped to attention. "Brother Vogel," he said softly, squinting his eyes and pursing his wet pink lips, "I have the answer, the key, the magic remedy for diabetes. Tell me, is this child on insulin?"

"Yes." John replied, rather defensively.

"Ah, my good brother, I never dreamed that we had this vile practice of the medical establishment going on under our very roof. Do you know what insulin can do to this child?"

"No." John admitted. "But I know so far it's helped her."

"Ahhhhhhh . . ." breathed the Goat. He came and took Julie's hand and looked at her face. "Blessed little one. Do you know what insulin will do to you? It will ravage your mind, wreck your body, and in the end, those beautiful eyes will be blind."

"Julie, run out and play." John said quickly, for once confronted by someone more eccentric than himself. "I think the other girls are right outside the door waiting for you."

Julie took one look at the light-eyed seedy face and flew out the door, terrified.

But the Goat was not finished. "My brother," he said, "there is no need to subject that precious child to the ravages of this evil medicine. There is a way, tried and proven, a natural way to health. It has been revealed to me and is documented in my book, *Health without Medicine.*"

How long the Goat pressed, or what he said, none of us knew, because we were told to leave the room and the decision was made in private. But that night John presented the Goat's plan to Anna.

She dropped her hands, and her eyes were wide with disbelief. "John, you can't be letting that insane man talk you into dropping Julie's insulin! The child will die!"

"Why do you always oppose me, woman?" John said angrily. "All he wants us to do is to experiment, to try his way. We've tried insulin, and you know how it works. Nothing is cured. She has to have the medicine injected every day, and he says it's harmful. Couldn't we try his method?" His voice ended on a pleading note.

"What is it?" Anna asked doubtfully.

"He says she should be put on a strict diet of natural undiluted grape juice every two hours, with a tablespoon of honey and herbs three times a day. He claims this will reactivate the natural balance of her body."

"Grape juice and honey? Why. John, she'll be in a coma before the week is over. I can't do that!"

"Try it for once, will you, Anna? I don't ask very much of you anymore. Just try this once. Dr. Forner says that if this is done while the rest of us fast and pray, a miracle of healing could be accomplished. Think what it would mean for this home, for proving the power of prayer, if we actually cured a diabetic. We could become a center of healing."

"But, John, we can't experiment with a child's life! Julie isn't a guinea pig! That man is crazy. He ought to be driven off the grounds!'

"And I suppose I'm crazy too! If you won't give her the grape juice, I'll do it myself!"

"Oh. Lord." Anna sighed. "Now what am I supposed to do?"

Julie was taken off insulin the next morning and put on large doses of sweet grape juice. For the first few times she was delighted to be drinking the forbidden sweet, and she lapped up the honey. Anna steadfastly refused to give it to her, so John set up a mixing center in his study. Dr Forner poured envelopes of natural food supplements into the grape juice and administered it to Julie, laying on his hands and muttering over her back.

"Over the pancreas." he said sagely, "is the most effective.'

The reaction of the group was divided. Some agreed to fast and pray with John and the doctor. Some went to the dining hall and ate, and watched Julie. Maxine was frightened.

The second day the patient became very drowsy. She curled up on her bed in the new house and fell asleep.

"The healing is taking place." The Goat nodded. "This deep sleep is a sign of healing."

The third day we were all called together for a general prayer meeting. Anna refused to come. She sat by Julie's bed.

John stood in the middle of the group in the dining hall. "Dr.

Froner says Julie's healing is trying to take place, but it is being stopped by the lack of faith in some of our group. God cannot heal unless we are united in spirit. The fight now taking place in Julie's body is the work of the devil."

While we were at the dining hall, Julie began vomiting, then had a severe seizure. Anna, who had not driven for several years, picked her up, wrapped her in a blanket, and laid her in the back seat of the car. The keys were in the ignition. She started the motor and gunned up the road.

John and the Goat heard the roar and rushed to the dining-hall window staring after her. She was gone, with their experiment.

The doctor in town was horrified. Anna was shaking and crying, completely undone. Julie was terribly ill. She was put in the hospital and the business of stabilizing her system had to be started from scratch.

When Anna came home, John was in a rage. "You . . . you stood in the way of God's power!" he accused.

Anna glanced at him and gave him a little smile. Then she went to her room and shut the door.

For several days a thick friendship was maintained between the Goat, John, and Nada. Then the Goat made a fatal move. He claimed that Nada had an unbalanced smell to her breath and needed to have his hands laid on her. According to John, he laid his hands on the wrong place, and with too much relish.

Suddenly the doctor was no good, was an immoral rat, and his companions were both his wives. Everyone became very cool toward them, and in a few days they left, the old Goat and his gray women, in the rattletrap.

No one ever dared mention them again.

We thought Forner was weird until our next strange visitor arrived, a nomad who came to our door one day for food and shelter. We never turned anyone away, so he too became our guest.

He said he was a preacher, and God knows where he came from. A taxi dropped him off one day, and he stumbled toward the study looking as if he had been assembled from spare parts. He was very tall, almost six and a half feet, and slightly stooped. His hair was blond and baby-fine. His complexion was completely beardless, soft and fair, and he spoke in a high-pitched falsetto voice.

"Just call me Preacher Peter." he crooned, extending his hand to John.

John looked at the hand. It was soft and delicate He shook it gingerly. "I'm John Vogel. What can I do for you?"

"Well, the Lord has sent me here. I don't know what He has for me to do, but I believe that will be revealed as time goes on."

We watched them go into the study, and we rushed to the house, barely able to restrain our laughter.

"What is *that*?" Maxine said. "A woman with a man's clothes on, or a man with a high voice?"

"I don't know!" Janey said. "How do we find out?"

It became a challenge as time went on and still Preacher Peter's instructions from heaven did not come. He moved into the study and took over John's spare room. It was no real hardship, since John now had a room in the Vogel house, and it certainly was no hardship for Preacher Peter to wait. He was all but starved, his clothes hanging on his long emaciated frame like rags on bones.

John tried to be kind to him. "You never know when you're entertaining angels unaware," he reminded us.

Preacher Peter had a curved cane, and with it in hand he shuffled to the dining hall and sat humped expectantly over the table. When the food was served, he consumed huge quantities, praising John for his generosity and God for sending him our way. But on the third or fourth day Preacher Peter was sick. He lay on the bed in the study, moaning and groaning in his rumpled suit, refusing medication or help. No one knew who should take care of him/her, John or Anna, and everyone was afraid to undress him for fear of what they would find. As long as he kept his clothes on, it could be safely assumed that he was male.

We were young and irreverent, and our curiosity was getting the better of us. We decided that if two of us were posted in the

NINETY BROTHERS AND SISTERS

dark outside Preacher Peter's window, sooner or later he would have to go to the bathroom and we could see if he sat down or stood up. The puzzle would be solved.

Janey and I were posted in the weeds behind the study. It was semi-dark and quiet, except for the night noise in the woods.

Suddenly the light jerked on, and Preacher Peter ran for the toilet. He retched violently, then let out a loud wail. Out of the study door he came, howling in his high crooning voice, "Halp, halp, I need halp!"

Janey and I, trapped, sank down lower into the weeds. As spies we were in no position to double as good samaritans.

John came out of the house buttoning up his white shirt. "What's the matter out there?" he called.

"My teeth. I urped up my false teeth! They're in your toilet! I'm helpless without them!"

By this time Janey and I were rolling in the weeds with laughter. We were nabbed, no questions asked, and made to fish Preacher Peter's big yellow dentures out of the pool of slimy vomit.

As for guessing his sex, it was a game nobody won. We never found out, and Preacher Peter's orders never did come. Fortunately he took it as a sign that he should be moving on, but for weeks afterward he was the butt of our jokes, the subject of our antics. Some nights at Gram's house the girls would ask me to do an imitation of him, and I would disappear into the bedroom, pull on Grandpa Will's suit jacket, hunch my back and shuffle out piping, "Hello, just call me Preacher Peter."

Yet at least our lives had a kind of balance. Mr. Sanders in Corbin was becoming a fast friend. After a day's shopping in town we were always welcome to come to his restaurant for a fried chicken dinner, complete with honey and ice cream for dessert, and his establishment gave our lives a touch of elegance, a chance to rub shoulders with the well-heeled travelers passing through Corbin.

In the ladies' lounge at Sanders' there was a sign next to the mirror. It said,

There is so much good in the worst to us
And so much bad in the best of us
That it little behooves any of us
To say aught about the rest of us.

I liked that, and I liked old Sanders, cussing a blue streak one minute and crying over the words to a song the next. In a flurry of gratitude one day I decided to paint a picture for him, and after thinking about it, I decided a copy of Solomon's head of Christ would be most appropriate.

I worked on the painting for days, matching Solomon's skin tones, the hair textures, the fall of the robe. The only thing I couldn't seem to get were the eyes. No matter what I did, one eye seemed to be looking heavenward and one earthward. It was maddening.

Finally I gave up and presented the painting to Sanders. He looked slightly astonished when he glanced at it, but graciously accepted it, praising my skill, my future, my long hair, and my family, and promising to hang it in his establishment.

It was hung in the ladies lounge, near the worst of us and the best of us, and completely ruined the poem for me. Christ, with his one skyward eye and one earthbound, filled me with a deep sense of embarrassment. Worse than that, the picture seemed to be a subconscious portrayal of something that was happening to me—a blurring of sight, an inability to focus. I finally slipped the picture off the wall, stuffed it under my coat, took it home, and burned it in the fireplace. No one ever asked about the missing art treasure.

But that episode was not Sanders' fault. He was unstinting in his praise of John, lavish in his encouragement of all of us as we grew. He wept over Carlita's piano playing, bought my attempts at art, and took carloads of us to the state legislature to increase our political awareness. On Christmas day he put up a CLOSED sign on his restaurant door and personally whipped up a turkey dinner big enough to feed over a hundred people. Red-faced and perspiring, he fed us, blessing us and trying not to cuss on Christmas. If Santa Claus had donned an apron, he could not have looked more like himself than Sanders did.

Other good men, like Mr. Haas, became interested in our home. Haas was an Illinois farmer on a big scale, but the excitement and risk of different religious movements ignited his imagination. He farmed for a living, but he lived to take part in big-scale religion. He was active in Youth for Christ, and he took our Galilean Girls group to Moody Church in Chicago to sing for a rally. He was a friend of the Billy Graham people and helped organize meetings overseas for their evangelistic tours. And he was a friend of the up-and-coming John Vogel, my father. His keen nose told him that this sprawling organization on the Bee Creek road was destined for the big time.

Mr. Haas was a huge fat man with an ordinary round face, but we loved him and thought he was absolutely beautiful. He made us feel beautiful, which was probably the reason why we attributed beauty to him. When he and John got in the car to go to town, we scrambled to go along, to listen to him talk of Glasgow and Berlin, of all the famous people he knew, and the big plans he had for us.

"First, you should get a Cadillac," he said to John. "If you had a three-seater Caddy, you wouldn't have to decide which of these pretty girls to take with you. You could take them all."

I leaned over the back seat listening, feeling young, innocent, and protected. John and Mr. Haas filled the whole front seat.

He turned around and grinned at me, his face jolly. "Hi, pretty face," he said, patting my head.

If I had been a kitten, I would have purred.

John followed Mr. Haas's advice, and placed an order with the dealer in Corbin for a three-seater Cadillac. Miss Smith shook her head, Anna sighed, and Nada tramped around like an angry cow, but John smiled to himself and quietly went through with it. The money prompted by the *Post* article was still coming in at a steady trickle, and besides, Mr. Haas had agreed to stand behind him financially. There were no posters or PRAY signs put up about this one. It was more of an investment with guaranteed results.

"Get on the road with those girls, and you'll recoup that money in no time." advised the businessman.

The three-seater was delivered to the garage in Corbin, and we giggled in embarrassment at its obscene size. John drove it home looking a bit uncertain, and it stood in the parking lot like a dark blue hearse.

"It's not that bad." John rationalized, looking it over. "We'll consider it a second bus, for the smaller group. It'll be an easier way to let people know about the home than taking the whole gang on tour, and less expensive too. Of course, sometimes we'll still take the whole group. We can have a choice of tours."

"How will you bill this act?" Nada asked sweetly. "Daddy Vogel and His Traveling Band of Beauties?"

I had the feeling that her smile was beginning to flash red.

But there was one good thing about the Big Clunk, as I came to think of it. At least it broke up the John-Nada automotive monopoly. That had been a bad situation for years.

Nada had a car when she came to join the home. John and Anna had a car as well, and Anna used to drive it. She had driven ever since she was a teenager, crazily lurching down Chicago's Michigan Avenue in her brother's model-T. But when Nada came, John's car suddenly became off-limits for Anna. No explanations. John and Nada made silly jokes about the cars, named them Aquilla and Priscilla, and parked them in the same garage. Then Aquilla and Priscilla were traded in and a new car was born under the joint ownership of John and Nada. Anna had been voted out of the conglomerate, and she had been stranded, a virtual prisoner in the forest. With the exception of the Julie incident, she had not driven for years.

But with the purchase of the Clunk, the smaller car was left to the women. John had other things on his mind and no longer cared. Anna was a driver again, and whenever things got too thick at the Vogel house, she sailed down the dusty road and off to town.

The office issued a ruling that all boys over fourteen would be sent away to boarding school. So the high school became a girl's institution.

A teacher had come to offer her services. She was an ageless woman, blond or gray, we could never tell. She had a Hummel-figure face, pink and white with clear blue eyes, and a Hummel-figure. She was it. She set up classes in the round-roofed log cabin, and we moved in.

Being in a classroom was a new source of confusion for me. I had learned to cope with the absentee teachers of the Calvert School, investing them with such qualities as I needed to project onto them. My English teacher, I decided, was a creative genius, since she appreciated me. The science teacher was definitely a young man of about twenty-one, with gorgeous eyes handsome and charming. I could fashion them all to my own taste, out under a tree in the summer or slumped over the kitchen table in the winter. But now I was confronted by this one woman, a single unit that smiled blandly, licked its lips, sat chin-in-hand and nose-in-knuckles, feet spread wide apart, watching us.

I had accumulated two years of credits since I started studying on my own and wanted to continue in the Calvert System. Since I was a class of one, no one minded. The only courses I shared with the others were typing and religion.

But the thought of learning to type made me wince. Anything that Nada did made me wince. I was going to be an artist, not some dumb little stooge sitting under Nada's tits in the office, like Janey. I refused to take typing.

John gave the five of us new typewriters for Christmas. "You'd better take it." he urged. "You never know when you'll need it. Typing is a skill that never hurt anyone."

"You'll need it when you go to college," Anna advised. "Where are you thinking of going?"

I glanced at John, but he looked away and said nothing.

But that was the future, and who but me was worried about the future? The present was enough, with the mob of comrades to relate to, the erratic adults, the excesses of spending, and the planned poverty. And why worry? There would be money in the mail tomorrow, and always somebody to drop into our lives to make us laugh or to cause us to wonder what living was all about.

The teacher did try, bless her, to make school exciting for us. One day she saw an advertisement in a religious magazine for a tract-writing contest. A prize of five dollars would be given to the person submitting the best tract. For a combination Bible and English assignment, she gave us a paper and pencil and asked us to compose a convincing argument for Christianity.

Usually I loved writing, but being told what to write seemed to dry up all my springs.

I stared at the paper, moving the pencil: "Yes, my friend . . ."

I stopped and looked around the room. I looked at the bare wooden walls and the common asphalt tile floor. I looked at the potbellied stove glowing in the corner, the last survivor of the central heating purge. I looked out the window and saw the study next door, with its riddle of the locked door. I looked at the teacher, alternately licking her lips and pressing her nose in her knuckles as she waited for us. I glanced at the paper.

"Yes, my friend . . ."

I looked around at the girls sharing the room with me. Carlita and Maxine. Arlene. Betsy. We, in a way, were the survivors of a purge as well. Everyone older than us had been banished, for some reason or other, to the deep dark domain of the world, the flesh, and the devil, the outside world. Hallie had been committed to an institution; Lethie had melted away, no one could remember where. Jessie had gone to live with Clara and her husband, Hank. Lewis and R. C., Ray and Homer, David and Troy—they were all mythical names now, one by one growing up and leaving. Even the good boys like Bobby and Eugene. Why had John sent all the boys away? How long was he going to keep us? Were we the chosen, or the prisoners?

"Yes, my friend . . ."

I scratched out the inane words and started over, but all I could think of was "Yes, my friend . . ."

At the end of the hour I handed in the three-word essay. I did not win the tract contest.

They continued to come tramping into our lives-the lost, the strayed, and the curious. Mr. Mac, a charming dark-eyed man with a handlebar mustache, was at least forty-five, with a wife no more than eighteen. She was his fourth wife. Mac sold Kirby vacuum sweepers, and it was in this role that we first met him. He sold John an expensive machine with a spiel so convincing that John could not resist it, even though we had no carpet. After that he came almost every Sunday afternoon. John said Mac had lost his job because he was an alcoholic, but he was never drunk when he came to see us. He was one of those rich dark-velvet men, bruised and battered by life for faults clearly his own, but so convincingly lovable that everyone except his three ex-wives forgave him. He had been a guitar player for the Grand Ol' Opry in Nashville, Tennessee, and we were fascinated by his guitar and tried to get him to teach us chords.

He held our fingers, showing us the positions, smiling with his velvet silken charm. When he left, John would be visibly agitated.

"You should never ask him to lean over you or touch your hands like that," he said. "You have to be careful of men like him. Mac's a good musician, but he's a corrupt, immoral, and lustful man."

It was impossible, even for John, to make this accusation against everyone charming. In fact some of our visitors woke a wistful look in his eyes because of their exemplary behavior, yet these people caused him a different kind of uneasiness.

When the Swanns drove into the parking lot one day, we watched them, fascinated as Floyd opened the gate for his wife, seemed to hover over her protectively, and all but cast himself on the ground for her to walk on. He was a big good-natured man from Alabama, and Ida Mae was one of those small dark soft-spoken southern belles. She touched his arm lightly as she walked beside him, and when she turned to speak to him her eyes lit with a small smile and her lips curved gently. We had never seen a relationship like theirs, and we were spellbound.

John was fascinated as well. I believe he even fell briefly in love with Mrs. Swann, not because he cared for her but because he craved the kind of worship she gave her husband. In a spurt of generosity, he suggested that Carlita, Maxine, and I take them on a walk to the river.

We swung along down the woods path, excited to be the scouts showing off our woodsy skills to these elegant people. Yet we stood and gaped when Floyd held a branch back so Ida Mae would not be hit in the face, and melted when she thanked him with that quick little smile. All three of us fell in love with them, with both of them and their charming courtship ritual. Most of what we had seen of marriage was either ugly, factual, tragic, or banal; but this was romance. We were infatuated.

We showed them the river and, seeing it for the first time through their eyes, it became a love poem, stirring and deep. Listening to the wind in the trees with their ears, it became a whisper, strong and intimate, speaking of warm passions. When they turned to each other with that light touch and smile, all of us wanted someone to turn to, to touch, to kiss. They were a walking argument against John's way of life.

John felt this. He took them to his table that evening and talked to them in private. "We have a very different life-style here," he explained, taking them into his confidence. "The girls who went walking with you today are all chosen servants of God. In the future they will not be interested in boys or romance, but will give themselves wholly to this work."

Floyd laughed, a big jovial smile lighting his face. "How are you going to pull that one off, John?" he asked. "They look like pretty normal kids to me. One of these days some good-looking boy is going to come in here, and one of them will be gone! They're going to fall in love. How are you going to stop that?"

John pulled his chair up and confided in them even more deeply. "I have a great plan for the future," he said quietly, "and I can surround these girls with so much affection that they won't feel the need to search for it elsewhere. My daughters and I are very close."

Floyd laughed and slapped John on the back. "Good luck, buddy," he chuckled. "I'd probably feel the same way if I had a daughter."

But Ida Mae laid her fork down and looked at John as though she wondered what he might not be saying but night mean.

The Swanns came often and were honored guests. Their presence always sent a quiver of excitement through the grounds; but none of us, least of all they, could have guessed the role they would play in our story.

John's plan would have startled Bob Long too, if he had heard of it. We first met Bob at a church picnic set up in the pasture at the home. He was one of the most influential people in the town of Corbin, a big hearty pastor in one of the local churches. The first day he arrived in our midst he was hugging everyone, carrying shoulder loads of little children, throwing punches at the boys, and drawing everyone into the circle of his personality. His favorites were Julie and Carlita, but he teased and played with all of us. He loved all the girls and walked about with his arms around us, two or four at a time, as many as he could reach.

He kidded Julie, whom he knew about through his friendship with the doctor in Corbin. She had made a comeback from the Forner incident and was even getting chubby from so much loving care. "Hey. Julie, I don't like girls I can't reach around."

We all thought he was funny. For once even John laughed. Bob Long was so obvious, so open, he could be up to no evil. But John winced when Long put his hugging arms around Carlita, and privately warned her to keep her distance.

"If people knew what goes on behind closed doors in pastors' studies," John said, "the churches would be empty."

As the home expanded, some of the familiar workers left and new ones came. Aunt Molly left because she met a man in a wheelchair and decided to marry him. She became Mrs. Oliver Boswell, Jr., which I thought was a lot better than living at the laundry. There were almost twenty-five adults now, all working for ten dollars a month plus room and board. The other money they received—from friends or family—was still pooled, and each received the same allowance, no matter how skilled or unskilled their work. Our living conditions had improved markedly, but the concept of communal living was the same. Even John, who handled thousands, seldom spent anything on himself. He was dressed in gift suits, hand-me-downs, and he had only Christmas ties. He bought only two items; one new Stetson hat a year, always gray and always broad-brimmed, and a supply of white long-sleeved shirts. I don't think anyone ever saw his arms bare, at least I didn't. I would have been embarrassed.

A baby was born at the county jail to a retarded mother, and we were asked to take him. The mother was a rape victim and the baby was tiny and sickly. It was a risk. If he had died we would have been in for some kind of investigation. But the baby lived, and no one ever inquired about him. His name was Jackie, and I watched him grow and become a beautiful child. Sometimes I stared at him, wondering how such an exquisite thing could come into the world under such horrible conditions. Was it possible that each life was a fresh start, a gift channeled straight from the beyond without regard to its surroundings? Did Jackie have a chance to grow up normal?

The question bothered me. Did any of us?

On the drawing board along the study wall John was compiling a sheaf of notes marked "Research." I contained my curiosity about them for awhile but one day when I was alone in the study I picked up the folder and began to read through the pages inside. Among them were stories he had written about the younger children, stories about the famous miracles that had now become part of our identity, and an apologetic explanation of our having spent so much money and yet not having built a church. But the pages that fascinated me most were John's personal recollections, jotted down during that first trip with the busload of children.

> Had I been a dreamer that night, I would have dreamed of my boyhood days. It was just a little way from here that God brought me into the world and took my father out. He had just finished his course of study at the Art Institute of Chicago and was beginning to be established, when he was stricken with pneumonia and died at the age of forty-two. From that time on I wandered. It seemed as if everywhere we went on this trip I had lived nearby in my boyhood . . . visited the Chicago airport. All the children went up the ramp to watch the planes as they roared in and out, but I looked at the ground. There where the metal monsters made their climb into the sky, I used to creep on my knees in the onion fields . . . also here my life was spared. Mother remarried and I was called home for a while. Stepfather and five children . . . We worked the farm for owner. . . . He had a truck farm, and it was customary to travel to the market with wagons and teams of horses. The driver told me I could go to the market with him, so I asked my mother if I could stay downstairs and sleep in the spare bedroom. She said no, and I went upstairs and slept with the others. I thought the market driver would forget me so after everyone was asleep I slipped back downstairs and crawled into the spare bed.

About midnight I awoke. The wall at the head of the bed
was beginning to sag, and the smell of my scorched hair had
awakened me . . . From then on I knew nothing. How I got
out I do not know. All I remember was the screaming of my
mother and stepfather, "Why didn't you call the others?
Why didn't you call the others?" There was nothing left of
the house. The other children were all burned to death. The
Purpose of God is strange, and His way past finding out . .
. ever since that day I have known. I have been called to the
lonely task of proving the power of God, even in the face of
opposition from society. I have been chosen, and am choosing
others . . . My plan at present is too deep even to commit to
these pages, but will in due time be made known. The Lord
God of Elijah reigns!

I stared at the familiar words, a strange shiver going down my
back. My father was cutting across the established order; he was a
man who dared to call black white, reason stupidity, and
intelligence nonsense. In his mind he was called of God, and to
seekers he gave the hope that some new thing might be found
under the sun. To the drifters on the road he gave the courage to
believe that they too might be favored by heaven because they
were abnormal, different. John had scorned all pretense of being
socially adjusted, and so far no one had stopped him. He was the
chosen . . . and he was choosing some of us.

CHAPTER EIGHT

For several years, fans of John's had been prompting him to write a book. The brochures he sent out describing life at the home were clever and full of human interest, and his public began requesting a compilation telling the whole story. He decided to comply. The "research" notes I had seen in the study were the beginning of this project. He had sorted out his jottings, organized past brochures into topics, and spread them on the drawing board along the wall. He settled in the study to tackle his book in earnest. He worked every evening and far into the morning hours, then fell asleep across his bed, often fully dressed.

Anna, alone in the Vogel house with her brood of girls, began to have a reflective look in her eye, the look that usually preceded a trip to Chicago. It was as though the situation built up for a certain number of years and days, and then suddenly she knew she needed the help of her family. I had grown accustomed to the patience and disillusionment in her expression, but when these became mixed with a shade of panic I knew a trip would be in the wind.

The invitation seemed to come about very naturally. Della's eldest daughter was getting married, and the whole Kingma clan would be together. It was assumed that Anna and I would come, and John would not.

There was heavy antagonism in the air as my going was discussed.

"She must go." Anna said. "She's been asked to be a bridesmaid."

"Whether she goes or not is up to her," John said subtly. "But she's not going to stand up in any wedding party."

"And why not"

"Who pays for the dress?"

"We do, of course."

"I don't have money for that sort of thing."

"You seem to have money for everything else."

"All right then, it isn't the money. I don't want her dressed in one of those low-cut slinky bridesmaid's dresses. Those things make me sick. Idiotic rows of idiotic people dressed in pink and blue and going through those idiotic forms. Tell me, How many of those weddings are a farce? Half of those girls are pregnant when they stand up, and the men will go on whoring happily forever after."

"Speak for yourself," Anna said shortly.

Anna wanted to take me to her sisters' to strengthen her ties with the past and the future, and I felt that she needed me. Yet I hesitated to offend my father. He was growing in power and influence, and I began to see that I was somehow involved in that circle of power.

Nevertheless, in the end I decided to go with Anna. Not to offend John or to side with her, but for my own sake. I was sixteen and had not seen the family for years. Last time I had been a child of twelve; now I was on the threshold of young womanhood. What difference would that make in the outside world? Here, being six or sixteen involved the same routines, the same aura of perpetual innocence. What was life like in Chicago? What were the cousins my age like? Could I still cope? Was I normal?

We boarded the train, now powered by a sleek diesel engine. Anna had packed my suitcase with dresses made on her sewing machine. There was a new air of comradeship and mutual respect between us. At sixteen and thirty-five, we were more like sisters who relied on each other. I was her remaining link with John, and she was my remaining tie with the world of ordinary common sense.

Chicago seemed very different. The streetcars were gone, and there seemed to be a great many men hanging around on street corners whom I had never noticed before.

Aunt Della's house was the scene of intense excitement. Her daughter, Ramona, was dark-haired and beautiful, and was marrying a big blond cherub of a Dutchman. Mamma and Pappa were ecstatic, and their happiness reverberated through the whole clan.

When at family gatherings I sought out the other cousins, now growing into young men and women, they were polite and self-confident, dating and talking of courtship, and I felt overdressed and over religious. I was treated with the deferential courtesy due a respected nun. I remembered John saying there was nothing in this world so ungodly-looking as a woman in pants, so I reached for some—a pair of jeans that belonged to a cousin two years younger and three inches shorter. They struck my legs at mid-calf and fit like a second skin. I walked around wagging my hips in a way that would have done John's suspicions justice, but they accomplished my purpose. I had traded my sainted image for a pair of blue jeans and felt it was a good bargain.

A persistent refusal to eat had become a matter of policy with me. Somehow I had the feeling that the ingestion of food was a trap, a method by which the gross fat adult world snared one into its greasy folds. If I were surrounded by a wall of fat, the light in me would go out, my keenness would be dimmed, and I would become gross and heavy. For me freedom was symbolized by thinness, by my persistent refusal to consume everything that was put in front of me.

The uncles and aunts, not guessing the seriousness of my aversion to food, pressed me to eat.

"Come on. Skeeter," teased Uncle Peter, the one with the big nose and the good voice. "even Hillbillies have to eat. You'll get T.B, and rickets. Or is it pellagra all those moonshiners die of?"

But I continued to nibble lightly and to swig at the ever-present bottle of Pepsi-Cola.

I found myself caught in a strange duality. While I had come to Chicago partly to get away from John's influence and was consciously fighting it, when people asked me questions as though I were "one of them", I answered defensively, and if anyone accused John of isolating us or denying us a proper education, I defended him. And in defending him I found myself more and more aligned with his warped psychology and his narrow interpretation of life. Thus, when Aunt Della asked me to be in the wedding party, I heard myself parroting John. No. I would not be in the wedding party. When the cousins asked me quietly if their parents were right, if my father was a little strange, I protested angrily. It was a shock to realize that against my will John had invaded my mind.

Set across the current of the cousins' lives, feeling withdrawn and shy, I asked Anna to show me where the Legendary Grandfather had been buried. Sensitively she realized the urgency of my request, and we took a bus to the cemetery on the other side of Chicago and went to find the grave of John's father. The cemetery attendant looked up his name and gave us a number, and we searched until we found a tiny metal marker with the number and the name, Frank Vogel, and the date of his death. There was no gravestone.

Anna left me alone, and I crouched over the marker with my eyes closed, touching the ground, trying to feel his presence—my guiding spirit, my genie. Where had I lost him? Why did he no longer speak to me, no longer stir my mind to be strong and free, vital and daring?

Tears began to drip down my face, falling on the ground. How could I get in touch with that clean hungry feeling again? How had I been snared into this contradiction, standing for what I doubted and defending what I hated?

The crazy portrait I had painted popped into my mind, the olive skinned Christ with one eye on heaven and one on earth—a sick imitation, a distortion, a parody of someone else's art. I was letting go of my first clear-cut perceptions of life, the search for meaning that was earthy and real.

I felt a sudden closeness to the ground on which I knelt. He had been absorbed into it by this time, the substance of his body passing into the rocky soil. I scooped up a handful of earth and put it in the pocket of the borrowed jeans.

Anna bought new dresses for us to wear to the wedding. It was a beautiful ceremony, romantic and dreamlike, but I viewed it as something alien and apart. Marriage was for ordinary people, people who wanted to have children and grow fat, people who wanted to appear respectable and whore around on the side. I would never marry. Instead, with money the aunts gave me I bought new oil paints and brushes, more determined than ever to be an artist. Someday I would have a jeep, a paintbox, and a typewriter. I would roam the Kentucky mountains as an artist and a writer, shooting any man who got in my way. If I ever did decide to mess around, there would be nothing sneaky about it. I would put a sign on my back that said, I am an artist, a writer, and a whore.

It was one of those conversations I was not supposed to overhear. Della had been busy before the wedding, and Anna had joined in the spirit of celebration, but when the honeymoon couple were on their way and the excitement was over, I saw them sitting at the kitchen table drinking coffee, the frightened look in Anna's eyes.

"What makes you think that?" I heard Della say.

"It's hard to put my finger on. He keeps dropping these little remarks to visitors: 'Oh yes, my wife isn't well' or 'My wife isn't able to take care of that sort of thing, you know.' He makes me out to be some sort of mental incompetent!"

"Anna, you know you've got twice the brains he has. You always did. Why do you let that sort of thing bother you?"

"Because he has this evil little way. He does it so subtly. He picks out a victim, drives the person to the point where he doubts his own sanity, spreads rumors and innuendoes, and then forces one to do something desperate!"

"Anna, whatever are you talking about?"

Anna put her hands over her eyes and shuddered. "Last year I was forced to be part of something that horrified me. Do you remember my talking about Hallie?"

"Yes."

"We took that child when she was small, eight or nine. We were responsible for her. Last year, partly out of fear of what she would reveal, he had her committed to a mental hospital. Even if she gets out now, no matter what she says about him or anyone else, people will shrug and say. 'Oh, she was in a mental hospital.' Don't you see? She threatened to expose him, and he destroyed her credibility!"

"But how could he do that?"

"It was shockingly easy. All he needed was a doctor's signature, a minister's, and mine, And now that he has the machinery, he could use it on anyone."

"Anna!"

"I feel it all the time, closing in on me. I can't describe it. I'm left home on trips with the group because I'm not 'well.' He's always alluding to some mysterious illness, to my ineptitude. He's driving me crazy. And one of these days when I start screaming he's going to pounce on me with the doctor, the minister, and the papers."

"Anna, Anna, you're overwrought!"

When we returned to Kentucky, the grounds had their usual look of beauty and peace, but in the study a new lock had been added. One now had to knock at two doors to proceed into the inner sanctum.

John was busy with his book. "I had to install a second lock," he said a bit apologetically. "I feel bad being so exclusive, but people come bursting in here all hours of the day and night. This way, if I'm working and don't want my train of thought interrupted, I simply don't answer the door."

He stopped mid-sentence, sensing my detached scrutiny of him. He was growing fat, and his face had taken on an unhealthy flush. There were bags under his blue eyes, and his hair looked greasy. His mustache looked scraggy, and I remembered he would be forty on his next birthday.

"You should wash your hair more often," I said.

He laughed mischievously. "You never waste any words, do you? How about it, would you like to illustrate my new book?"

He was doing it again, involving me. I was aware of it, but this was too big an opportunity to pass by. It might even be a step toward reaching my own goal.

"What kind of drawings?" I asked.

"Watercolor . . . pen and ink. You could do a couple, and we could get the opinion of the publishers as to which would reproduce best."

"You have a publisher?"

"Sure. That happened while you were gone. You shouldn't go away; you might miss out on something important. I wrote the publisher in Grand Rapids, and they're enthusiastic about the project. They might even come down here and pay us a visit, do an interview and the works."

"Wow!" I said. Nothing like this was happening to any of the cousins in Chicago.

By now visitors were a fact of our daily life. Every day, and especially on Sunday, cars drove up to the parking lot and people asked to be taken around the grounds. In his brochures John had invited the public to come and see the "Galilean Miracle," and they came, sometimes in droves.

Our life was organized to accommodate these people. Regular tour groups left the parking lot every hour on Sunday afternoons and followed a set course, telling set stories and pointing out set objects of interest. The rooms, always clean, now had to be immaculate. They were not only the place we lived, they were the showcases for a living miracle.

The Galilean Girls group was stationed in the dining hall. We spent the time between tour groups in practicing, and when they arrived we formed our circle and performed. When the group left, we went back to practicing until four o'clock, at which time we began setting the tables and fixing a light supper for around a hundred people. At seven thirty we met again in the Vogel house, in the cathedral-ceilinged living room, to rehearse new music. This get-together was originally meant to be a Sunday evening prayer meeting, but most of us felt we needed singing practice more than public prayers. Public prayers, we discovered, could be dangerous. Although we presented a united front and stuck together to perform, there were many divisions and antagonisms among us. These tended to leak out in prayers.

Carlita and I had become deeper rivals and antagonists. She felt that as chief musician she should be in charge of the singing group. But I had started it and had no intention of handing it over to her. Maxine sided with me, and the three of us lived in an uneasy enforced closeness. Janey had an unimportant voice and worked at the office, so she was neutral. Pearl was Carlita's sister and stuck with her. They both sang well, the best high voices in the group, and had to be humored. If one of them had a headache or a grouch, we were off. Zula, with her deep bass voice, was one of the most talented and the touchiest of all. If I didn't look at her the right way while facing the group or frowned while I was concentrating on the harmony, she would begin to sulk and burst into tears. All the girls with humdrum voices seemed to be stable and well adjusted, but the big talents were all pains in the neck and had to be coddled. It was a strain to be the leader, but I had learned at this point that a big bra was not the only key to power. Assuming responsibility and being involved also helped and were perhaps even safer.

With all the visitors and all of us teenage girls, it was obvious we would sooner or later come into conflict with John's design for the celibate life. When young men asked our names and if we were allowed to date, we were as shocked as if we had received an indecent proposal, and melted into the woodwork while John made his speech about our having given our lives to God, and romantic involvements not being in the divine plan for us. When the puzzled young men were gone, we collapsed into laughter, feeling protected and unreachable.

One Sunday afternoon during our regular performance a blond young man sat near our group in the dining hall. He was eighteen or nineteen, not particularly handsome but tall and good-looking in a big-adam's-apple kind of way.

After the singing he came up to me and extended his hand. I looked up at him apprehensively.

"Do you remember me?" he asked.

"I don't think so," I said, my heard pounding. John would not like his talking to me.

"Our fathers used to work together, in the American Inland Mountain Mission, on the London Pike." He smiled.

I went white, a feeling of horror spreading over me. Was he the little boy whose weewee I had pulled?

"Uh, what was your name?" I stammered.

"Baker, Bill Baker." he said. "We used to play together."

I nearly died of relief. The other kid's name was Harry.

"Nice to see you, Bill" I said, regaining my composure.

"When can I see you again?" he asked. "Just the two of us? Could I come out some afternoon and get acquainted?"

"Oh, any Sunday," I said, knowing I would be busy all day.

He left, and I collapsed into a chair. The girls were all laughing.

"How are you going to explain that?" Carlita goaded. "You invited him, you know. Daddy says a guy never comes around unless he knows he's welcome. How are you going to explain that?"

"Did I invite him?" I asked. I was so rattled I didn't even remember what I had said.

He came the next Sunday, an event that would have been considered right, good, and normal anywhere else. For me it was a catastrophe.

I told John I was sick and couldn't lead the singers, started to go to the bedroom and lie down, and then realized that my bed, my room, my house were on tour. Unless I wanted five hundred people staring at the bottom of my feet. I would have to find some off-the-tour place.

Under the Vogel house there was still an old fruit cellar where Anna used to store canned goods. Now that we had enough money to buy food, it had become the repository of a lot of old junk. It was almost directly under the original cabin that had become the new living room, and I hid there for the afternoon. After a while, enjoying my confinement, I began to rummage through the dusty junk. In a corner I found an old guitar-like instrument in a plush case, its strings rusty and broken, but with a good bow. I resined the bow and looked around to see what else I could discover. On the shelf behind me, among spider webs and old green mason jars, lay a saw. It was a common handsaw, but it looked interesting, so I picked it up.

From someone among the floaters and drifters who came to our house, I had picked up the rudiments of playing a saw. Bending it between my knees and hand, I pulled the bow across the smooth side and produced a loud tremulous wail.

Overhead chairs scraped, and male voices spoke and responded.

"I'm sorry, she's not here now. She might be back this afternoon."

"Thank you. I'll wait."

I ignored them, working away on the saw. Braver and braver, the tremulous wail rose to a loud full-throated warble, prodded by the bow. I almost had "Sweet Hour of Prayer" perfected when I heard the chair scraping again.

"What is that strange noise?" asked a young man's voice. "It seems to be coming up through the floor!"

"What strange noise?" John said. "I don't hear anything."

"I'd swear I heard something."

"Waaooow!" shivered the saw, and the chair upstairs scooted again.

Someone cleared his throat nervously. "It seems to be coming up through the floor. There, don't you hear it?" he said excitedly.

"Waaoooow!" shivered the saw. I was working on "When They Ring Those Golden Bells," and the long-range spacing was giving me trouble.

"There!" he said. "There it is! I hear it!"

"Hear what?" John said. "Are you sure you're feeling all right?"

Soon afterward the poor fellow left. I peered through a crack between the old foundation and the new house and saw him glancing back apprehensively over his shoulder. It must have taken him a week to recover.

Everybody laughed about poor Bill Baker and the "ghost" under our house, and I didn't mind. I didn't particularly like him anyhow.

Eugene came roaring into the parking lot one day on a motorcycle, splendid in boots and goggles. He had left the boarding school in Canada where he had been sent two years before and found a job in Cincinnati. Now he was a man of the world, curly-haired and good looking. Forgetting the tightness of his old home, he offered a ride on his motorcycle to his childhood sweetheart, Carlita. They had taken one spin around the parking lot when John went into a tantrum and drove the astonished young man off the place.

"Who does he think he is?" he raged. "I spend my whole life raising up you girls to be pure, and he thinks he can come roaring in here on a motorcycle and carry you off, just like that! And you'd let him too, Carlita. You wanted to go with him, didn't you? Oh, my God." And he rushed to the study with Carlita hot on this trail. The study door slammed, and we heard a long loud exchange of Carlita's denials and John's accusations. Then it was quiet.

At last Carlita emerged looking like a wounded bird. For once I almost felt sorry for her.

"Why does she put up with that?" I asked Maxine. "Why doesn't she just tell him off? "Beats me," said Maxine. "I sure don't know. Why don't you ask her?"

But something kept me from asking Carlita. When a visitor came to see me, John acted as if it were funny, and we all laughed. When Eugene paid attention to Carlita, John behaved as if it were a catastrophe. It occurred to me that the reasons for our being "protected" were not the same. And, whether I wanted to admit it or not, Carlita at fifteen was getting beautiful. She was tall and slim, with fair skin, dark hair, and kittenish blue eyes. She was a total spellbinder. I hated her guts.

· · · · ·

John's publishers were brothers, both dark-haired with touches of gray at the temples, important-looking. They had been high school friends of John and Anna, had started a publishing business, and were now among the most successful religious publishers in the Midwest.

They sat in the study talking to John, toured the grounds observing the places mentioned in John's stories, and they smiled at each other. When they saw the children, played with them, let the little ones climb on their knees and sing songs for them, both of them lost their heads and their hearts.

Pat, the younger brother, picked up baby Marcella, an adorable eight month-old. "How about it, John?" he said. "Could you spare, one for me? I'd give her everything in life she could ask for."

John grinned his self-conscious grin. "Pat, I can't give away my children."

"But you've got so many, you wouldn't miss one."

John shook his head. "Can't do it, Pat," he said. "These are my kids."

Pat was clearly impressed. Later several of us sat in the padded booths of our big kitchen at the Vogel house talking about the book. John had already written twenty-five of the seventy-five short chapters planned, and Bernie, the older brother, was flipping through the pages, reading snatches aloud in a dramatic voice. We were fascinated. We were going to be in a real book, a book that people would keep for a long time and not just throw away like a magazine.

Pat took the manuscript from his brother and turned to the first page. "To my dear wife. Anna." he pronounced. "For the love and sacrifice she has given all these years."

John looked over Pat's shoulder, startled. The page was blank. Pat glanced sideways at John without another word.

"The book will be dedicated to my oldest daughters," John said. We were all tense. Anna looked embarrassed. No one dared say anything. This damned tangle of relationships contaminated everything it touched. I had half expected John to dedicate the book to Nada for "the love and sacrifice she had given at the office," but if he didn't dare mention Nada, perhaps we were the logical alternative. Anything done for the children seemed to be okay. I had learned that much in this game. And I remembered the notes in the study. None of them had anything to do with Anna. Was he really going to try to discredit her? I thought of the conversation at Aunt Della's, and wondered who would end up defeating whom.

With all but four credits in my high school course completed, I concentrated on the sketches for the book. There were to be seventy-five. The closer the end of high school came, the more work John piled on me, forestalling the college question. I drew at the sloped drawing board in the study, and although I was proud to be a part of his project. I could not shed the feeling of resentment.

"Why don't you want me to go to college?" I asked bluntly one morning.

"College is a waste of time for girls." he said. "You'll go away, and in one year's time you'll have lost your senses over somebody, got married, and it will be the last I see of you. You'd probably marry some fat stupid Dutchman and have a dozen kids."

"Some great opinion you have of me," I said, rinsing out my brush.

"On the contrary."

I glanced at him. He was quiet and looking at me very strangely. "Well?" I said.

"Will you promise me something:" he asked softly.

"What?" I said, not looking at him. I felt my heart start to pound with the old mixture of love and fear.

"Promise me you'll never leave me?" he whispered.

"What do you mean?"

"Promise me you'll stay here forever, be my helper, my right hand. I need you. I love you."

"Forever?"

"I have a brilliant future planned for you. Do as I say, and someday all that is here will be yours."

My knees were shaking. I felt as if the devil were taking me to the top of the mountain and asking me to sell my soul in exchange for the power he offered. "I . . . I really don't know." I said. I'll have to think about it."

I washed the brush clean and left the study.

John had leaned heavily on the local color around us, and I drew pine trees, square log houses, picket fences and potato patches, cliffs and giant oaks, hoot owls and oxen, fox hunters, moonshiners, mules and wagons. I made drawings of funerals, shotguns, mired-down model-T's, fireplaces, the river, the mountains and the moon in the pines, boats on the river, rugged men with crosscut saws, a sawmill and buildings in the process of construction. There were the millshed school, the Pepsi-Cola plant in town, the jailhouse in Williamsburg, a mule being dragged to the altar during a revival meeting, the country post office, the voting house, the new bus, Barbara under the porch eating out of a pig trough, the billy goat, and the cow. I put everything in our life into pen and ink sketches. Almost everything. And as I worked I wondered how I could put on paper some of the feelings which were as real as a goat or a cow—my confusion about the future, the real fear I sometimes felt in John's presence, the mystery of the building I was sitting in . . .

But I shrugged and did my work. Everyone had his bag of troubles, and sometimes they were the most interesting part of a person's life. I thought of the story I would write to go with these sketches. It would be quite different from John's.

The publishers had written asking me to do an oil painting for the book jacket. I was to be paid a hundred dollars for it. The hundred dollars meant nothing, since it would go into the communal fund anyhow but I was excited about the chance to do a jacket. It was to illustrate the opening scene of John's book, at a place called the Flat Rock, on the land between the Hensleys' and ours, with four men seated around an open fire listening to their foxhounds chase.

I was finally becoming a real artist! John's plans and mine were merging. The rest of my schoolwork was laid aside, and I put on old clothes, fitted out my paintbox, and hiked up to the Flat Rock. I worked every day, painting the mountains and the forest, then posed the men one by one. The leader was old Bill Godsey, smoking his pipe. I felt like Norman Rockwell incarnate.

Uncle Bill looked at his portrait. "Shore 'nuff!" he said unbelievingly. "I'll be durned! Looks so much like me it right near scares me!"

No other girl at the home would have been allowed to sit on the Flat Rock painting a man's picture, alive or dead. But I was in the rule-immune area of the artist, and I was suddenly allowed to live outside the strictures of ordinary mortals, to stare intently at the curve of a mans nose, the slope of his shoulder, the folds of his overalls. It was a giddy freedom.

The oil was barely dry on my picture when we packed the thirteen girls of the Galilean group into the Cadillac and headed north for a new tour. But the jockeying for position was in no way left behind. It simply intensified in the cramped confines of the car. The three Chosen Disciples sat in the front, the Best Voices in the middle, and the masses in the back. We three in front took turns sitting next to John. Sometimes, as we drove through a town, a passer-by would look at us, do a double take, explode with laughter, and point, yelling something at us. We must have looked like some apparition, a huge blue Cadillac crammed with thirteen girls and driven by a man with a mustache. Furthermore, we were no longer ragged backwoods girls but were dressed in the latest style. John had personally taken us shopping, and bought us the best.

In one washroom, the attendant looked us over. "You girls entertainers or somethin'?" she asked.

"No," we told her. "We're from a children's home."

"Orphans?" she asked incredulously.

"Well . . . yes."

"My Lawd," she muttered, "the orphan business shore must be pickin' up!"

It was. We were treated like royalty everywhere we went. Once again other young people crowded around us at the meetings as though we were stars. It was intoxicating. In our navy blue suits and white blouses, we sang standing in a half-circle, clapping our hands and swaying to the music, belting it out in four-part harmony. Sometimes Pearl and I or Zula and I sang the lead while the others chanted in harmony, but no one ever sang a solo because John was afraid of creating star personalities. We were a team, and what we did was done for the group. Yet it was hard to avoid audience favorites. People came up afterward and praised Carlita's high clear voice, Zula's deep rich tones, or Maxine's beautiful eyes. John usually smiled and hustled us out the exit to the basement or changing area. He decided that on our next tour we would wear long full robes to keep people from staring at our legs. I didn't care. I had knees like Aunt Ren anyhow.

John himself looked quite a character standing behind the podium, with his tanned face, dark wavy hair, and sincere blue eyes. His whole body shone with a charismatic power that made people fall under the sway of his words without hearing what he was actually saying or perceiving the dangers inherent in it. "Let it be remembered," he would declare solemnly, "that most children's homes are the product of circumstances. Children are dumped and a home must be found for them. But our home, from its inception, has been different. We have been established to prove the power of prayer, and the children are the medium. What greater medium could one use? Children are the greatest in the kingdom. And our children do not come and go. When a child is placed in our home as one of God's chosen, we keep that child and finish in him or her the work of grace."

A few astute souls may have winced at the notion of using children to prove a point, but the great majority thought of John as a remarkable man of faith, a daring pioneer, and a friend of God. Others, ready to follow the latest trail to a miracle, never even thought at all.

Before, on trips of this sort, we had stopped at friends' homes, sleeping in piles on the floor or staying in a borrowed cottage. Now, thanks to the generous offerings we received, we began to stay in motels. At night, fresh and glowing from the adulation of the audience and the clank of money in his pocket, John would make the rounds to kiss his singers good night. If one did not kiss Daddy good night, her loyalty was suspect. Since he always slept in the room where I was, I realized slowly that as his only "real" daughter, I was cast in the role of chaperone. More than once I awoke to see him on Carlita's bed giving her kisses which were more than fatherly. I would turn away, a sick angry shame burning through me.

Back down to the south, stopping at drive-ins, thirteen girls munching hamburgers and smelling like mustard, falling asleep all over one another, sleeping and waking, singing and quarreling, stopping at gas stations wrinkled and smelly, the constant butt of jokes.

"Man, them all your kids?

"No. I got fifty more at home."

"Fifty more? Not all with one woman!'

"No, there are around twenty."

The gas station attendant would scratch his head and wonder if he had had a hard day until John laughingly explained. Then we would be treated to free pop and go away feeling that people were nice, even if they did live in the soiled domain of the world, the flesh, and the devil.

During the trip we had delivered the last of John's manuscript, my jacket painting, and my sketches. Now, six months later, finished books were ready. John scheduled enough meetings to pay our traveling expenses, and we drove to Chicago to pick up the first copies.

I can't say how anyone else felt, but as I looked at the words and pictures I was terribly excited. I had seen something created from ideas, paper, and ink. Yet as we drove the highways toward home, I had an even deeper feeling, a strong intuition that the book should not have been written so soon. This Happened in the Hills of Kentucky, with its simple assumptions and lighthearted stories, showed only the surface action, beneath which the stage was being set for a much more serious drama.

At Christmas that year the tree in the dining hall was almost embarrassing in its overload of gifts from groups and individuals. Gone were the days of the aluminum soap boxes. We had everything now. There had to be a huge boxed-in area under the tree to keep the presents from falling all over the floor. There were toys, clothing, books, and cosmetics; but the books were still censored, the clothing had to have sleeves, the cosmetics were thrown out except for powder and perfume, and all the card games or games with dice were taken away.

Maxine, Carlita, and I were given special presents. John took us to the jewelry store in Corbin and let each of us pick out a ring with our birthstone. Maxine and I picked out ours, and John helped Carlita. She put it on her left hand, third finger.

"Not there, dummy," I said. "That's your wedding finger!"

She looked helplessly at John.

"It's too small for her right hand," he said. "Maybe we can get it sized later."

"I wouldn't wear it there." I said pointedly. "People will think you're married or something."

John shot a glance at me, the glance that meant shut up, and I did, and thought no more about it until later.

But glancing at my own ring, I felt a trifle strange about it. It was a lovely bar of amethysts and small diamonds set in gold, but it made me uneasy. In the beginning our life had been hard but simple. I had always helped take care of the smaller children, washed socks, settled fights, scrubbed floors, ironed, and done dishes. I had planted potatoes and stripped cane, had husked corn in the fall and picked berries in the summer. It had all been fun, a game, a part of growing up.

But now I was growing up . . . to what? What use did I have for expensive jewelry and fancy clothes, for plush surroundings and big cars? I was an artist, and would have preferred bare feet and blue jeans. Somehow that ring, and my acceptance of it, made me one of the corrupt elite. I began to have misgivings about all it stood for.

A tall cement-block tower was constructed in the middle of the area that had been pasture, between the Vogel house and the dining hall. It rose against the trees, gray and shaftlike, with a bluntly pointed roof. Speakers were installed on the top floor, and an over-sized double manual Hammond electric organ was set up in the music room at our house. Carlita was put in charge of all organ playing and spent long hours practicing with the outside speakers shut off. On Sundays, or when guests of special importance arrived, the organ echoed over the forest with an eerily beautiful sound. John loved the music and sat listening to it with his head in his hands, often weeping quietly.

The little children crowded around him.

"Daddy, why are you crying? Are you sad?"

"No . . . just crying for happiness," he said, scooping them up and hugging them.

I tried to organize the sprawling area called the art room, decorating its walls and setting things on the too-generous shelves, but no matter what I did, the place always resounded with emptiness. I also clipped from a magazine an ad for an art school in Connecticut and wrote for information about taking courses. A few weeks later two men turned up asking for me. John met them in the parking lot and brought them to the art room. They looked at my work and asked if I would like to enroll in their classes. Before I could answer, John had courteously escorted them out the gate, telling them on the way that I had a gift from God which was not to be interfered with by men's teaching methods.

They must have left thinking we were all insane, and I ground my teeth in pent-up rage.

"Did you send for those men?" John asked, white-lipped.

"I asked for information. I didn't order two men!"

"I'd rather have you dead than in art school. Those places are the pit of hell."

"Your father went to one. You brag about that!"

"That was different. Art school is no place for a girl."

I went back to the empty, echoing art room. Where was the place for a girl?

In this bleak mood, I turned again to Aunt Kay. She was teaching other children in the upper grades now, but she had never lost touch with her original group. Every Friday night during the summer she took us out in the woods for cookouts, and Friday nights in the winter she had a craft class with us. Both were only organizational shells around her real purpose—to give us an opportunity to talk, to discuss life, to find ourselves and discover meaning as we grew. It was the one forum of free discussion available to us. Yet for several years, because I sensed John's vague mistrust of her, I had kept my distance, out of loyalty to him. She was one of those who had avoided his Truly Spiritual Soul Society of unquestioning followers. But now I needed help. I began first by indirect, then by more direct means to send out distress signals.

One Friday night up at the Flat Rock, not far from where I had painted the jacket for John's book, we built a fire and began to roast wieners, sitting around the blaze, talking and listening to the tree frogs and whippoorwills sounding in the darkness. We discussed growing up, and futures, and all the things that did not exist in John's mind except as he saw them.

"But how can you know what's right to do and what's wrong?" I asked, as usual jumping into the middle of the question.

Aunt Kay looked into the fire with a little smile. "Don't you think you can usually tell that?"

"Sure, I can tell what I think is right, but that's only where the problem starts. Some things seem right to me, but by doing them I would offend someone else's sense of right. Then how does one choose?"

"You mean, if the person happens to be a parent or an authority?"

"Right."

"That's difficult to sort out when you're young. Younger people usually have to live within the bounds set for them by older people, at least until they are old enough to make mature judgments themselves."

"But what about a young person who sees wrongdoing? I mean . . . are we responsible when we obey people in authority who lead us into wrong?"

Aunt Kay was silent for a moment, weighing her answer. Pearl and Carlita, Maxine and Janey were listening intently.

"I believe," she said slowly, "that in the end each individual, and certainly a person as old as you girls are, is responsible for his or her own actions and decisions."

"But sometimes," Carlita interrupted, "sometimes if a person speaks up, it will cause trouble! They will be punished!"

"Give me an example," Aunt Kay said.

Carlita hesitated, looking around the circle of faces. "Uh, well, uh . . . like the Garden of Eden." Carlita finished the sentence rapidly. She had heard nothing but Bible stories since she was small, and it was the only example she could think of even though the analogy was not clear. "Sure. Eve had the free choice of whether to do something or not, but when she did it she was punished!"

"I thought we were talking about speaking out against wrong," I said. "What does that have to do with it?"

"Carlita is thinking about the consequences of making any choice," Aunt Kay covered kindly. "And that is to be considered.

When we're old enough to choose, we are old enough to accept the consequences."

"I wonder if they were ever sorry afterward?" Carlita asked, staring dreamily into the fire. "Do you think they wanted to leave that garden, and the only way they could do it was to disobey and get kicked out?"

"I never thought of it that way," admitted Aunt Kay.

Carlita's question startled me. I had never heard her say anything sensible before.

"I'll bet . . ." I agreed, warming to the idea as I said it. "I'll bet they were bored silly in that garden."

Aunt Kay smiled and poked up the fire. "You're getting close to some very basic problems." she said. "And I can't give you all the answers. The only thing I can tell you is that there are many things we don't know. Life is a search."

I listened to her quiet voice with the wideness of the night sky behind her, and felt a wonderful sense of release. Nothing was finished, nothing was too late. Life was still open for us to discover, and the decisions were ultimately ours.

Even in this paradise.

CHAPTER NINE

The Laurel River floated idly past, the pink of rhododendron blossoms reflected in its smooth brown pools. In a few places rocks or fallen logs stirred it to foaming white resistance, but for the most part it glided past, brown, sluggish, compliant.

I sat on a rock halfway out in the river studying the cloud patterns reflected in the water, the action lines created by resistance, the surface and the depths. How deceptive water was! Colorless in the hand, yet adapting itself to every color in its setting. Was water brown or pink or blue or green? It was all of them, none of them. Yet somehow, if one laid down the pools of brown on the canvas, with blobs of pink and swirls of green, water appeared, water transferred from the river to the canvas. It did not need to be understood in order to happen. In fact, trying to understand it inhibited the process. Logically, if one took river water and spread it on the canvas, it should look like river water. Actually, all one would have was wet canvas.

Whether instinctively or in deference to his father's memory, John respected art and my desire to be an artist, and for the past two years painting had been my escape from the bewilderment and strangeness surrounding me. But a new struggle was going on beneath the surface: Would he use me for his purposes or would I use him to get what I wanted? I was catching on to the fact that "using people" was the name of the game, and the two of us played it hand over hand.

When his book was officially published, a Corbin department store offered us a window for display purposes and asked me to paint a backdrop of the hills and valleys with the original log cabin nestled in the pines. I was to use fall colors; fall leaves would be piled at the foot of the painting, and stacks of the book would be set up among them. John and I were both delighted. He wanted me to do it to promote his book, and I wanted to do it so I could stay in Corbin for a few days, free of supervision.

I felt a huge sense of freedom. I walked boldly past that forbidden place, the Hippodrome Movie Theater, and glanced into its dark doorway. I dared admit to myself that the buttery odor of the popcorn coming from the theater smelled good and did not stink. I walked past the Catholic church and even tried to smile at a black-garbed nun, but it was more than I could pull off. I could brave the power of Hollywood, but the power of Rome was more than even I could face. When the jukebox played in the City Café, I could tap my foot and listen to the words. Not that they were much to listen to, but at least I could if I felt like it.

At the corner drugstore I leaned on the counter and talked to Mr. Dyche, the gray-haired druggist. He had often given us curious glances when we came in with John and company, and he seemed glad to have a chance to talk with one of us alone.

"I'll bet a girl like you has a lot of boyfriends," he teased.

"You'd better bet on something else!" I laughed. "I can't even have one. We're not allowed."

"How does your daddy manage that?" he asked. "It didn't seem to make much difference what I told my kids. They just grew up and did as they pleased. How can he make you all do as he says?"

It was hard to answer him. Perhaps, I thought, it was because we had not yet come to any ultimate clash of wills.

My first taste of independence had left me eager for more, and I was glad to go back to Corbin when Gram got sick and had to go to the hospital for tests, and John asked me to stay with her. He probably wanted a few days without my candid remarks, and I wanted another stay in town to try my wings.

Gram was not really sick, but the work in the dining hall had worn her down. Hardly five feet tall and barely ninety pounds, she'd been wrestling huge thirty-quart kettles, preparing gigantic meals, and rushing around the kitchen with her eyes flashing and her corseted back ramrod straight, bossing the work crews. She was totally exhausted, and, besides, she looked worried.

"I hope your father knows what he's doing," she said in veiled words. "I love him, and he's my son, but he sure doesn't use his head sometimes. I made the remark to Grandpa Will just the other day that I can't understand why . . ."

I sat and listened to Gram, brought her magazines and Pepsi-Cola, and when she fell asleep I walked down the creaking hospital stairs to the street.

The street—the wild and worldly whistling and bustling Main Street. But what was there to do? I had only enough money to buy food. The clothes in the shops looked fascinating, but I couldn't buy them. I tried to think of a way to invest the few food dollars I had to earn more.

In Belk-Simpson, the store where our book was displayed, I had noticed men's neckties with colorful printed scenes and other pure white ties. On a hunch, I talked the clerk into selling me a dozen white ties on credit, and then in the art goods store I bought a set of textile paints. Back in the hospital waiting room I dug up all the old magazines that had outdoor pictures and began laying out designs. I painted the ties one by one until I'd done half a dozen, left the hospital, and went up and down Main Street calling on the shopkeepers, offering them hand-painted ties for ten dollars a piece. It was an outrageous price, as much as the adults at home got for a month's allowance, but I sold all six, paid for the dozen I'd bought, painted six more, and walked into the best shop in town. My luck held and I found a glorious gray denim skirt and jacket with a red striped shirt and a jaunty cap that became my identity badge. I wore it whenever I needed assurance that staying at the home was my own choice, that if I ever wanted to live in the outside world I could survive.

We all came home sick from the next trip. Christina had been doubled up with pain and fever in every motel, but we were on tour and John told her to straighten up, we had no time to mope around. She was assigned to the middle of the back seat so she wouldn't show from the window and create bad publicity, and we went on. A day after we returned home, she turned a deep yellow. We were in for a round of hepatitis.

In the unpredictable way that hepatitis spreads, it skipped from dorm to dorm, one victim at the boys' cottage, two at the girls'. I was the only other teenager at our house that caught it, possibly from taking care of Christina, and I found myself fascinated by the high-level pain and fever. Physical suffering was almost a relief after the unnamed anxiety I'd been living with. I could simply relax and have hepatitis. I didn't have to wonder what was the matter.

The fever soared, and I began to hallucinate. I was building a model of the Garden of Eden for visitors to go through. At the exit, each person would have to choose whether or not to eat the fruit, which was in some vague way sexual. If evil won, it was supposed to prove something. I never could get the thing concluded, but lay with it spinning, around and around in my mind. Then I too turned a deep yellow. When the fever dropped, I felt curiously cleansed, aware that some battle had been fought deep in my mind, in regions that were strange even to me. I felt new and vulnerable, uncommitted. As yet I had neither eaten the fruit nor refused it.

But nothing could have prepared me for the day I met temptation head on, the day John had not planned on. It was an ordinary dull December afternoon. Snow had fallen and melted, leaving the grounds a sodden mess. It was Friday, the day set aside for art classes in the empty wilderness known as the art room.

I felt foolish teaching art to kids younger than myself. It was one of those wheel-spinning activities John had given me in the hope of keeping thoughts of college out of my head, but I knew it was a farce. What I had learned I knew by practice and intuition, and I did not know how to pass it on. It embarrassed me to pose as a teacher. But every Friday a roomful of eager young students gathered, wanting me to show them the secret of becoming an artist. All I could do was encourage them, give them drawing materials, and share with them the excitement of creating.

That day the group of would-be artists were deep in the excitement of creating twenty-five versions of a billy goat when I saw a car coming down the road and parking in the lot. Relieved that I was occupied and would not be called on to act as a guide, I ignored it. A little later Carlita came swishing into the adjoining room and switched on the electric organ. The music began floating majestically from the tower, and I wondered what personage of importance had arrived. I heard them coming through the house, through the library, and into the music room. Aunt Kay was taking the group around.

I concentrated on the children, feeling nervous about being observed. Organ music on Friday. I could see it. This would be some professor from an art school, and I would be caught teaching twenty-five kids how to draw a billy goat twenty five wrong ways.

I looked up, and Aunt Kay was standing in the doorway. With her were two women and a tall young man in his early twenties. She introduced them, and the names escaped me. People came and went by the hundreds, and what did a name mean?

Then I realized the young man was watching me closely. He had fantastic shadowed eyes. His face, besides being extremely good-looking, had a quality that made me do a double take. There was something open and fresh about him, something that was hard to believe. I studied him covertly, wondering if there really were such people in the outside world. As casually as I could, I showed them around the room.

Between classes I had been working on a chalk drawing, a view of the breathtaking mountains that appeared when one rounded the bend approaching the home. The young man stopped in front of the drawing, looking at it in a preoccupied way. Then he looked directly at me. "Is it exciting to work here?" he asked, a host of questions in his searching eyes.

"I . . . I guess so!" I said, laughing a little. No one had ever asked me that before.

Then they were gone, out of the room and down the stairs

before I realized that I didn't know his name, and a name might mean more than anything in the world.

Maxine came into the room as I was sweeping up after class. "Did you see what I saw?" she whispered excitedly.

I nodded at her and kept on sweeping.

"You should have been in the study," Max was still whispering. "You'd think we were being attacked by the enemy! When he walked in, Daddy looked like he was seeing a ghost. I was supposed to take them around, but one look at that big tall guy and he picked up the phone and called Aunt Kay. I never saw him move so fast! He didn't even let him sign the guest book. He got a separate sheet of paper and asked him to write his name and address."

I laid the broom down and looked at her. "Why?"

"I don't know."

"Where is it?" I asked quickly

"In the study, in the office basket."

"Is anyone there?"

"No, Daddy's gone, checking around the grounds to see that nothing happens while he's here."

I left the rest of the sweeping and ran to the study with Max. We dug out the piece of yellow paper with the name and address written on it in brown ink. Gordon DePree, Zeeland, Michigan.

I gazed at the paper in my hand, wondering who and what he was. One thing was sure. With a name like Gordon DePree from Zeeland, Michigan, he was Dutch. The fact tingled like a peppermint.

They accepted John's standard invitation to stay for supper, and I, caught in the familiar ambivalence, decided not to go. But when the last bell rang, I found myself putting on a red jacket and running toward the dining hall like life was going out of style. I sauntered through the boys' section, trying not to look at him and hoping he was looking at me. He was sitting between the two women he had come with, and I wondered if one of them was his girlfriend. I hoped they both were. It would be safer.

After supper it was beginning to snow again, silver flakes floating through the half-dark air. From a distance I watched him put on a blue jacket and slip into his boots. Everything he did seemed so clean and uncomplicated. Then I followed the gang of girls and we piled into the red jeep with John, ready to go home. At that moment I saw Gordon coming toward us, boots undone, long legs striding through the snow. He reached the jeep and bent down. From where I sat, crushed in the pile of girls, I could see his face just beyond John's tired profile—young and alive, close-shaved dark beard, white teeth.

"Say, you wouldn't need any volunteer work here during the summer, would you?" said the deep voice. "I'd be glad to help, dig ditches or anything."

Johns slack facial muscles stiffened. "Thanks, that's very kind of you, but we're fully staffed for this coming summer. And as for volunteers, we really don't have a place for a single fellow to stay."

Gordon got into his car with the two women, and they drove up the hill. The jeep motor roared. John shifted gears viciously, and we shot ahead. Huddled in the crowded darkness, no one said a word.

How in the world I ever had the nerve to brood about him all that week, I'll never know. All the excommunications, the people who had been banished to the black unknown for committing the unpardonable sin, the curses of God on former offenders—all seemed to disappear into an unreal mist when confronted by this warm tide of feeling. I was in love with Gordon DePree, and all the rewards of heaven and the fires of hell failed to reach me. Telling myself I was crazy, I lay awake at night dreaming of him. I recalled his eyes, his smile, heard the deep voice—but it was the look in his eyes that I conjured up over and over. What did it mean? Who was he, and what was his life, and how could I ever know? I tossed unsleeping, caught in a delicious fever.

I thought of writing to him, then knew I could not. Besides being unladylike, I would be killed.

When his letter came, one glance at the brown ink on the envelope made me think lightly of both death and ladyhood. I had not imagined it. Something magic had happened to him as well. Of all the people at the home he was writing to me.

I hardly dared open the letter, afraid it might say something ridiculous or too extravagant or less than my dream of him. But his words were polite and cautious, measured and gentle. He thanked me for showing him around the art room, and conveniently asked a question that would require me to answer him.

"I'll have to admit I'm an old man of twenty-two," he wrote., "and in my first year of grad school. Could I ask a favor of you? I have to do a paper on getting ideas across to children. Since you teach a class once a week, would you share some pointers with me?"

I sat holding the letter and sighed, the strong strange feeling gripping me. I could see his eyes again, and I shivered. Then I almost laughed at the thought of explaining how to get the idea of a billy goat across to my "students"! What could I say? "I'm trapped here, and I'm a rotten teacher.?" Hardly the line. I would compose a very ladylike letter, telling him that the most important element in relating to children was sincerity (it produced sincere-looking goats) and hoping he could read between the lines to learn that I felt he was the most genuine looking human being I had ever seen. John would surely read the letter before it was mailed, and I dared not say anything quotable.

John did mail the letter, grudgingly, and I was torn between hoping I would and hoping I wouldn't hear from Gordon again. But when the second letter came I knew I wanted it more than I had ever wanted anything in my life.

We were going out to Cumberland Falls Lodge that night to celebrate a birthday, and we were dressed and waiting when John came from the boys' dorm with the letter. I could tell he had been keeping it in his pocket. It had a worn, crumpled, worried-over look. There was fatherly resignation in the way he handed it to me, as if to say. Well, here you are. What did I expect?

I took it and went into the bathroom, the only private place in a household of twenty-two girls. I opened the envelope with shaking fingers and read the brown ink message. He *had* sensed what I was saying between the lines. He was warmer this time, and a trifle bolder.

" . . . I've been wondering what the dating situation is at the home," he wrote. "I imagine you are all considered brothers and sisters there . . . Do you ever date outsiders?"

I stood in front of the mirror, my blood thumping from my feet to my throat. *Gordon, dear far away mysterious Gordon, can you possibly comprehend a life like mine? Is your life really a simple choice of dating whom your will? My friend, my love, even the word date sends my sainted father up the wall. What can I do? I can't even use your words to answer you. They're red flags from the pit of hell.*

I closed my eyes and held the letter to my face, kissing it gently. I would find a way. I would risk all the anger in the world to know this man.

Dinner that evening was a warm haze, a golden glow. I walked the cobblestone floor of the candlelit lodge thinking of how it would be to come here with Gordon. Everything would work out all right. It had to. It was right. John could be a grouch at times, but when it came to ultimate decisions, he usually gave in and let me do as I chose, with that little defeated, indulgent smile on his face. Actually, I was quite free. I could even detect a glint of humor in his eyes—as though he thought me quite a young devil.

We were in the ladies' room at the lounge before I caught the first hint of trouble, but I was enveloped in such a cloud of love that I chose to ignore it.

"Are you going to write back to that guy?" Carlita asked while we were combing our hair.

"Of course I am," I said. "Why wouldn't I?

She looked at me as though I were breaking the eleventh commandment. "You'd better not," she said. "There'll be trouble."

"What kind of trouble? What can anyone actually do?"

"If you have a boyfriend, I'm going to have one too."

"Suits me. You'd probably be a lot better off if you did."

"What do you mean by that?"

"I mean that you're eighteen and I'm nineteen, and we're not kids anymore. We've got to grow up!"

Carlita looked down at her fingers and twisted the ring. It was still on her left hand.

Without too much trepidation, I gave John Gordon's letter the next morning and went back to my room to wait for his permission to reply. As far as I was concerned, it was a polite formality on my part, and I was being considerate in asking his approval. I seemed to have conveniently forgotten that in making this request I was negating years of indoctrination. My mind raced ahead, thinking of the possibilities of love. Gordon and I would carry on a correspondence all winter. Next summer when the world was warm and green, he could come from Michigan and help on the grounds, and I would get to know him, to understand all those questions in his eyes. We could drive to Cumberland Falls and walk the paths, holding hands like the other strolling lovers . . . and in some quiet corner we could stop and kiss. And what if it all came true, if we fell in love, deeply and for all time? We would marry and both work at the home. We could be John's future helpers together, and there would be no rebellion, no pain. It would be paradise, with apples for breakfast every morning, and there would be no sworded angel to drive us out.

Carlita came into the room, crashing into my pleasant daydream. "Daddy wants to talk to you," she said.

I looked at her, but she avoided my glance. Her face was red, as though from crying, and there were weltlike puffs under her eyes.

"Did someone hit you?" I asked. "Your eyes look funny!"

"It's none of your business!" she said, going into the bathroom and slamming the door.

Still blindly dreaming. I walked along the gravel path between the hedges and knocked at the study door. John let me in. His face was red too, and there was an angry hunch to his shoulders.

"You wanted to see me?" I asked.

He sat down behind his desk and fiddled with a pen. "About

the letter," he began. "Did you actually intend to answer that fellow?"

"Yes," I said steadily.

"You know you girls are not allowed to fool around."

"I don't consider this fooling around."

"Then that's even more serious. Do you know what this means?' Each one of you has your place here in the future, and if one of you breaks it, everything will be broken. If one of you defies me, the whole chain of discipline will be destroyed. Even if I wanted to be lenient with you because you are my child, it is impossible. There is a principle involved, and I'm afraid you're forcing me to set a choice before you."

"But why does it have to be a choice?' Why can't I have a boyfriend and still help you here?"

"And what if he doesn't want to work here?"

"That's all so far in the future! All I'm asking for right now is a chance to write to him. I might even decide I don't like him. You never can tell. Don't you think it will all work out for the best? Don't you trust my judgment?"

"In some things, but not this. There'll be no exercise of judgment. Don't try to fool me! If he so much as lifts a finger in your direction, you'll fall for him. I'm not that stupid. Answering his letter is not the simple thing you pretend."

"Why isn't it? Why does everything around here have to be so all fired complicated? Give me one good reason!"

John cleared his throat and looked away. "There are certain factors here which you have been very slow to comprehend. No one knows the strain under which I work, the complexity of my life. Maybe someday you'll understand, but for now I have to lay it on the line. If you decide to answer his letter, you leave. You will walk down the road and never come back. It's up to you."

I went to him and put my arm around his shoulders, using the name I seldom spoke. "Daddy, do you always have to chop the world in half? Do things always have to be so broken?"

His shoulder muscles stiffened under my arm. "You heard the

choice I've put before you. If you choose this man, your usefulness
to God is finished."

"Why did you get married?" I asked quietly.

"Married!" He said the word like a curse and got up suddenly,
knocking me halfway across the floor. By the time I had collected
my senses, he was already in the next room with the door locked.
The letter lay on his desk. I took it and left the study.

The prayer room in our house had always seemed like a clammy
little box to me, and I seldom used it, leaving it for more formally
pious souls like Carlita. But now it seemed the right place to go,
the only authority higher than John.

I closed the door and knelt by the wooden bench, too confused
to formulate a prayer, letting thoughts and feelings rush through
my mind. On one side I felt the fears of the past closing in on me,
the nightmare that John would in some way sacrifice his only child
for this cause, dread of being banished forever to the black unknown
that we had been taught to hate and suspect, revulsion against the
thick wall of submission growing around me like a layer of fat. At
the same time I glimpsed the hope of the future opening to me,
my yearning for a life that was creative and free, my longing to
rebel thoroughly and finally against John. There was no middle
ground, no room for compromise. Either John would win or I
would.

The questions fought one another in my mind. What had
caused his sudden change of attitude? Why did he pretend I had a
choice and then snatch it away? Why did he give me the letter at
all? Some piece of the puzzle was missing, but one thing was certain,
there would be no reasons given. John did not deal in reasons. I
would have to make a decision based on what I knew.

Face red and eyes swollen, I sneaked out to get a piece of paper
and a pencil, then ducked back into the sanctuary of the stuffy
room. One by one I checked off the issues on two lists, STAY and
GO.

When I had written down everything I could think of, I stared at the lists, the truth slowly sinking in. At nineteen I was madly in love with a perfect stranger. I knew nothing about him, nor he about me. For this will-o'-the-wisp I was considering forfeiting a future with a nationally known and well-respected organization. I would be disowned; I would break up what was left of the family; I would be booted out penniless and friendless into a world with which I was not too well prepared to cope. Yet I would risk it if this stranger and I were not strangers, if we really knew each other. But as things stood, what could I do? Go knock on his door and say, *My love, my dream, for you I have given up heaven and earth. Take me!* If he had any sense, he would run.

For hours I crouched at the bench, torn with a gut-wringing pain. If only I could talk to Gram, could ask her again what it was like to run away and marry a man one adored at the cost of everything. But her story was different. Mine was even more shadowy. He might consider me only an interesting curiosity, and I would make a terrible fool of myself.

No, in the end it was not John's opinion I was worried about but my pride. I could get hurt by making a decision when this friendship was so green and tender. This was not the time to decide. Staying was the opposite of deciding. If I stayed, maybe someday, somehow, the right thing would happen.

At night I came out of the prayer room and walked toward the study feeling light and hollow, as though my whole body had been purged by fire. John was sitting at his desk, his head resting in his hands. He looked up when I entered, and I saw a strange look on his face, a look of hope and shame and eagerness and deadness.

"Okay," I said hoarsely, "you win."

The next afternoon Janey came from the office fresh with the news that John had dictated a letter to Gordon and Nada had typed it. I felt relieved that at least he would have some word, would know that I was alive if not free. Then in a final act of cleansing I tore up the two precious letters and threw them away. I was determined to force the whole affair out of my mind. How had I been drawn into this whole mess anyway? How had I ever been tempted to swerve from my original intention to remain aloof from men? They were a curse, not worth the trouble.

Carlita stood in front of the long mirror in our bedroom preening and giving me sidelong glances as she combed her hair. I knew she was in some way to blame. Clearly she had some power over John that I did not, and I hated her more than ever.

That winter all the hallowed spots were accursed. The snow falling in the twilight, the glimpse of a blue jacket, the memory of his face. I switched my materials to the other side of the art room, unable to stand where Gordon had stood. The thought of him was still a searing pain.

At Tripplet's store in Corbin, I was struck by Andy Tripplet's face. He looked like Gordon. Andy had been married for several years, and I had hardly ever spoken to him, but his eyes had that same shadowed quality, that same haunting look when he smiled. I watched him sometimes as he walked across the parking lot, tall and good-looking, with a limp that on him was attractive. He had been an unconfessed idol of mine for years. His face had always fascinated me, and now more than ever.

It was that haunted quality, that bruised look under the classic features that startled me. He had been an only child, loved and favored by his parents, headed for a medical career, when he was stricken with polio. And now he was married to a pretty girl and had a son and worked in his father's grocery store, a big and profitable business, but not what he had dreamed of.

Sometimes I sat in the car waiting for John to buy groceries, waiting for time to pass, for the sun to go down and the moon to come up, for the world to dissolve and explode in a melting heat, for some token of divine justice, and I would see Andy walking across the parking lot carrying groceries for someone. I'd watch his rugged sensitive face and want to talk to him. I wanted to ask him, What is it like, Andy, five years after your dreams have been broken?

Are you still alive in there? Does it still ache? Is it all right now, or do you still cry in the darkness?

But Andy was a grown man, out of my class, and I was too shy to speak to him.

The home continued to grow and prosper. A large storeroom was built next to the dining hall, and we acquired freezers and storage areas. Once a week a wholesaler delivered cases of canned goods, and the frozen food man came on Tuesdays, sliding trays of rigid meat and fish into the freezers. The bakery in town made up a special order for us twice a week, stone-ground whole wheat sweetened with honey. It was so wholesome that even Miss Smith ate it. John was the dietician and Gram was the cook, and between them we ate royally.

The dining hall was elegant. The boys' section was solid cedar with amber lights, and the girls' was wainscoting and blue, with a wishing-well fountain in the center. A piano with a Solovox attachment stood in one corner of the girls' section, and every noon after Carlita had eaten, she played organ-piano solos. Toward the end of the hour John stood up, read from the Bible, and prayed poetic prayers while Carlita gave him a soft musical background.

In these prayers John asked for dedication on the part of the staff. He prayed for more obedience from the children, for a spirit of self sacrifice so that the work of God might go on. He prayed that we might be spared the temptations of the flesh and given the singleness of mind to make the greatness of the home a worldwide reality. And all this was prayed to the tune of Carlita's seductive music.

The booths in the dining hall were soft and padded, and I felt that they were going to smother me. Sometimes when I heard the music begin I would excuse myself, swing over the booth, go out the back door, run down the steps and up the hill to Gram's house. There were just so many times a week I could stomach what to me was mush. Yet as I sat at Gram's house thinking about it, I knew I had chosen this mush over a real-life risk. Was my choice final?

Deep inside I knew nothing was settled. I would bide my time and see how things developed. There might still be a chance of getting out all in one piece.

But one thing I knew was that the kind of religion I saw around me had begun to rankle. The hardware store in Corbin was owned by a man named J. P. J. P.'s business was not doing well, and he decided to spend some money advertising on the local radio station. Many merchants sponsored local preachers and advertised at the end of their sermons. J. P. asked John if he would be interested in a weekly program.

"Bring all those kids in and let 'em sing!" the hardware man said. "And you can get in a little preachin'. I think the people of this here area would enjoy that!"

We were not exactly slated for primetime—seven o'clock Sunday morning when all but insomniacs and fanatics were sound asleep. We had to get up at five to get everyone ready, and before it was light streams of us converged on the yellow school bus. Most of us went back to sleep on the long curvy ride to the radio station, but when the bus door was yanked open we all poured out.

The station was small, two studios and a control room, and our gang filled one studio to capacity. On signal from Rufus at the controls, we hummed while John introduced the program. Then we sang, John delivered a five-minute talk, and we signed off while J. P.'s commercial went on. While we filed out, a man and a woman with a guitar started singing in the other studio. Then the woman preached. It seemed she preached the same sermon every week.

Looking at her, I could understand the prejudice against women preachers. She was a hard-bitten wrinkled old bag, alive with the wrath of God. Every time I looked at her, I hoped the world would be lucky and she would convert no one to her way of life. But there was one comforting thing about people like her. They all hated one another, which saved me the trouble of having to do it.

One Friday evening that spring, when the world was warm and wonderful and bursting with new life, we went on a hike with

Aunt Kay, tramping across the fields fragrant with blossoms to the whispering pine forest over the hills. We set down our basket of food in a clearing called Bald Rock, and then with a whoop and a swing we were on our way down the path to the creek. All of us were grown now, seventeen, eighteen, nineteen. Janey was even twenty. We were getting old.

Back up the hill, we gathered wood for a fire. The whippoorwills were beginning to sing their plaintive lonely song. The frogs croaked in loud choruses, and the moon was coming up over the ridge. Somewhere in the distance a lone foxhound howled, and a hunted fox barked its choking cough. The fire crackled and sparkled, lighting up the gray mossy rock. Around us the trees closed in, dark and shapeless in the night. It was as though this were a continuation of all the other summer Friday nights, but now that we were getting older the questions were getting deeper.

As always, we roasted hot dogs on sourwood sticks and toasted sweet rolls with peanut butter. We kicked off our shoes and sprawled on the rock and ate too much and asked all the questions never supposed to be asked, except on Friday nights. If any of us had ever repeated the things that were said on those nights, all of us would have been incriminated; but there was an unspoken agreement which none of us had ever violated.

I was roasting a hot dog for aunt Kay.

"Did you ever write back to him?" she asked quietly.

"No. My father won't let me."

"I don't see how he could possibly object. Such a prince of a man. I understand he's doing his graduate work in theology."

"I know," I said, dismay straining my voice.

"Why do you say it like that?"

"He just didn't seem to be the type."

"What's the type" she asked curiously.

"Oh . . . just not very free. Thus saith the Lord and if you don't like it you can go to hell—sort of that attitude. This guy looked like he still had a few questions."

"Don't you think ministers have questions?'

"They can't afford to. It's called doubt."

Somebody poked the fire and it blazed up.

"Don't you think doubts can be good?" Aunt Kay asked.

"I've never had a good one. Sometimes they can really pull your world apart. If I could have one wish, it would be that everything I know and everything I believe would all fit together, that it would all make sense."

"But don't you think believing in God helps you put life together?"

"No. I think the way I've been taught to believe in God rips life in half!"

"Really? Why is that?"

I sat quietly staring into the dancing flames, trying to crystallize my thoughts, to reach back to that long-ago time of innocence when I and the Green God, creator of the green goodness, were friends.

"I don't know where to start talking about it, but I know one thing that bothers me—this thing about miracles. Miracles really make me nervous."

"Nervous? Why is that?"

"I like a world I can depend on. I like a God who creates and then follows His own rules. I like wonders like seeds sprouting and babies getting born and the sun coming up in the morning. But a lot of people don't even think of these as being done by God. Something strange or anti-natural has to happen before people see it as a miracle!"

"But you still haven't told me why miracles make you nervous."

"They scare me! There's nothing you can depend on. Pray, and blood will flow from a tomato. Pray, and it will rain up from the ground and green grass will grow down from the sky. Pray, and if you're heard, the whole world could be turned into a giant lunatic asylum, with no lines between what really is and what one imagines!"

Carlita and Pearl, Maxine, and Janey had joined us now and were listening.

"Don't you think," Aunt Kay asked, "that all of life is a combination of fantasy and reality?"

"Sure, a combination." I said. 'But when the fantasy gets control of the reality, you're in trouble! You're crazy!"

"Oh?" she said.

"Not you personally!" I qualified, and we all laughed.

But Aunt Kay wanted to take the discussion further. "How do you feel that too much fantasy and too little reality affects you?" she asked.

"It's hard to tell the difference between right and wrong," Max said.

"Sometimes you feel lost," Carlita added.

"But how does it affect the way you feel about yourself?" Aunt Kay probed.

The words "feel about yourself" suddenly touched my mind like a glowing coal from the fire, lighting up a dark corner where six little girls lay crowded in bed telling scary stories.

"Ohhhhh!" I groaned, covering my face and half laughing. "I could tell you something about that! When I was just a little kid, I thought I was somebody very special. I had a silly feeling that my parents weren't really my parents, that they just took care of me, and that I was the child of someone much bigger and more important, whom I called the Green God, and there was this sense of mystery and magic about me. I guess in a way I thought I was a little bit holy, or at least very good. Then two things happened all at once. I found out that I was born because my parents did the same thing dogs do to have puppies, and then, bingo, it was Christmas, and I heard that Christ was born pure and holy because he came straight from God and Mary didn't have a man. Talk about feeling undercut! He had been born clean, but I was no more holy than a puppy."

"And you saw this as a split between real life and believing?"

"Not then, I didn't. I believed, but I was crushed. I tried and tried to figure it out. I was hoping they'd made a mistake writing the Bible. I knew lots of kids without fathers, and that was no problem, but Christ being born straight from God with no help from Joseph, and being the only pure one, that completely wrecked any thoughts I'd ever had of myself as good. I was embarrassed about being born, like I'd had a dirty start."

I paused, out of breath and a little frightened by what I was saying. A branch burned in two and fell into the fire, and Carlita breathed a deep sigh. Her mouth opened as if she wanted to say something, but the words didn't come out. I looked at her face, wistful and different in the firelight, and wondered what she was like under that hostile surface. Did she really feel lost, like me?

Aunt Kay shook her head, an amazed smile on her face. "I never know what you girls are going to come up with," she said. "And I must admit, coming from a very logical background, most of these thoughts never occurred to me. Maybe by the time you're my age you'll be relieved to have a little miracle now and then, something even more miraculous than a sunrise. In your search for a world where knowing and believing fit together, leave room to grow. Remember, you don't know everything. Don't limit your ability to believe to what you know. Part of life demands a grasp of reality, and there I would agree with you, but part is projected out beyond us . . ."

I listened to her voice, as I had for so many years, and watched the flicker of the firelight on the other girls' faces. Black behind us were the dark reaches of the sky—mystery. If only I could come closer to comprehending the realities of my life, perhaps the unknown would not trouble me so deeply.

There was a stifled sound in the quietness. I looked across the fire and saw Carlita crying.

That summer the flowers bloomed as if they had been fertilized by an army of dead men, and I felt as if I were every one of them. Dead. Spiritless. I tried to paint, and the brush fell out of my hand. Then I began to write poetry, to blister my notebook with scorching lines against loneliness, injustice, and warped religious attitudes toward love. I wrote down every angry thought that flashed through my mind, tore it out of the notebook, and threw it away. It was one safe way to stay sane.

Once I wrote a calm letter to Gordon telling him everything, and hid it in the lining of my purse. I would mail it the next time I went to town. Then I remembered that I had promised not to write. If I ever wrote to Gordon I would march into the study and tell John so. I would not, if I could help it, become a part of the duplicity around me. But even if I did write, and he wrote back, what would come of it? I would still be faced with the same brutal choice, the same dangers. And where would I go? What would I do?

Sickened, I realized that for all my good resolves, I was falling into the same trap as Anna.

CHAPTER TEN

The day the letter arrived from a movie company asking permission to make an hour-long sound and color movie of the home, John was excited, but some of the children were puzzled. A crowd of youngsters clung to the red jeep as John roared across the pasture to the dining hall at noon. Among them were Phyllis and Winston, now ten and twelve.

"Movies are bad!" Winston said, wrinkling up his nose. "Why does Daddy want to let them make one of us?"

"This one isn't bad," Phyllis assured him. "It's Christian!"

John explained it to all of us at lunch. A religious film company was going to do the story of the home. "We will be taking the instrument of the devil and using it for the glory of God." John said. "When this film is made, the work of the Galileans will be known worldwide."

Frankly. I was a little disappointed. I wished that the filmmakers had been the real thing, demons straight from the pits of Hollywood. If we were going to use the devil, why not meet him straight on?

But when they came, these watered-down devils were exciting enough. Two men breezed into the parking lot one day, short-sleeved and sunburned. Ken was a tall blond Swede, and Ralph a dark intense German. Ken had written a series of children's books that all of us had read, and he was a live hero. Ralph was loaded with the mysterious equipment of a cameraman—filters, reflectors, makeup, sound recorder, and all kinds of magic. We were completely in awe of them, and they enlisted our willing help as a free production crew.

It was the idea of entering the world of the forbidden that intrigued us most. A few of the children could remember going to movies before they came to the home, but most of us had never seen a motion picture. John had been instructed both by his Calvinist background and by the teachings of his later religious affiliations that motion pictures were anathema, and it was one of the random beliefs he had chosen to keep. The drive-in outside Corbin was described to us in the most ghastly terms, and we were expected to shield our eyes when we passed it at night. The theater in town was unthinkable, and our few affluent friends who had television sets were asked not to turn them on in our presence. Where movies were concerned, our eyes were virgin.

To relieve our complete innocence, Ken and Ralph had brought along their latest film, a story set in East Germany. It was a suspenseful thriller about a boy who was trying to escape from some evil power. The first time they showed it, we sat riveted to our chairs, unable to believe the moving images on the screen. When Hans was being chased by the one-eyed Von Ribbentrop, some of us got so excited we started shouting. "Go, Hans, go! Run, run, run!" And when the film was finished, we all clamored to see it again. They showed it three times before we were satisfied.

"You people are good for the ego!" Ken laughed wryly.

"Yeah, but don't let it go to your head," Ralph reminded him. "That was a simple chase story. This one isn't. At least it's not so clear to me what we're chasing."

The original plan had been to make a movie more or less based on John's book, but when Ken, the writer, actually began to take the chapters apart for structure, he decided that would be impossible. This produced a touchy situation.

"It's a great story, John," Ken said, "and I'm sure you'll have a good response to it, but it's no movie script. A script has to have a strong story line and suspense to pull people along. You have to wonder what's going to happen to X, and if Y will get there before Z, or nobody's going to sit and look at it for an hour."

"Never mind, X, Y, and Z," John told him. "The book has all you need to make a top film. It has all the stories of answered prayer, the incidents of faith and miraculous answers. They're the essential message of this place!"

"Let me tell you something, friend," said Ken, shoving his horn-rimmed glasses up on his nose. "People aren't going to care what the essential message of this place is if they're bored off their butts. To the public the appealing thing about this place is the kids and what happens to them!"

Ken retreated to a quiet little house on the old Hensley farm to write his script on location. He pored over John's miracle stories one by one and shook his head in bewilderment.

"There's no way I can use this material." he said. "It looks bad enough on paper, but it's going to look worse on film. I've got to get some other angle, something to convince people that this place is for real."

"What do you mean for real?" John argued. "There's no convincing to do. You make me sound like a fraud! This place is real. Just tell what happened."

"Okay now. John," Ken said. "Let me give you rule number two in writing a script. A story must be built on believable assumptions. Now let us understand that unless my name is DeMille or yours is Houdini, I cannot have you praying one minute and pulling a thousand dollars out of a hat the next—not as an assumed part of a story. People won't swallow it!"

"Then scrap the whole film." John said angrily. "Because there is no other story here!"

"Now not so fast, not so fast." Ken checked him. "There are lots of stories here. Every kid who's come here has a story. Think of the pathos in the lives of these eighty-some kids. Say, would you mind if I took a look at some of your files? Do you have background histories of any of the families?"

"We have case histories on all the children," John said coolly. "You can go to the office and ask Nada for anything you need."

Ken's script was finally written, based on the composite histories of several families. He wrote a story about a boy and girl he called Fin and Becky Tazewell, whose father was killed in the mines and whose mother was dying of T.B. The Tazewells lived in a broken-down cabin in the mountains. They were discovered by a social worker and brought to the Galilean home. The young Tazewells, shy and backward, were introduced to their new surroundings by Daddy Vogel. They saw the splendid grounds, heard the organ and the choirs, toured the buildings, and met the other children. Becky was greatly impressed and loved everything she saw, but Fin was not so sure. He viewed the new splendors with one eye on the woods, and the first time he ran into difficulty, he headed for the hills. There was a terrible storm, and Fin was lost in the woods. Becky was worried. In her concern, she was told to trust in God, and she accepted the faith of the other children as easily as she had accepted everything else. But to compound her worries, she heard that her dying mother wanted to see her children once more. Having now been converted, Becky was worried about her mother's standing with God, and she rushed to talk to her. In a stirring death-bed scene, the mother's soul was saved before she died. Fin was found camping in a mountain cave, and they all returned to the home to live happily ever after.

With the script written, Ken and Ralph chose the leading characters. No one was surprised at their choice of Phyllis and Winston to play the parts of Becky and Fin. They were both intelligent children who were poised and self-confident. Phyllis had large liquid brown eyes and silky long hair. Winston looked much younger than his twelve years, a cute compact kid with a turned-up nose, big white teeth, and green eyes fringed with long lashes. Andy Tripplet played the social worker, and John insisted on playing himself.

Although few of us could have leading roles, we were all eager to help in any way we could. I was given a chance to sit with the headphones on, watching the needle for voice modulation on the sound recorder. I listened to the lines, repeated over and over, wondering about some of them. The beginning of the film had genuine drama and charm, but as it went along the story seemed to fall back into assumptions just as arbitrary as those in John's book. I wondered how Ken could doubt that John prayed and got a thousand dollars in the mail, yet could believe that Becky prayed and the angels carried her mother's soul to heaven. It seemed a toss-up to me. Perhaps the only difference would be that the audience would believe the one because they had heard it so often, and disbelieve the other because they had not. I sat with the earphones on, watching the needle swing, wondering about the line between truth and fiction, between fantasy and reality. Was truth always measured against what people assumed was true? If that was the case, in a way the whole world was as illogical as the place where I lived.

I saw the needle swing to the high side of the sound gauge and turned the knob down to center it. Surely in the outside world some people could handle religious ideas within a livable framework, unlike John, who took every idea in the Bible to fantastic extremes. It was no wonder, in sound-gauge terms, that he had shot clear off the dial and was out of earshot.

Photographing the younger children was no problem. They were unself-conscious, uncomplicated, and John allowed the cameraman complete freedom with them. But when it came to scenes involving the older girls, all the old conflicts surfaced. For one thing, John would not allow us to wear on-camera makeup.

"Not on your life!" he told Ralph. "I've never permitted any of my daughters to smear their faces with paint. Once they put all that garbage on their faces, they might decide it looks fine, and then what would I have? A crowd of harshly painted hideous-looking women. God forbid!"

He looked as though he were going to burst into tears. The cameraman sighed and shrugged his shoulders, then turned to us. "Why don't you kids at least go out in the sun and get some color on your faces, huh? Some nice good natural all-American God-given sun!" And he went off mumbling that he should have taken the job he'd been offered in California.

Suntanning as a way of inducing color had never occurred to us since our berry-picking and cane-stripping days had ended. We tried it and were delighted. The whole sun deck outside the art room was strewn with bodies—not in bathing suits, God forbid, nobody owned a bathing suit—but with girls with elbow-length sleeves rolled tightly to the shoulder and skirts hiked to the knee. But the sun shone freely on our bare faces, and it was there the color was needed.

John viewed the mass sunning scene with disgust. "Look at what you've done to them now," he accused. "There will be no end to this vanity. Before you know it they'll be slipping down to the river and sunbathing nude."

Maxine and I tanned gloriously, but Carlita's skin did not respond to the sun. Her face was clear white and pink, and her eyes were blue blue. She seemed made to match the colors of the music room, rich deep wines and gold. Her hair was dark, and when she dressed in the right shade of blue she was a perfect photographer's model. Ralph took a good deal of footage with Carlita playing the double-manual organ. Then one day when the light was a bit off, he took out his makeup kit and quietly suggested she put a little pink on her lips.

"And one more thing," he suggested politely. "Uh, your ring is great, but I'd like to get a close-up of your hands on the keyboard, and all those rubies and opals take away from the nice line of your hands. Do you mind slipping it off for a minute and putting it over here?"

Carlita, conditioned to obey whoever was in authority, did as she was asked.

Ralph was immersed in his work when John walked into the room. John took one look at Carlita, and his face went tight.

Ralph, unsuspecting, turned around and winked. "Quite a beauty you have here.' he said admiringly. "I might enter some of these stills in a photography contest. Would you mind? Say, John, why do you need all these pretty girls? Couldn't I take just this one home with me?"

"You're married," John said dourly.

"Ah, aren't we all. But it's always nice to have an extra girl around the house. How do you manage it?"

Ralph was squinting into his lens, making photographer's jokes and conversation to keep a light in his subject's eyes, but to John it was no joking matter. He looked from Carlita's face to her hands. "Where is your ring?" he asked, an icy chill in his voice.

"I asked her to take it off," Ralph apologized. "I didn't think you'd mind. You know, you get all these girls gussied up in rubies and diamonds in your film, and nobody is going to give to this place."

John swung around and walked out of the room. Carlita hastily locked up the organ, smiled apologetically at Ralph, and picked up the ring. Then she followed John to the study. That night Ken and Ralph were locked out of the study and Carlita was locked in. It was a repetition of the Eugene episode. We could hear loud cries and angry accusations, and no one dared enter.

Ken and Ralph were baffled. None of us had any concrete explanation to offer, so Ken went to Anna. "Could you tell me what in the world is going on here?" he asked.

"I do wish I could," Anna said, smiling placidly. "I really don't have any control over that situation. I go to the study as seldom as possible."

"Do you mind if I ask you some frank questions?"

"No."

"Do you and John get along?"

"In our own way."

"And what's with the little French babe, Nada?"

"I'm sure you spent enough time over there during your research to know what the score is. Maybe you know more than I do."

"Damn it!" Ken said quietly. "Excuse me, I mean darn it. If I'd had any idea what a nuthouse this place was, I'd never have accepted this assignment. You know, there's something here that's definitely off color. I can't put my finger on it, but I have this premonition that I should burn every roll of film we've taken!"

"Why don't you?" Anna asked.

Ken looked down at Anna and shook his head. "I'm in it too deep now, lady. My company's given me twenty-five thousand dollars to make this film, and I've used over half of it."

They stayed most of the summer, and we got to know them well. I turned twenty. It was a black day. I was perched on the edge of oblivion, growing up to nothing, old before I'd had a chance to live.

Ken tried to offer his condolences. "Just take a few aspirin," he said in his mock-serious voice. "The pain won't go away, but you'll learn to live with it."

"What pain?" I asked, wondering if anyone had told him about Gordon.

"Oh." he waved his hands, "just the pain of living, of finding out what you are that you didn't know you were, and what you aren't that you thought you were."

I looked at him blankly. "Would you say that again?" I asked.

"Finding out what you are that you didn't know you were, and what you aren't that you thought you were," he repeated.

I still looked at him blankly.

"Oh, never mind." he said, waving his hands again. "It happens all the time. You'll recognize it when it bumps into you. It's called the philosophy of oshmopishpop."

"Of what?" I said, wondering if he spoke English.

"Um. I can tell you're going to succeed in this world. You catch on to things in a hurry."

I laughed, trying to remember one thing he had said. "Are you what you thought you were?" I asked.

"Oh, its a very sad story," he said. "I keep thinking I am, and then by some dirty trick I keep finding out that I'm not quite . . ."

"Not quite what?" I said, completely lost again.

"That's exactly the problem!" he said. "I'm not quite what I intended to be!"

"What did you intend to be?" I asked, grateful for some shred of something I could understand.

"Oh, it's too late now." He sighed sadly. "Take my advice and do it while you're young."

I left laughing, not quite knowing what he had said to me but somehow appreciating it.

When the movie makers left at summer's end, John sat in the air-conditioned study brooding over what he considered their exploitation of his resources. His farewell to Ken had been chilly because his book had been ignored and his favorite miracle stories omitted from the film, and he was still angry at Ralph over the Carlita incident. Frustrated with the whole movie experience, he cast about in his mind for some way to exercise more control over his kingdom.

A few years before, a widow who had no way to earn a living had brought us her two daughters and signed them over to the home-legally. Later she remarried. Her new husband had a decent income and a fair house and consented to her bringing her children to live with them. When she came to the home and asked for the girls, John refused, saying they were his by law.

The mother went to a lawyer in Williamsburg who was already somewhat skeptical of the Galilean operation and who took a great interest in the case. It came to trial, and in court the girls' mother stressed her former poverty and her present chance for a new start. John argued that the whole structure of his home was at risk if a legal document, signed and notarized, was not binding. Any parent could come at any time and snatch away his charges, creating an atmosphere of insecurity and fear. He announced his intention of keeping all the children up to the age of eighteen and some even beyond that age. The trial was played out to a packed courthouse, and in the end the circuit court judge, a man named White, ruled that the children should be given back to their mother. John's lawyer appealed to a higher court, but the ruling was the same.

Now White was again running for circuit court judge, and John had become obsessed with the idea of defeating him. White's opponent was a man named Bill Thorn, and John sent word to Thorn that he would like to see him.

Thorn came to the study, a rotund rosy man with a nice face. He was nervous as John invited him in. We wondered what it was all about and stuck around until John asked for privacy.

"Well, Thorn, what's your stand on liquor" John asked.

"Sir, I'd like to see the county stay dry."

"And on roadhouses?"

"Well, sir, I'd like to see them all closed down."

We went into the other room and heard no more of the conversation until they came out a good hour later. Then we heard John say. "All right, Bill. You do your best. Run an honest campaign, and well back you up. If it's God's will. He'll give you the judgeship."

When Thorn was gone. I asked John if he'd made a deal with him.

"What do you mean, a deal?" he asked warily.

"I mean, did you say you'd try to get him elected if he'd make judgments in your favor when he's circuit court judge?"

"Well . . . not in so many words, but more or less."

"But isn't that tampering with the law? Isn't that sort of obstructing justice!"

He looked as if he wanted to belt me one. "Spread that around, and you'll get me in plenty of trouble," he said. "I swear you're getting more like your mother every day. Let it suffice to say that if God wants this man in office, he'll be elected. You can't argue with that."

But John did not leave the matter in divine hands. Everywhere he went, in the countryside and in the town of Corbin, wherever the election was being talked about, he spoke against White. He said White intended to destroy the home, that White was an instrument of the devil sent to obstruct God's will, that he would have children snatched from the arms of the Savior and thrown back into the pits of sin and drunkenness they had come from. Young children would be given back to moonshining fathers, and young girls would be forced back into situations where they would be subjected to the temptations of the flesh.

Andy Tripplet heard John raving against White one day in the store. "Hey, Brother Vogel, you better not get mixed up in Whitley County politics," he warned, laughing. "You don't have any idea what a hornet's nest you're sticking your head into. Why, you make a political enemy today, and ten years later if he's got a chance, he'll sting you!"

"I have to protect myself," John argued.

"Aw, come on now, relax." Andy smiled, putting his lanky arm around John's shoulders. "There's plenty people around here willing to fight for you. We know what White did to you, and you don't have to tell us. Anybody's for that home ain't going to vote for White no how!"

But John became more and more determined to make sure of the election results. A week before the voting he asked Thorn to come and see him again. Thorn sat in the study fidgeting, hat in hand like an overweight schoolboy.

"Bill," John began, "I've decided to go on the air on your behalf."

Thorn looked startled. "Now look, Brother Vogel, that won't be necessary. You're going to make enemies that way. We all have to live together in this county once the election's over. I don't want you getting hurt for my sake, and besides that, I'm not sure how I feel about preachers getting mixed up in politics. As you said, I've tried to run a clean campaign. I hope I'm the best man and will win."

"I'm not saying you need my help," John countered. "And in most cases I would agree with you about separation of church and state, but in this particular instance I feel there is a definite overlapping of interests. People all over the county have heard that I oppose White, and some of them aren't sure why. This could cause misunderstanding, cause talk that I'm just meddling. My speech would not be so much an endorsement of you as a clear statement of my reason for opposing White."

"Well, Preacher, if that's the way you want it, I'm sure I can't stop you. Just don't get hurt for my sake. Politics is a rough game for preachers to play."

The next morning John went on the local radio station with a paid political broadcast. He told the story of the two girls. Judge White, and the effect that this ruling would have on the future of the Galilean Children's Home. He urged all the home's faithful supporters to vote for Bill Thorn, and to defeat Judge White. Then he closed with a poetic prayer that God's man would win.

The next morning the Corbin Times-Tribune printed an article by Judge White in which he said that he had only interpreted the laws of the state of Kentucky as he understood them, giving preference to the natural mother of the children, and that he had made his judgment in the cause of justice without pressure or for political reasons. His article implied that Thorn, if elected, would never have that same option.

But when the votes came in from the towns and the country polling places of Whitley County, Thorn had won. John was jubilant. It was the first time he had ever tried to influence county politics, and he had succeeded. It was another stone in the wall of security he was building around himself. But Bill Thorn had never been a religious man, and being cast as God's choice made him nervous. That weekend he joined the Baptist church in Williamsburg and was baptized. And John felt that his whole scheme—known and unknown—had been justified by the salvation of a politician's soul.

I found an empty notebook and began an allegorical tale, full of disguised anger. Every few days I wrote a chapter and tested it by reading it aloud to the crowd of children Phyllis' age who congregated on the art room steps. They laughed at the funny parts and cried when the mean guy killed the good guy's sweet little dog. It was a tearjerker and, in one of the mad-hatter definitions I had picked up from Ken, bad enough to be worth something.

I sent it to a Chicago publishing house, copying the address out of one of the books I had read as a child. They accepted it, paid me two hundred and fifty dollars outright, and commissioned me to do my own illustrations for another hundred dollars. The money meant nothing, except as a tangible validation of my worth. I gave it all to John. What mattered to me was that I was one step closer to being an artist and a writer. All I needed now was a jeep.

But trusting any of us with vehicles was more than John could take. Hs made a token attempt at teaching me to drive the red jeep, pronounced me unteachable, and forbade me to go out on country roads alone.

"But I have to do the sketches for my book, and I need some country scenes and people that we don't have on the grounds," I said. "I have to go over across Whippoorwill Hollow."

"Then take one of the workers with you."

"I can't get anything done if I have to sit and talk to somebody all day."

"Take Fanny. She hasn't seen much of the countryside. She's quiet and won't bother you."

I thought for a moment. Fanny was the newest worker at the smaller boys' dorm, a tiny blue-eyed woman with many of Gram's physical characteristics. But John was right. She was quiet. Her distinguishing mark was her ability to stand in wide-eyed wonder and believe absolutely everything she was told. She was John's sort of woman, the kind he wished we all were.

Fanny and I crossed the creek, and I made the sketches. She was not bad company, but I began to feel things closing in on me again. Would it be possible to be an artist and a writer in this environment? Written words had to be guarded, art had to be chaperoned. It was not exactly the giddy air of freedom one needed to create in.

John's book was on the market, and a film was in the making. With all this on his mind, he began to plan a grand tour. Word had come from Muskegon that the first parts of the film had been processed and were being edited. The color was beautiful, much better than they had dared to hope, and the acting was superb. Winston, who played Fin, was as professional as any child actor they had seen. With all that was happening, we were becoming too high class to travel around in a tarpaulin-covered school bus, and John began to plan on buying a new luxury-liner coach.

The project took no small amount of his particular skills. In such decisions he no longer worried about asking advice, or getting support from his staff but considered the larger and more important matters his private affair. As long as he had the approval of God, he did not even notice, much less ask for, other opinions.

The day that he announced in the dining hall that we were going to get a new Super-Dura-Liner coach, Nada stomped over to him. The dining hall was noisy with kids leaving, and John could hardly hear her.

"John, how can you do this to me, you naughty man," she simpered. "You didn't even tell me! You know we owe the work crews over a thousand dollars in back wages. How can you-" She stopped mid-sentence. John was watching Carlita play the piano-organ and was not even listening.

"John!" she snapped. "Did you hear me? If we don't pay the workmen by the end of this week, we'll have to lay them off! There is, I repeat, there is no money!"

John looked at her, as if returning from some long flight of fancy. "Oh . . ." he said. "Okay, Nada. I'll tell them."

Nada's head snapped back in what used to be her smile. It had now become more of a grimace, an expression of aggression. She turned and walked across the room, and I noticed with satisfaction that she shook both above and below the belt. Nada was getting fat and forty.

To John, his reasoning in regard to the coach was flawless. The Bible said, Delight yourself in the Lord, and He will give you the desires of your heart. John had been delighting himself thoroughly in the work of God, and believed therefore that heaven would give him his new desire. It was perfect logic. He laid out what he always referred to afterward as his Four-Step Plan of Faith, and decided that once these four steps were successfully achieved, he would consider himself approved of God and correct in acquiring the coach.

The first step was the workmen's wages. John agreed with Nada that they should be paid first. He needed a thousand dollars to pay their wages, and he began to pray. Within a week the bank in Corbin notified him that a railroad engineer in West Virginia had deposited two thousand dollars to our account. The workmen were paid, there was cash to spare, and Nada said no more. John was ready to go on to the next step.

Meanwhile, to whet his appetite, he visited the Fitzjohn Motor Coach Company in Muskegon, driving up to the factory with a carload of girls to inspect different coaches. He selected one that seemed suitable to him, and when he came home he hung a picture of it in the dining hall, with a $16,000 price tag on it, and the word PRAY. Anna and Miss Smith passed each other in the dining hall, rolling their eyes. John had finally flipped.

But he forged ahead with his plan. The second step was to sell the ton-and-a-half farm truck for $1500. He advertised it for sale in the Corbin Times-Tribune and spread word around the countryside, but there were no buyers until a stranger came to the parking lot one morning.

"How much you asking" he inquired, looking the truck over.

"Oh, uh, maybe I'll take eleven hundred for it," John said apologetically.

The man looked at him disapprovingly. "Don't sell that truck for eleven hundred," he said. "I've got a sales lot up in Lexington, and if you bring it up there I'm sure I can do better for you than that. I can't promise, but I'll try."

The next day Boyd the bus driver drove the truck to Lexington. No price had been agreed on, but in a few days a check came for exactly $1500.

John was beside himself. "Exactly to the penny what I agreed with God!" He smiled, all but clapping his hands.

I watched, wondering what the third step would be in this deal with heaven. Before long I knew. The school bus was to be sold. In this case John's agreement with God was that he would get three thousand dollars for it if he was to consider himself guided to go on with the coach. Since the market for school buses was naturally limited, he contacted the county superintendent of schools, who came to the home and gave the bus a good once over. He was the same county superintendent who had sent us the old desks and used books years before.

"What's your price?" he asked.

"Three thousand," John answered. "And I won't take a dollar less. It's in perfect condition. We don't allow our kids to scratch initials in the seats; we take good care of the motor; it's as good as new."

"I'll give you twenty-five hundred," bargained the superintendent.

"Can't do it," said John, and the man left. So John got in touch with the fellow who had sold the truck. He agreed to put the bus on the lot as well, and Boyd drove it to Lexington and left it.

A few weeks later, the county superintendent returned. He got out of his car and walked to the study. John met him.

"Brother Vogel, I guess I've been unfair with you," he apologized. "When I told the school board members what you asked for your bus and what I offered you, they said I ought to be ashamed. They reminded me that you take a big load off the county's hands, feeding and educating all these kids. They said I should offer you the three thousand."

John grinned a slow triumphant grin. "Okay." he said. "I'll get your bus for you tomorrow!"

That night he sat at his desk counting up the tally. He had $4500. There was only one more step in the deal. From some source he still had to obtain five hundred dollars over and above the living expenses of the week. Before the week was over, the five hundred extra dollars came in the mail, a bit from here and a bit from there. John had his five thousand down payment in hand for the luxury coach, and the complete nod of agreement from his God. Like a boy who had saved up his allowance for a new toy, he gathered up a few of us and took off for Muskegon. He walked into the Fitzjohn Motor Coach Company with his money in his pocket and was ready to pick out his favorite.

He was called into the business office.

"What financial security do you have for meeting these payments, Mr. Vogel?" the dealer asked him.

"Security? Nothing but my word that I want the coach and will pay for it."

"You realize that we can't do business that way. Can't you get your local bank to finance this deal?"

"That's not our policy."

The man coughed. "Uh, this children's home. How much does it take to operate a month?"

"About five thousand dollars."

"And how much assured income do you have?"

"Three hundred fifty-seven."

The man looked up, ready to laugh, but John was not laughing. The dealer straightened his face.

"I read the literature you sent, and it all sounds wonderful," the man said doubtfully. "But frankly I don't see how we can ever put this deal through."

"I believe you will," John said calmly.

We drove to another town to stay with friends while the company thought it over. In a few days John was called to the phone. He was to come to the office of the company president to discuss the purchase of the coach.

The president looked at John reproachfully over his glasses. "Now how can I make a deal with a man who has a fixed income of three hundred fifty-seven dollars, eighty-seven children to feed, and expenses of five thousand a month?" he asked. "How are you going to meet payments of five hundred eighty-five a month?"

"I don't know, but I will," John assured him.

The president looked at him and shook his head. "Well, since you do so many crazy things, I guess I can at least do one." He smiled, extending his hand. "The deal is on!"

John handed over the five thousand dollars, and his order was placed. In two months he had his coach, with plush seats, air conditioning, indirect lighting, luggage compartments underneath, and the name THE GALILEANS in the destination window. We could travel in style. But most important to John was the assurance that he was in direct contact with heaven. He needed the approval of no one, the censorship of no one. God was on his side, and which of us would have dared deny it?

The number of people touring the grounds daily had grown

to a torrent. To make sure that they understood the purpose of the home, John arranged for a sign painter to make rustic signposts at every important miracle site and building. Old Ben Stromberg had turned up one day, so fragile he looked blown in by the wind, and offered his services. He was paid the same ten dollars as everyone else, and old Ben's delicate script began to appear everywhere, on scripture signs, no smoking signs, no-women-in-slacks signs, signs with the names of buildings, and historical markers. But old Ben's prize work was destined never to be on display.

In all the hassle of buying the coach, John had not noticed that Grandpa Will was ailing. He came to the study one day for help. "I feels me not so good," he said to John. "Maybe I better go to the doctor."

In Corbin the doctor checked his heart. "Not too much I can do for you, Gramps," he said, "You're wearing out, old feller. Better take it easy, take a few more naps, hoe a little less, smoke a little less."

Gramps clutched at the back pocket where he kept his pipe. No one was supposed to know. Despite the no-smoking signs on the grounds. Gramps loved his pipe and couldn't stop smoking.

Now he decided for sure that life without a pipe and a hoe wasn't worth living, and he went back to work.

Old Ben came past the flowerbeds one day and asked Gramps how he was feeling.

"I don't know,' Gramps said reflectively, leaning on his hoe. "Sometimes I read those words in the Bible: 'Put your house in order, for you shall die and not live.' You know, maybe those words are for me."

That was when old Ben got out his best silver paint and made a sign for Gramps lovingly lettered in Old English script: SET YOUR HOUSE IN ORDER FOR YOU SHALL DIE AND NOT LIVE. And he proudly brought his gift to Gramps, who accepted it graciously. But the sign was stored in the back bedroom with the picture of the five children who had died, and never hung in the living room as Ben had hoped.

"That old fool!" fumed Gram. "Give a man a stupid sign like that! Hah!

. . .

John went on with his plans for the grand tour, the tour of all tours, with two choirs, books to sell, a movie to show, a television program in Chicago. Welcome Traveler had asked us to appear on their program. The whole world was opening up to us. And John wore his Stetson with a new rakishness. His strides between the study and the jeep were long and confident. Nothing was too large or too small for him to tackle. He was becoming invincible.

A nearby country church invited the Galilean Girls group to sing. Ordinarily John would have considered this too unimportant for these hectic days, but the invitation came from an old friend to whom he owed a favor, and he accepted.

"Wear your robes." he instructed us. "I don't want all those country hicks staring at your legs."

We went to the tiny backwoods church dressed in formal robes.

The floorboards were bare and creaky. The benches were homemade, decorated with decades of initials. The piano had ivories missing, and the church had been bypassed by the electric line. Two kerosene lamps sputtered at the front, giving a soft candle-lit glow. The traditional funeral parlor fans were tucked in the hymnal racks, reminding one of the imminence of the hereafter.

I sat in the rustic church thinking of days when our life had been simpler. Had it been better then? Had it ever been better? The absence or presence of material things had not made that much difference. There were questions so much larger, so much more basic than the acquisition of land and buildings and cars, even through prayer. Did John ever think of these things? Would he ever?

A country man in overalls was making the announcements. Mothers with babies in their arms dotted the church, seated among tired-looking men and squirmy children. In the back row a few young people sat whispering and exchanging glances.

"We thought this here would be a good night for a testimony meetin'," the announcer was saying. "And Brother Vogel, we're mighty proud to have you and these fine lookin' girls with us tonight. We was wonderin' if they'd like to come up one at a time and give us a little word of testimony."

I nearly froze to my seat. We were trained never to do anything alone, always to function as a group. What on earth would I say?

John was caught, but rose smilingly to the occasion. "I'm sure my girls would be glad to do that," he said. "Why don't we start at the end of the row and go across. Just a brief word about your service to the Lord."

Obediently, one by one, we filed up. Pearl said she wanted to be a nurse and work at the home. Carlita said she had given her musical talent to God and wanted to work at the home. Janey talked about working at the office, and another girl said she would work at the home even if all she could do was scrub floors. Closer and closer the line came to me. I was terrified. I wasn't very good at lying, and what I had to say would be hideously out of keeping with the other speeches.

I stood behind the homemade podium, my knees pure jelly. "I . . . I want to grow to be the best person I can, and use my life in some good way. I'm sorry I'm not sure how yet." I gulped and dived for my seat, my face crimson.

Maxine squeezed my hand. "You're probably the only one who told the truth," she comforted.

"And I'll probably get hell for it too," I whispered.

But the particular kind of hell would never have occurred to me. When it happened it left me deeply shocked, guilty, and confused.

I went to the study a few days after the church fiasco to ask John about music for the tour. We had been on quite cool terms since the testimony meeting, and I was hesitant to face him.

"Go with me," I begged Max. "I don't like it in there alone."

"You go ahead," she said. "You probably need to have a good talk with him before the trip, and you won't talk if I'm around."

So I went by myself.

John was in his inner room, sprawled on the couch, dreaming dreams and seeing visions.

"I think we'll start on the church building again," he said to me. "But if we open it up to the public, we'll have to put the whole place under twenty-four-hour guard."

"Guard? Whatever for?"

"I have valuable treasures here," he said. He reached up and pulled me down beside him. "Do you know that you've grown to be very beautiful?"

"Oh, average," I grinned.

"No, many men tell me you're very beautiful. You have a lovely body. I get upset when I see men looking at your body. I was upset the other night."

My heart was pounding crazily. I felt afraid of him. "Why were you upset?"

"All the other girls seem so committed to me. Why are you so hardhearted? Why are you so slow to commit yourself to God?"

"Because there are so many things I'm not sure about yet. I don't get direct answers from heaven like some people. I believe in God as much as you do, but He seems to make me figure things out for myself."

His eyes had a glazed look. He reached up and put his hand on my breast, then pulled me down and kissed me on the mouth, a soft wet warm kiss. I felt the tip of his tongue and shuddered.

"Does that make you feel strange?" he asked, his eyes half closed.

A warning sounded in my mind, and I shook myself loose with a crooked grin. "Why should it?" I asked hastily. "You're just my good old father, aren't you?"

With my heart thudding painfully, I made a quick exit from the study. What would Anna say if she knew what John had done? I wanted to tell her, yet I knew it would only add to her grief. And yet by not telling her, I became a part of John's conspiracy. Was that what he was trying to do—enlist me among the company of the faithful?

Shaking with shock, I locked myself in the bathroom with Maxine and told her.

"Don't worry about it." She shrugged. "He does things like that all the time. You just have to know when to stay out of his way."

"Good grief!" I said. "I wonder what would happen if a person didn't get out of there?"

At last the day arrived when Ken and Ralph came driving down the road with the finished film. We congregated in the dining hall, the projector whirred, and there we were on the screen. Corbin and the slow train, the mountain scenery on the way to the home, Grandpa Will's flowers and the floating flag. The children's faces, John's gentle smile, the rustic buildings. Then the story focused on Becky and Fin, and Becky was sweeping the porch of her tumble-down mountain cabin, brushing the long silken hair from her lovely child-face. Andy Tripplet, handsome and kind, took Cinderella and her adorable brother to the home, where they would be given love. The screen was awash with love, and I felt a little ashamed that I had questioned the story. It carried a tremendous emotional wallop, and the photography was stunning. It was all devastatingly beautiful, and we cried. Gram and Gramps cried too, and when the lights came on even Ken and Ralph were in tears. Everyone hugged everyone else, and felt wonderful.

No one doubted that *Shelter in the Cumberlands* would be a success.

CHAPTER ELEVEN

We rolled into Grand Rapids in the spring of 1954, all gleaming aluminum. We were the Galileans, the people with the message that the Lord God of Elijah was still on His throne. All who doubted need only come and listen to our words and they would be transformed. John paced restlessly up and down the aisle of the Super-Dura-Liner coach, his Stetson cocked over his face. He bent down and smiled here, patted a head there, gave a word of reassurance to the best singers, checked with Miss Smith, took my list of songs for the Galilean Girls group. He was the focal point, the guiding spirit, the father of us all.

That first night in the auditorium of a large nondenominational church was in truth pure miracle. John stood on the platform, splendid in a dark suit, radiating his unique combination of shyness and magnetism. The audience was clay in his hands. Then he called his children to the platform to sing.

Forgetting the tragedies and comedies of our private lives, we gave the audience a show to remember. Some power seemed to lift us up, singing through us, and the microphones translated our voices into magnificent sound. Then the room was dark and hushed, and the movie flashed on the screen, wringing the spectators' hearts until they wept. By the time Phyllis and Winston come on stage to take their bows, the audience was hysterical. An offering was taken while the girls group sang. It amounted to several thousand dollars.

John stepped to the mike, visibly shaken.

"I just want to thank you," he said humbly. "What you have given will be our coach payment for this month. We have purchased this coach on faith, and you have been God's answer for the first payment."

His words were drowned in a sea of applause and amens.

But at the resort in Charlevoix, Michigan, things began to come apart. Admirers of the home had offered us accommodations in their lakeside motel for as many nights as we needed to stay. It was a beautiful spot, where winds rippled across the lake and rustled through the Michigan pines. It may be that we were tempted by its charm to stay in one place too long and without the old familiar props. John was the only male, and all his women were in a holiday mood, all demanding his attention at once. Anna, Nada, Carlita, and I were all on hand, but our specific duties and occupations had been left at home. We turned on him. He was like a man on his way to heaven with a pocketful of devils, and the train was going too fast for him to jump off.

Anna, who was quiet and retiring at home, took her stand, "You should at least stay in my room while you're traveling," she warned, "if you value your public image at all. People notice such things. And I think you should arrange to sit near me, at meetings. At least not obviously near someone else."

I listened, wondering if she was protecting John or herself, or if she even knew anymore. Perhaps it was a matter of blind survival by now, without too many reasons.

Whatever the problem was, John must have felt it could be solved by sitting on our beds all evening. In the pine-finished motel room he sat on the edge of Carlita's plaid bedspread, staring soulfully at her and whispering quietly. I was embarrassed, but never really upset about it until the night he offered to read to us before we went to sleep. He opened his worn Bible and read that passage from the annunciation in which Mary replies. "I am the handmaiden of the Lord. Be it as you say unto me."

"In Biblical times women were not afraid to be used by God to accomplish His purposes," he said, looking directly at Carlita, "and used in whatever way He chose. I don't see why we are so hesitant in our day to make our bodies a living sacrifice."

I looked at him and saw the strange glazed expression in his eyes.

Something about his face made my flesh crawl. Carlita began to cry, and Maxine and I glanced at each other. Then John kissed us all good night and left. Carlita turned her back to us and went to sleep.

I lay in the darkness that night trying to sort out the terrible conflict I felt in the room. Why did I want to get up and bash Carlita's head in? Why did I shiver when I looked at her as John sat holding her hand?

Was I competing with Carlita for his attention? Was I? After all, he was my father, and besides that he had made me give up Gordon to stay with him. He owed me something. Or did he? Had I honestly given up Gordon, or was I only waiting like Fin in the film, with one eye on the woods, ready to run? No, on the nights when I watched the film over and over, it was not Becky the angel I identified with. It was Fin the rebel. I did not want John. Carlita could have him. The revulsion I felt was something stranger than straight sibling jealousy.

But regardless of how I or anyone else felt about John, Carlita had come to think of him as her exclusive property—at least until the afternoon she walked into the bathroom at the motel and found his arms around her younger sister. Pearl was half dressed, and John was kissing her.

"Oh, excuse me!" Carlita said and slammed the door on them. In a moment John emerged, red-faced. Carlita sailed past him, tore into the bathroom, and started slapping her sister. They pulled each other's hair, screaming and fighting like two cats.

"I told you to stay away from him." Carlita shrieked. "Stay out of his way, do you hear me? If you let him get anywhere near you, I'm going to tell our . . ."

"You leave me alone! Who made you my boss?' And anyway . . ."

"You'll be sorry, you stupid little fool!"

John reacted, as usual, by bursting into tears. I looked at him as he lay sprawled on the bed sobbing and shaking his foot, and found it hard to connect this craven creature with the figure of my father strutting proudly in his Stetson. There was something unnerving about it.

"Let's get out of here." I said to Max.

The two of us went down to the lake and sat by the boats watching the breeze send peaceful ripples over the water. Up by the highway the resort was dotted with playing children, and the gleam of the coach shone through the trees.

"Our problem is that we look so good, so innocent, so peaceful." I told Max. "Who would believe us, even if we told them the sort of things that go on?'

"But . . . what exactly would you tell?" Max asked.

She had a point. Standing up and saying that Daddy kissed Pearl in the bathroom would hardly bring the city police running.

One thought had excited me during the whole trip, and that was the possibility of seeing Gordon again. It was only a wild dream, a crazy chance, but every time I thought about it the trouble around me seemed a little less important. We were, in fact, scheduled to appear in a church in Zeeland, Gordon's home town, and I lived in a fog of yearning and dread every time I thought of it.

The church in Zeeland was like the one in which John and Anna had grown up: Dutch and Calvinist. Even though John had pulled away from his traditions and refused any help from or connection with these churches, they often called him to come and present his program. He had a kind of prodigal son appeal, the black sheep who had dared to stray from the family. There were even those who envied him, and thought that he might bring a breath of fresh air to the stuffy old Dutch ways.

But since each generation rebels against the last, the stuffy old Dutch ways represented stability and security to me. The night our aluminum Super-Dura-Liner pulled into the town of Zeeland, I stared out the bus window looking at another world. It was a little Michigan Dutch town, with one main street and rows of well-kept houses on tree-lined lanes. Towheaded children rode bicycles, and a young woman pushed a stroller down the sidewalk. I wondered what it would be like to live in a town like this, with someone you loved, just a quiet life, with nothing to prove, maybe raising children and going to a dignified church on Sundays.

We drove down one of the quiet streets, and I looked at the red
brick church looming up beside the coach. This might be his
church. He could be here. We filed out and went into the basement,
where a meal was being set out on long tables. In a dream I poked
down a few bites of food and put on my long blue robe. I listed the
songs we would sing and gave the list to John. One of them was a
song that gave me a chance to turn around and scan the audience.
Pearl and I sang the lead together, while the rest of the group did
a background chant in harmony.

The meeting began. It had been more than a year since I had
seen him. Could I have forgotten what he looked like? No, if I saw
him I would know, just as I had known that first day.

Pearl and I were facing the audience, singing:

> When the world seems cold, and your friends seem few
> There is someone who cares for you.
> When there are tears in your eyes,
> Your heart bleeds inside,
> There is someone who cares for you.

I searched the rows. Was he there? Would he decode my
message?

The performance ended, and John stood by the back door
shaking hands. My whole body was shaking. I was still searching
the crowd for his face, working my way toward the back.

The audience was congratulatory, adoring. A tall dark-eyed
woman took John's hand, and there was a straightforwardness about
her that suddenly made him flinch. Her face showed none of the
worshipful awe, only a knowledgeable little smile.

"Hello . . ." John said uncertainly.

"Yes, Mr. Vogel. I'm very interested in your work. I've read
your book and enjoyed it."

John looked at the face. It was in some way vaguely familiar.
"Thank you! Uh, what did you say the name was?"

"De Pree. My son Gordon visited your home a little over a
year ago. You might remember him!"

John's smile dropped like peeled plaster. I felt rooted to the floor. She was his mother, and he was not there.

"Oh, yes, yes, yes."John said, pushing her along with his handshake. He reached for the next person in line and struggled to reposition the smile.

"Ohhhhh!" breathed the next lady. "You're such a wonderful man! You just make me get goose bumps! God bless you!"

We were hustled out the exit, with orders to change and get back on the bus immediately. As we were peeling off our robes, John came downstairs. He pulled Carlita aside.

"I don't know!" I heard Carlita say sulkily. "Ask her!"

But John said nothing. What was there to say? All our words were for the crowd, not for one another. I took off my robe, still shaking with nervousness and disappointment. Gordon could have married and forgotten. It had been a long time.

After that night things were a blur. We sang on a radio program in Grand Rapids, on television in Chicago. Events that would have filled me with excitement a few years before now seemed like one long nightmare. Stand here . . . move there . . . put your robe on . . . take if off. Sit here, eat, sing, go to sleep. Get up, hurry up, get on the bus. Now smile, sing. Push the button, and out comes the smile, the song. In goes the button, march off the stage. Find a quiet place. Are there no quiet places anymore? Stand, sit, smile, sing, walk, sit, smile, sing. Don't think. Don't find a quiet place. Just keep moving, this way please.

See what they have given us! Prizes! There are prizes for all Daddy's good children. Lunch at the Palmer House. Thousands of dollars. Yes, now walk on camera. Stay in the chalk lines. Now the giant suitcase will open, and out you walk! Sing, girl. They're giving us a dishwasher, gas stoves, cases of food, and a stainless steel heated and refrigerated cafeteria counter!

Applause, applause.

I sat staring out of the coach window on the way back to Kentucky, knowing I had come to the end of something. I had begun to hate songs like "Someone Who Cares." I felt I could never sing them again.

Grandpa Will was hoeing the flowers along the road when we drove in. He seemed tinier than ever, far below the high aluminum windows. He waved to us merrily, bobbing like one of his petunias. We drove into the parking lot, not exhausted this time from bouncing in a wagon or truck or school bus, but emotionally drained by the high-pressure strains of the trip. We were quiet as we gathered up the piles of luggage from the generous baggage compartments, strangely silent as we divided up and started back toward the now luxurious dorms. It was ironic. The easier life became the less heart we seemed to have. There was no physical wilderness to overcome now, only the nebulous new battleground being drawn up in our minds.

Back in the old routines, the battle took on a new intensity. Over Carlita's strong protests, John had suggested that Pearl take over the study chores. He said his purpose was to free Carlita to spend more time in organ practice, but Carlita was angry, and her younger sister eyed her smugly.

Pearl was a strange-looking girl. She was attractive in a way, but her eyes were very close together and her brows were bushy, giving her a beetle-browed look. She rolled on the balls of her feet when she walked. She was always meticulously dressed and powdered when she came to the study. We all laughed at her.

"Wow, you really get all primped up to do your scrubbing, don't you?" I teased.

"Don't laugh at her," John said. "She's insecure enough. She's always lived in the shadow of her older sister, and I'm trying to help her develop confidence in herself. That's why I'm encouraging her to go into nursing. I think she has great potential in that field. She has a very gentle touch."

"But how will she study nursing? I asked. "Are you going to let her go away to school?"

"I'm thinking about it."

"How come she can go to nursing school, and I can't go to college?"

John looked uncomfortable. "You can't make the same rules for everyone," he said. "She's going to start nursing school by correspondence, and then if it becomes necessary for her to go away to school, we'll have to arrange it."

"Necessary for her to go away?" I said, blinking.

John turned to his work and did not answer. Pearl began to spend long hours in the study, but instead of becoming more self-confident, her face grew more and more closed, and her shoulders hunched over like an animal's afraid of being kicked.

It happened on the way to the barn early one morning. Gramps was walking with Stumpy and the other boys past the water tower on top of the hill when suddenly he gave a little cry and fell. The boys picked him up gently and carried him back home, but he was dead before Gram saw him. She rushed to the phone and called John. He was awakened out of a deep sleep to hear his mother say, "John, Will is gone."

John was deeply shaken, as all of us were. It was the first time anyone close to us had died. The undertaker was called, and John picked out an expensive maroon velour casket. Gramps lay in our cathedral-ceilinged living room, clean and stiff against the white satin lining. Stumpy came quietly and put a single red rose in his hand. Gram sat beside him, straight-backed and tearless.

"It was for the best," she said when we offered our condolences. "Will was a good man, and it was his time to go. It was for the best."

It seemed to me a strange thing to say, but it was hardly the time to question her.

Gramps had given Gram detailed instructions for his funeral. He wanted the service conducted in the flower garden and the girls group to sing his favorite Dutch psalm from the Psalter. We had never heard it, but Gram had an old Psalms hymnal saved from her Chicago days and we learned the song for the occasion, the solemn Calvinist music sounding strange and majestic against the backdrop of the blue Kentucky mountains. It was difficult to sing, and most of us choked back the tears as we harmonized. Grandpa Will was a good man, an honest hard-working simple man who lived what he believed and prayed and swore in Dutch. We loved him.

Gramps wanted to be buried near the church. The workmen dug a hole in the sage-grass field and lowered his body into the rocky clay soil behind the partially finished building. I watched them cover him with the mound of earth, wondering who had been more important in my life, this grandfather I had known, or the one I had never seen.

Afterward his death lay like a pall over the grounds. The younger children were content that Gramps had gone to heaven, and the older children could accept death as a part of the mystery of life, but John seemed deeply disturbed by the event. The confrontation with death seemed to have thrown him into a mood he could not shake off.

"When Gramps died, did it make you think of your father's death?" I asked, trying to help him. But he rarely answered a question directly. Instead he looked at me vacantly and asked,

"How old am I? Forty-four?"

"Almost forty-five."

"My father was only forty-two when he died. What if I don't live long? What would happen here if I died? Could I count on you to carry on?"

I patted him on the back, trying to cheer him up. "Come on, that was back in the days before they had proper medication. He probably died of something that a good shot of penicillin would cure now. You're not going to get out of life that easily. Come on, now, Father John, you've got a long time to live!"

"I don't know," he said, shaking his head. "I've got a feeling that it would be far better to be in heaven than to bear the trials of this present world."

He began to lay out papers and draw up new plans. There was to be a large new reception hall for visitors, where the choirs would sing, art and handwork would be displayed, and the book would be on sale. For those who had time to linger, there would be regular showings of the film. There would be an overnight guest room, and the study would no longer be used for this purpose. His plans for the study were the strangest. He tried to explain them to me.

"There will be a series of rooms opened by electronic controls." he said. "And there will be an electric buzzer system with a flashing red light to tell me when someone is coming. It will be possible to reach me only when the red light has flashed in my inner room and I press the electronic controls to admit whoever is coming. I never have a private moment to myself anymore, with everyone tramping in and out of here. It's like a . . ."

"But why?" I interrupted him. "Why do you need so much privacy? And flashing red lights with electronic controls? Good grief, are you sure you don't have a fever or something?"

I laid my hand on his forehead, but he turned away. And I began to wonder. Was it real or did I imagine it that he was not well? Should someone be consulted, someone who could help?

I went to the art room and began to rummage around in my materials. If I got outdoors and got to work, maybe I could think more clearly.

Up at the Hensley farm I breathed in the quiet peace of the summer day. Snow Hensley had smilingly given me permission to paint a scene on his land, and in John's muddled state of mind I had even managed to get away without a chaperone. I set up my easel. I had to be alone. The apple trees had well-formed summer fruit, and the warm green smell of the orchard grass rose around me. The tree under which I sat dipped a branch into view, giving the corncrib and the wagon parked in its shadow a three-dimensional frame. I squeezed out the oils and began to work, waving to Snow and Sary Jane sitting across the road on their front porch.

I marked the line where the shadows fell across the logs of the corncrib, knowing they would change with the sun. The leaves in the foreground were disproportionately large—and they would be that large in a photograph—still the old problem of making the real seem believable in art. It seemed to confront me wherever I turned. I turpentined the leaves out and began again.

I was hard at work when a shadow fell across the canvas. I looked up, and Boyd the driver was standing over me, his hat pushed back and an impish grin on his face. He had been a good friend for a long time, and I was glad to see him standing there.

"Hey, you'll scare me, sneaking up like that," I laughed.

He looked at me, still grinning. "It's a wonder your daddy lets you out like this by yourself, and him so strict," he said.

"Oh. I sneak away once in a while."

Boyd was silent, watching me rough in the background. He was one of those men who spoke in eloquent silences, and it took him a long time to say what was on his mind.

"Things ain't exactly right at your house, are they?" he finally managed to say.

"You might say that," I answered, working.

"It worries me. I don't think your daddy's very fair with you."

"Aw, I guess I don't have to put up with it if I don't want to," I said. "You know the good old saying. 'I don't have to do nothin' but die.'"

Boyd laughed, a quiet gentle chuckle. "And what if you decide someday you ain't puttin' up with it no more?" he asked.

"What would you suggest?"

Boyd shuffled his feet and tipped his hat back precariously far. "All I'm sayin' is, if you ever need any help, you know where to find me. I'll do anything I can for you, and I mean that, even if it costs me."

I looked up at him, and there were tears in his kind eyes. I had an urge to give him a good hug, but I thought Sary Jane might wonder what was going on.

That week John lay on his bed in the study with his face turned to the wall. Light of any kind seemed to bother him. His complexion was a purplish red, and he clutched his Bible to him. Sometimes he had one of us read a psalm for him. Since Gramps' death he had read the psalms day and night. The words seemed to soothe him.

> *In you. Yahweh. I take shelter. Never let me be disgraced. In your righteousness deliver me, rescue me. Turn your ear to me, make haste. Pull me out of the net they have spread for me, for you are my refuge. You God, have seen my wretchedness, and known the miseries of my soul . . . take pity on me. Yahweh. I am in trouble now. I hear their endless slanders as then combine against me, plotting to take my life away. Rescue me from the hand of my enemies and persecutors.*

By the end of the week he was in such a state he let Anna persuade him to go to the doctor.

"Maybe just a little overworked. What have you got now, ninety kids?" The doctor smiled good-naturedly. "Blood pressure's a little high. Why don't I check you into the hospital for a good rest? You'd be surprised how many of my patients never get a good vacation unless I put them in the hospital."

Corbin had built a new municipal hospital since I had stayed with Gram, and we drove up to the black-topped parking lot feeling foreign in our own town.

They gave John a droopy white hospital gown and put him to bed. Anna offered to stay and take care of him.

"Maybe you could stay one night." he said uncomfortably. "And tomorrow some of the girls could come. Since I have a private room, I don't think anybody would mind if I have a few children around."

The children he wanted were Pearl, Carlita, Maxine, and me. Anna sighed and left.

The four of us became known as the "bodyguard." We slept in John's room, two by two, ate our meals in the hospital cafeteria, and sat talking or reading to John during the day. Carlita and Pearl were one shift. Maxine and I were the other.

At home, life went on as usual. The sun came up, and the meal bells rang, one for wash-up, two for line-up, three to come in. It was summer vacation, and the teachers cleaned out the classrooms in the new school. Gram stood straighter than ever, cooking the meals and serving them from the new stainless steel heated and refrigerated cafeteria counter. Nada was getting fatter and Anna was getting thinner. The sun went down, and all the little children gathered in their pajamas, their faces clean and shining, ready for a bedtime story. On the surface it was all as it had been in the beginning and would be forevermore, world without end; but underneath, there was terminal sickness, a malady unto death.

Carlita and Pearl were on duty in John's room when the rotund Mr. Haas stopped in, having heard that his Kentucky friend was ill. He visited for a while, then drove out to the home, where he went directly to the boys dorm and had a long conference with Nada. When he finished, he came to the Vogel house and looked me up. I was in the art room, trying to finish up the Hensley painting.

He waddled into the art room, and I felt a rush of relief at the sight of him. I ran to him and was half crushed in his big bear hug.

He led me over to a chair and set me down. Then he stood in front of me and looked at me directly. "Now, young lady," he said, "would you do me a great favor and tell me exactly what is happening around here?"

"I don't know, Mr. Haas," I said truthfully.

"Okay then, another question. How are you doing?"

"Not too great."

"What can I do to help?"

"I don't know yet. I can't make up my mind what to do."

"What are you now, twenty?"

"Twenty-one in a few weeks."

"You, my dear, are getting to be an old maid. Are you going to sit here all your life?"

"What can I do about it?"

He started to say something, then closed his mouth with a snap. "Well, I don't want anyone to blame me for putting ideas into your head," he said slyly, "but if you ever need help, just you call on your old friend Haas, you hear?"

That was my second offer. I stored them both away for future reference.

John came home from the hospital rested in body but like a caged animal. He paced the study, back and forth, making plans for the addition at the back. Every morning workmen came to put up the superstructure of the new addition. I was completely baffled by it and wanted to ask more, but John had other matters on his mind.

"The brochure." he said weakly one day. "We haven't sent out a brochure since before Christmas. It's been half a year. If we don't get one in the mail, the money will drop off."

"But we don't solicit money."

"I know. I know. It's just a reminder. People get a brochure, and they remember to send something."

"Are we in the red?"

"Not exactly, as far as current income is concerned, but I've had a problem. Can I confide in you?"

I hesitated. Was I to be considered loyal, with the mass of conflicting ideas that were surging through my head?

"I won't repeat it," I promised.

"You know J. P., the sponsor of our radio program?"

"Yes."

"Well, a few months ago, just after our tour, we came back with a lot of money. I guess you knew that."

"I never knew exactly how much."

"It doesn't matter. But J. P. came to me a few days after we returned and asked if he could borrow some money. He said he had the chance of a lifetime to invest in a trucking line, and that if the business went well he would turn a good share of the proceeds back to the home. We even talked about it becoming a sort of subsidiary business, with J. P. as manager. He said to do this he needed twenty thousand dollars quickly."

"Twenty thousand dollars! Did you give it to him?"

"I did. He's been so good to us. I couldn't turn him down. The bank wouldn't approve a loan, and it was such a good opportunity. But now he tells me the deal has somehow gone wrong, and he's bankrupt. He's lost every cent of our money!"

For some reason I felt an enormous sense of relief, as if I'd expected to hear something much worse. "Don't worry about it," I said. "Money has never been a big problem around here. You taught us to believe that if our hearts are right with God, everything will work out. Don't you believe that anymore?"

He turned his face to the wall for a moment, then looked at me with misery in his eyes. "Will you write the brochure?" he asked. "I can't seem to do it. The material is all there in my notebook. Take a look at it and see if you can put together something that sounds interesting. If you can write a book, I guess you can do a brochure."

He looked at me with an expression half dominating and half frightened.

I picked up his notebook and walked toward the door. "I'll see what I can do," I promised.

"Remember to tell about Grandpa Will," he said, and began reading the psalms again. Sick or not, he still knew how to hook me by handing me responsibility baited with power.

I took his notes to the art room and spread them out on the big palette-shaped table that had been built for me. I had long wanted it, but now that it was there, its presence weighed on me like a huge obligation that filled the whole room.

I sat looking around me. The art room contained everything I had ever asked for, everything I needed to become a good artist, except one thing—freedom. There was a terrible hollowness about the lovely paneled walls and the lavish equipment. It was as if all the colors of the rainbow had been handed to me, and someone had tied a bag over my head. What could I paint? What was there to say about life until I knew about love, about good and evil, about human temptations and emotions? And what if I became a famous painter, reproducing every wart and wrinkle on canvas, what would that be compared to falling in love and creating another live human being? Was painting itself to become my imitation of life, my excuse for not living?

I pushed the questions out of my mind and spread the notes out on the table. The fact still remained that John, my father, was sick and needed help. For now I would help him.

But the notes were as confused as John's mind. I stared at them hopelessly, wondering how to arrange his non-facts into a readable brochure.

"First meeting, several thousand dollars . . ."

No, I'd better not mention how much money had been collected on the trip. Most of it was gone, because of John's lack of good judgment. Nada must be furious about that. I wondered what Haas had been talking to her about, and where she fit into the power structure now. Well, scratch that one. We'd better not praise God for money that had slipped through somebody's fingers.

"Marvelous accommodations on Lake Charlevoix . . ."

Weren't they, though? And marvelous intrigues and mysterious goings-on. The chagrined look on Anna's face the night Nada was screeching like a bat out of hell and her attempts to explain it to the hostess the next morning.

"I'm afraid John gets himself too involved in all these people's lives," Anna said apologetically. "And there are conflicts of interest at times."

"You're a better woman than I am," said the motel owner's wife. "I'd claw my husband's eyes out if he had as many women hanging around him as yours does."

I shook my head, thinking that might make a good story but not a very proper brochure.

Well, scratch than one.

"Tour through Michigan . . ."

I sat staring at the words, the old familiar pain tightening my throat. Yes, I could write a nice heartbreak story for John. Classic scene of the jealous father hovering over his only child. Enter handsome prince. Only this time the handsome prince didn't even enter. Enter handsome prince's mother. Prince's mother gets move-along handshake. Only child goes to basement with great loss of face. Handsome prince has probably married someone else. Frustrated only child goes home and writes brochures for jealous father.

A good story, but again John's public would never believe it.

Notes, notes. What was this? Guests of Welcome Traveler. As far as I was concerned, the sooner that TV interview was forgotten the better. John had insisted that the three of them, he, Nada, and Anna, be seated together and featured equally. But the script had been written only for John and Anna. John's insistence on including Nada because it was essential that she be introduced to the public had created a scene embarassing for all. Anna offered to let the two of them do it, but the script wasn't right for that. She finally took her place next to John, feeling and looking as if she had been bashed in the face. The director of the show suspected the root of the problem and made jokes.

Oh, Lord. Didn't anything happen on the trip that turned out to be good? We did get a stainless steel heated and refrigerated cafeteria counter, a dishwasher, two gas stoves, and a walk-in freezer, and all we traded for them was standing up singing a lie night after night, singing songs which were beginning to sound more and more like discord in the dark. The music was losing its melody, its harmony, its words, and becoming one long scream . . .

I banged my fist on the art-room table and shook my head, trying to shake the horrors out of it. Concentrate, you fool. Find one good thing. Pick out one you can write about without having to tell a lie or pile on the crap. There must be something.

There's Grandpa Will. He died, which has got to be the most normal thing anyone has done around here for the past six months. I decided to start by writing about Grandpa Will. I tried to pin him down in my mind as someone who would fit neatly into one of John's brochures, someone saintly, dead, and departed, but living pictures of him kept creeping into my mind. I saw him standing in the flowerbed near the no-smoking sign, his back pocket slowly smoldering from the not-quite-extinguished pipe hastily stuck into it.

I saw him coming in from work, hanging his flat Dutch farmer's cap on the wall, and giving Gram a smack on her corseted fanny, and then sticking a blue wildflower in her gray hair.

I saw him sitting in his living room the night we surprised them, the night we dressed in crazy get-ups and knocked on their door. I was a character named Jimbo, dressed in forbidden pants with a chalk mustache, chewing a whole package of gum and strumming my four chords on the guitar. Max was dressed in a slimy satin shawl, and Carlita and Janey were dressed like old men. We put on a music show for them, and I even got the spirit and started huffing and puffing like a mountain preacher. And I loved Gramps that night for understanding us, for being reverent in his own way, yet being able to laugh with us.

Dead! No, I was mistaken. Grandpa Will was not dead. It was the rest of us, who were dying on our feet. Gramps was surely somewhere making friends by passing out a pocketful of peppermints, or chatting with the Old Man Upstairs, trying to find a fold in his robe to hide his pipe.

John was in the study waiting for me to write something that would fascinate the public, would solidify our image as one big happy family. He was waiting, Bible in hand, for me to write an apology for his way of life. It was the tract-writing contest all over again.

Yes, my friend . . .

No, there is nothing to say, my friend.

My friend, my father.

John.

CHAPTER TWELVE

How can one tell the exact moment when night becomes day, when darkness becomes light? One second there is no horizon, only a blank blackness, and with the next stirring of the wind there is a line, an earth, and a sky, and it is morning.

Anna was bustling around the yellow dorm kitchen mixing a cake batter and cutting chicken to fry. It seemed good to see her in command. For years I had almost felt like her mother, worrying about her safety, protecting her from John, and shielding her from disturbing information. But now it was my twenty-first birthday, and she was giving a party.

"Is your father coming?" she asked.

"No, he said he'd let us celebrate alone."

"Do you know what's the matter with him?"

"Not really." I said, sticking my finger into the spice cake batter and licking it. "Do you mind if I ask you something?"

"Anything goes on a birthday."

"Maybe it's not too nice a question, but what good does it do you to be married to him when you are such strangers?"

Anna was silent for a moment, running water over her hands. "That's just the way it is," she said, and I half expected her to add, "Rome wasn't built in a day," even though it would no longer be appropriate. It was not the building of John's kingdom that was a concern now, but its maintenance, publicly and privately. The struggle between my mother and my father had gone on for years, like an endless arm wrestling match and I wondered who would snap first.

It was an uneasy birthday party. John stayed in the study, refusing to come out. Carlita appeared at the last moment, looking flustered and red-faced. Anna was nervous and kept licking her lips and drumming her fingers. I was in such a divided state of mind I thought my head would split down the middle.

One by one they came and took their places around the big table. These people were my friends, my sisters, my classmates. They combined all the roles usually played by many people. All of us had been everything to one another. If I did decide to leave, what would life be apart from them? And the little ones, peeping in the window at our "big girls' party," Phyllis and Julie walking through the room every few minutes to get a look, Winston and David, who were like loving little brothers, Stumpy, Gram—all the people I had known forever. Could I give them all up at once, never to see them again?

Yet what would happen if I let these relationships blur my thinking? Added to my other shadowy concerns was the growing awareness that the violence I had sometimes feared at John's hands might never explode in one merciful blow but would express itself in slow psychological torture that would leave me able to function physically but dead in spirit, a walking zombie.

I looked around the table. Janey. It was starting to happen to her already. The youth was going out of her face. She had a short permed hairdo and a wrinkle across her forehead, and her eyes had the dull look of absolute virtue. She was turning into a drone, a slave to a good cause. Her face frightened me. She had turned twenty-one and shrugged it off. Was I going to do the same thing? Would we meet every year like this, celebrating twenty-two and thirty-two and forty-two, until a collection of old crones sat around the yellow padded booths? It was like a nunnery, a dedicated holy order. Only something had happened and it was becoming an evil order. Was I ready to give my one precious life to something I could not wholeheartedly believe in?

That was the basic problem, not the cost of the decision but the result. In basic human terms, and stripped of John's strange jargon, I was being asked to trade love, marriage, children, education, and freedom for an investment in a very risky venture— an institution with an absolute dictator as its head who was lying in a room with his face to the wall, surrounded by mysteries and riddles.

Suddenly, I knew. Looking around at the cake-eating girls what had to be done was suddenly clear. The mysteries and riddles of John's life were going to remain just that unless someone acted decisively, and that decisive action would have to be taken without knowing all the answers. It would have to be a leap in the dark, a leap toward what I hoped was right. As far as the cost—the book and the film, the crowds and the applause, the coach and the organ, the rich friends and the padded security, the plush buildings and the Cadillac, the clothing and the jewelry—I did not want it. I was twenty-one. I had served my time. I wanted to be free. I was leaving.

The party was over.

In the downstairs room facing the garden I began drawing up secret plans. I had no money, nowhere to go, no way to get there. Anna would approve, but as usual would be helpless. I would have to start at zero. Having nothing left me free to do anything. It was a clean feeling. The wildly possible future careened crazily before me. There were two people who had offered to be bridges, big Haas and good-natured Boyd. How could I fit them into a rescue unit and use their offers?

I found a piece of paper and began writing.

> *Dear Mr. Haas,*
>
> *It was great to see you last time you were here! Do you remember you asked me how things were going, and I said not so hot? Well, they certainly haven't improved, and if the offer of help stands good. I need it now. This may shock you, but I'm leaving the home. I want to go to college, and you know my father. This is an all or nothing decision, and I'm burning my bridges.*
>
> *The kind of help I need is this: I've heard you speak of*

knowing the president of Wheaton College. Could you
somehow arrange to talk to him, tell him that the situation is
getting very repressive here and that I need to get away? I
would need help in finding a place to stay, work to do, and
maybe some special assistance to become enrolled in college.

I stopped scribbling and bit my lip. There was the very real
danger that this letter would never make it through the regular
mail channels. It would be ripped open in the office for censorship,
and that would be the end of plan one. It would also be the end of
my one-upmanship After all these years I did not want to get
kicked out of the home by a snooping old bitch like Nada. I wanted
to leave in dignity, with my head held high and my eyes full of
self-righteous tears while they begged me to stay.

But who could help? Boyd, of course. He was the perfect
solution. His incoming mail did not pass through the office as
ours did. He got his mail at home.

I finished the letter:

As you can see, I've written Boyd's Bark Camp address as the
return. Please use it. This is important. Thanks a million,.
Mr. Haas. You are saving my life.

I addressed the envelope and went to find Boyd. I could hear
the high-pitched whine of the cut-off saw up at the mill shed and
knew he would be there. With only a few words of explanation, he
sensed the urgency of the situation, and he stuffed the letter in his
pocket with a slow wink. "You can trust the Boyd express," he
promised solemnly.

I waited for the answer for a full two weeks, eaten with
restlessness. All day my face burned with a mysterious glow, and
at night I lay awake pondering what I had done. What if Mr. Haas
had not meant what I thought he meant? What if he would be
shocked by the enormity of my request and turn my letter over to

John? What if John had only used him as a spy to find out my true feelings? What if I were too old to go to college? What if I had forgotten how to study? There were two credits I had never finished, and I had no diploma from high school, which, when I thought about it, had probably been planned by John. Would any college accept me? Were there entrance exams one could take? Over and beyond all this, would Dr. Edmund, the president of Wheaton College, be reluctant to get mixed up in a battle with a powerful man like John Vogel?

Had I stirred up a situation in which I would be dropped by everyone? "I don't care," I whispered to myself in the middle of the night. "I don't care. At least I'll be free."

Meanwhile, a feeling of danger was in the wind. John seldom stirred from the study, and in his absence everyone and everything seemed changed. It was as if all the old rules were suspended, as if nobody had the power to enforce them.

Stumpy brought me a birthday present. It was the first time he had ever given me anything, and I was pleased. I opened it to find a small music box that played "I Love You Truly." I listened to the tinkling little tune, thinking of all Stumpy and I had lived through together, from the first days of the home. He was a real friend, and I would miss him.

But the next time I passed Stumpy on the dining-hall path, he called me aside, and the situation began to get more complicated. He was almost as tall as I was, if I stood on the down side of the hill, and there was a new look of nervousness on his face.

"Did you like your present?" he asked hopefully.

"I did, Stump. That was real sweet of you."

"I meant it," he said, all seriousness on his face. "I meant them words on the bottom of the music box. I've wanted to tell you for a long time, but I didn't dare. I was afraid you'd think you was better than me. Can I, uh, can I call you my girl?"

His words took me off guard, and I stared at him, not sure whether to hug him or laugh.

"Oh, Stumpy, you are sweet! But you're like my brother! I love you too, Stump, but not like that. Come on, Stump, let's shake hands and promise to be friends forever." I couldn't tell him yet that I was leaving and might never see him again.

He looked at my outstretched hand, shook his head, and kicked his toe in the dust. "I should've known better," he said, walking away.

"Hey Stump, don't be mad, buddy. Its okay."

"Maybe its okay for you." he called over his shoulder.

"Do you want your present back?"

"No, keep it!"

I stood on the path, stung by the sound of tears in his voice. Stumpy in love with me—what would happen next?

It was during that same week that the Swanns turned up from Birmingham. They drove into the lot, and I ran out to meet them. They were as exciting as ever, and I led them to the study bursting to tell them about the whole terrible state of affairs. But they were admirers of John's, and I was unsure how they would react if they knew what I was doing. How many of John's friends would still be my friends when this was all over?

As usual, the study door was locked.

"The Swanns are here!" I called, banging on the door with my foot. The air conditioner roared, but there was no reply.

"That's funny," I said apologetically. "I know he's in there."

"Never mind," Mr. Swann said politely. "He might be having a conference. Well go out in the car and wait."

"There's no reason why they can't open that door," I insisted. "I know Pearl's in there. Sometimes the air conditioner is noisy and they can't hear. Let me go around the back and knock on the, window."

"Oh, no, no, no! We'll wait!"

Then John was at the door, apologizing profusely. I'm sorry. I was resting." he said. "Come on in. I haven't been feeling too well."

I let them go on in without me. I had the feeling that if I

walked into the study I would have a heart attack. What went on inside I don't know, but the Swarms cut their visit short and left that evening, instead of staying two or three days as usual.

"You'd better get some rest, John. You sure don't look very well," Mr. Swann advised.

John again felt the compulsion to confide in the Swarms. "I can't sleep very well these nights," he said. "In fact, I lay on the floor in the girls' room until about five o'clock this morning. Only the Lord knows how I struggle with Satan in the battle for my daughters."

Mrs. Swann put her arm through her husband's and looked at John carefully. "I think we should be going, Floyd," she said gently.

It was two weeks to the day when Boyd met me on the front walk. He gave me a slow wink and patted his pocket. I nodded and passed him. Later, when John was safely at the office and Boyd was working on the car motor, I ran out to see what news he had.

"It's my pocket," he said. "The corner's sticking out. Take it. My hands are greasy."

I pulled the corner and folded the letter small enough to fit in my hand.

"Thanks," I whispered. "I'll remember this when I'm rich and famous." Then I walked away, as if I had been involved in such dangerous intrigues every day of my life.

In the depths of the locked bathroom, I shared the contents of Haas's letter with Maxine.

Dear Lenore,

I have known for a number of months that something was radically wrong at the home, but I was powerless to do anything until one of you came to me for help. The offer certainly stands good and you can depend on me.

I've called Dr. Edmund and briefed him on your situation.

He is most sympathetic and will cooperate. If you can arrange
to get to Wheaton, I'll have instructions left for you at his
house. Go there, get word where to stay, and get settled in.
I'll be in touch with you as soon as I can.

He added a telephone number I was to call collect and signed
the letter "The Haas family."

Max and I stood with our arms around each other, crying from
relief and excitement and happiness and sadness.

"Don't worry, Max," I promised her. "When I find a place I'll
send for you. I'll get a room somewhere, and then you can come."

I knew that telling Father John of my decision would precipitate
a battle, but I was hardly prepared for what did happen. I had
barely spoken to him for two weeks, knowing something would
show on my transparent face. When he slept in our room, I took a
blanket and slept out on the sun deck, feeling oppressed by his
presence. I had had time to build an emotional barrier between
us, and as I walked to the study, it was not in any sense to ask his
permission. I had my mind made up to leave.

It was a hot late-summer afternoon. I knocked and was
admitted. The study was the same as ever, filled with the thick
sultry air of dead-end secrecy. I realized as I entered that it no
longer mattered. It was not mine, nor any part of my future.

John was lying on his bed, propped up, reading the psalms.
He looked up surprised.

I took a quick breath, adrenaline suddenly pumping through
me in terrifying spurts.

"How are you feeling?" I asked with false calm. "Better, thank
you," he answered formally.

There was a brief pause. I tried to steady myself. "Uh, I, uh. I
have something to tell you."

"Yes?"

"I'm leaving."

"You're what?"

"I'm leaving. I've thought it over very carefully, and I have to go. I wish it didn't have to be this way, that I could leave home as people normally do, go to school, and come back to see you, but I don't have that choice. If I'd had more freedom, I would have stayed. But it's not good like this. It's not good for any of us. I'm sorry. Goodbye, Daddy."

I leaned over and kissed his forehead. He was silent, his eyes blinking and sending small ripples down his cheeks.

"Then go," he said hoarsely, turning his face away. "And God will judge you!"

"I'm willing to take that judgment."

"And don't expect five cents from me!"

"I don't want anything, except the right to live my own life . . ."

He did not answer. I turned and opened the baffling study door for the last time. It clicked behind me, and I walked down the gravel path, the old fear that I might be damned for disobeying John lurking around the edges of my mind. Let me be damned. It was a toss-up. I might as well have hell later as right now.

I was in the closet, pulling out the clothes I'd need. Anna had promised to brave John's wrath to drive me to Wheaton.

"Are you going to take this?" Max asked, holding up the dress I had worn the day Gordon came. I hesitated a moment. The dress had taken on the character of a national monument, celebrating glory won and dead.

"I'll take it," I said, "but I'll probably never wear it."

Moments later, when I was in the bathroom, Carlita tapped on the door. "I've got to talk to you," she said.

"Yeah? What is it?" I asked, opening the door. Not even Carlita could bother me anymore.

"I've got to leave too," she said abruptly.

"What are we doing? Playing follow the leader?"

"No. I'm serious. Please don't joke. I've needed to leave for a long time, but I've been so scared. If you break away now, I'm going to do it too."

"Look. Carlita, I don't want to get blamed for your leaving!"

"Please listen to me. I . . . I have to tell you something." Her face had gone white and she was breathing hard. I thought she was going to faint.

"What is it?" I said, shaking her. "Say something!"

"Just a minute. I'm so scared I can't talk. I don't even know how to say it. Maybe you know already. Your father . . . Daddy . . . He's been doing things that are terrible and wrong."

"Doing what?" I pressed.

"Doing it. He's been doing it to me for a long time."

I found myself suddenly cool and clinical. "Would you please be specific?" I asked. "I'm tired to death of this guessing game. What has he been doing to you?"

"He's been kissing me and feeling my breasts and sticking his thing inside me . . . for a long time."

"Why did you let him, you stupid fool?"

"Because . . . listen, believe me. I didn't know." She was crying. "I was just a kid and I didn't know what he was doing. I trusted him. I didn't think he would do anything wrong."

"But don't you know?"

"Of course I knew when I got older, but he threatened me. He said I would go to jail if anyone ever found out, and he told me not to worry, that for the two of us it wasn't wrong in God's sight. He said he had given my life to God when I was just a little girl, and I was . . . like married to God. That's what this stupid ring was." She began twisting it off her finger and held it out in her hand. "I couldn't tell anyone, because I was so ashamed."

I stared at her, the cool clinical feeling turning to ice. "How come you never had a baby?" I asked.

"He used things. But I'm scared now. I've been scared to death for a whole month. I looked it up in Pearl's nursing book, and I haven't had my period for almost two months."

"Have you told him?"

"He'll kill me. He acts like a crazy animal."

I felt my cool breaking, the ice turning to fire. "Where's that ring?" I demanded.

She held it out to me. I took it and laid it on the floor, jewel side down, and crushed it flat with my heel.

"Here," I said, "go give him that!"

It was hot, but I was shivering when I sat on the cool tiles of the bathroom floor. *I could see him, in his long-sleeved white shirt and broad-brimmed Stetson, doing it fantasizing that he was God himself. I began to shake, clamping my teeth together to keep them from chattering. My father—my father—how could he do that? How could he do that? How could he do that when he was so strict with us?*

Suddenly I was filled with a terrible lightness, a feeling of floating in space, a space where John could no longer reach me. He and I lived in two different worlds. I no longer needed to be worried about his moral judgments. I could do better than that without trying.

I hunched on the floor, my head slowly clearing. What had seemed like the ultimate shock a few minutes before now gathered in my stomach like a ball of strength. I leaned back, a slow smile spreading over my face. I no longer needed to fear John's curse, nor being damned for defying him.

Maybe, for once, God was on my side!

But it was too terrifying to tell Anna, too close. I went to find Aunt Kay. She listened to all I had to say before she spoke.

"And you decided to leave before you knew all this?"

"I didn't know a thing!"

"Isn't that strange! But you're absolutely right, my dear. You've got to go. Don't worry about the other children, there are plenty of adults here who have chosen to come and serve. Go and get some sense of distance from all this, and then, who knows, you might even come back some day. I'm not worried about you."

She gave me a warm comforting hug. "Are you going to try to find a certain young man?" she teased.

"I don't know. I'm not leaving because of anyone else except me, this time. I've got a lot of sorting out to do."

"I understand." she said.

The next morning Carlita was in bed burning with a fever. She called Anna and whispered something to her.

Anna lifted the bed covers, and her eyes went wide. "My Lord, girl," she said. "You've got to get to the doctor! What happened?"

Carlita turned away and began to cry. Anna threw a robe over her and helped her walk out to the car. The motor started, and the car zoomed out of the lot in a cloud of dust.

The study door opened, and John came out. He guessed what was happening and ran to the Cadillac. Before Anna was out of sight, he was chasing her up the road. Up the hill and around the bend the two cars raced.

"Good grief, what's that all about?" I asked

Maxine took me to the bed where Carlita had been sleeping. I stared at the pool of blood.

I never knew what happened until Anna told me later.

The two cars raced each other all the way through the woods, out on the Bee Creek road, and into town. Anna was going over a hundred miles an hour, and John was bearing down behind. She could see him in the rearview mirror, screaming and cursing, trying to run her off the road. The faster she went, the faster he followed.

Finally they reached Corbin. Anna swung into the side street where the doctor's office was and rushed Carlita in. John dropped behind and stayed out of sight.

The doctor took one look at Carlita, spread out on the table, and shook his head. "Either an attempted abortion or terribly rough handling of some sort," he said. "Who the hell did this to you?"

Carlita refused to answer, staring at Anna.

"I said, who did it?" the doctor repeated roughly.

"Daddy," Carlita whispered.

The doctor stripped off his gloves and threw them in the sink. "That son of a bitch," he said.

The news spread around the grounds as every other scandal had, but this was different. This was the final battle between Good and Evil. It was Armageddon. God had plummeted from the heavens and committed the devil's sin. There was no reason, no order, no justice in the universe. The sun was dark, and the stars were falling from the sky. The devil was loose in the garden. There were wild terror, murder, insanity in the air. It was the last day, the final judgment.

When we heard John's car coining down the road, I ran out of the house, terrified of encountering him. I ran across the pasture and crouched behind a boulder quaking with fear. I had double-crossed him, and Anna had proclaimed his shame in public. He might be truly mad, crazy enough to kill.

He drove into the lot and staggered toward the study with a heavy gait, like a drunken man. He looked straight ahead. No one spoke to him or offered a hand or looked at him. It was as though someone had pushed a button and we were operating like robots. By his command, such people as he were not to be seen, not to be spoken to. By his own teachings, he had committed the unpardonable, sin, and he was to be banished. The institution he had established could not tolerate his continuing.

That afternoon Anna picked up the telephone and called the boys' dorm. "Nada," she said, a new firmness in her voice, "could I talk to you? Okay, why don't you come over here?" She hung up the phone and called me. "Lenore, are you ready to go?"

"I'm all set. How soon are we leaving?"

"I'm sorry, but I can't leave your father like this. The man is dangerously out of his mind."

"Mother, what do you owe him? After twenty-two years of . . ."

"Lenore. I've got to get professional help for him. I'll get someone else to take you. You can make it on your own. Your father needs me."

When Nada came staggering into the room, her eyes were red. "Oh, Anna!" she wailed, putting her arms around my mother's neck. "To think that all this time he was fooling us both! Oh, I'm so sorry, Anna, sorry for all the grief I've caused you. I know how you feel now. That evil, double-crossing man! He said he loved me, that you no longer wanted him, and I thought he was an honest man! Oh, my gracious, and here he was playing around with these children. The man is mental!"

Anna unwrapped herself from Nada's sticky embrace.

"He is," she said coolly. "Please don't overwhelm me with your true confessions right now. We've got two things that have to be done. Lenore has to be driven to Chicago, and John has to be taken to a hospital . . ."

"Oh, spare me the sight of him." Nada sniffed. "I'll drive mademoiselle to the north, and you take care of your husband."

An hour later Pearl had come to the Vogel house and told Anna the same story as her sister Carlita, and other girls were divulging similar tales. Still shaken, I picked up my bag and walked to the car. Nada and Maxine were there, ready to go with me, and a crowd of confused children stood around the parking lot asking when I would come back. Aunt Kay and Miss Smith were wishing me God-speed. John my father was in the study crying and moaning, his voice rising and falling in weird crescendos. Carlita was in the hospital. Gram was kissing me goodby. I was leaving.

We were in the car, driving away from the familiar grounds, the place that had been home. The houses on the Bee Creek road flew past, powdered in late-summer clouds of dust. Fifteen years before. I had decided to run away, and now I was finally leaving. If I had left those fifteen years ago, I would have missed a lot—a lot of fun, a lot of life, a lot of love, and a lot of hell. I was glad I had stayed. I was glad I was leaving. Whatever it had been it was over. Now all I still faced was five hundred miles in a car with my best friend and my worst enemy.

The doctor in Corbin had told Anna he wanted to see me. We

stopped at his office on the way through town.

His face was kind as he sat across the big desk. "That must have been a rough scene," he said, shaking his head. "Believe me, I've been around a long time, and I've never seen anything like this. Your father's a sick man. But don't let this affect your own attitude toward sexual relationships. This is definitely abnormal behavior, definitely psychotic. Just try to forget it. I guarantee you, you'll never run into anything this crazy the rest of your life!"

I smiled at him, still too numb to feel any pain. "I'm not scared at all," I said. "Just glad to be out of that mess. I'm anxious to see what real life is all about."

"That's the spirit!" He smiled. "And listen, don't go hungry. If you ever get in a bind, or need help, you know where we are. Here's a little something from the wife and me. Maybe it'll help you get started."

He placed a check in my hand and kissed me on the cheek. I went to the car, assured that the great unknown would be the best place I had ever been.

That night the three of us stayed in a motel. It was the first motel I had ever been in without John. Everything seemed new, different. Nada was uneasy. She tried to be one of us, erasing the years of hurt with sudden friendship.

"Your papa really had me fooled," she confided. "He actually gave me the impression—I wouldn't say I could quote him, but he always gave me the impression—that your mother was mentally incompetent, and that it would only be a matter of time until she would have to be hospitalized. He felt there would be less blame on him that way than with a divorce."

"He talked about a divorce?" I asked.

"For years he said he wanted to marry me. That, he said, was why he wanted me to become familiar to the public, so the transition would be smooth. That evil old schemer! Well, he'll get his now!

Anna will be the one to drag him off to the funny farm. He's gone nuttier than a fruitcake!"

I studied her face, a bit overwhelmed by this juicy information. As usual, she was smiling cheerfully, but there were deep dark rings around her eyes. When Max and I were out of earshot we exchanged a few quick whispers.

"How do you feel about traveling with ol' Big Tits?" I mouthed.

"We would get stuck with her. Do you think she's really changed?"

"I don't know." I said suspiciously. "You never can tell when she's putting up a big front!"

It was the old familiar trail up through Indiana, marked with motels famous for fights and restaurants remembered for moody silences. Up through the outskirts of Chicago and over to the west, but this time my thoughts and feelings were radically different. At the end of the road there would be no warm smoky gathering of Anna's clan, no adoring crowds ready to give money and applause. There would be a request to make at a college president's home, a request for asylum, for work, for lodging, and a chance to begin life over again.

By the next morning, Max and Nada were, gone. I awoke in the guest room across the campus and went to the window. The tall elms lining the sidewalk arched above the quiet street. Red brick buildings dotted the velvet green of the campus, and students walked along the paths in groups or singly, clutching armloads of books. It looked like heaven.

And I, who had been ready to search for freedom at any cost, who had been ready to be damned if necessary to find my own soul, found myself overcome by an extraordinary sensation. Here on this verdant campus I felt a presence, a sense of the Green God whom I had lost in my submission to guilt and fear. Here there was no fear. There was no anger, and in the vacuum created by their absence I felt an inrush of a powerful love. I gazed out the window, my raw spirit touching life. It was good. I was free. Heaven with its harps and robes could be someone else's concern. This was all I needed.

I dressed and walked across the campus, smiling and ready to get acquainted with everyone. The student center manager gave me a job, presented me with a uniform, and before noon I was punched in and behind the counter stacking plastic trays and making friends. Meals were free, and I would earn sixty-five cents an hour. Compared to ten dollars a month, that was a fortune. What more could anyone want? By the end of the day I had a date for an upcoming football game, and after a few days campus housing put me in a house on Washington Street with a gang of girls in the junior class. They were a gum chewing, clothes-swapping group of wise women who showed a personal interest in my adjustment to normal society. It had been decided I should wait a semester to start classes, so for the first four months these young American citizens took it upon themselves to introduce me to the customs of a country I had never known.

"You mean you've never dated?" blond Wilma said incredulously.

"No, not yet!"

"Well, for heaven's sake, why not? Are you scared of guys?"

"I never had a chance."

"What do you mean, you never had a chance?" I told them the story of the home and John, to assorted laughs, hoots, and groans.

"Oh, my God," said Sandy, a rotund freckled girl who was always trying to diet. "How ghastly! Doesn't all that scare you?"

"Not anymore. It's all over now."

"Are you going to date on campus?"

"I've got a date for the football game already," I said smugly. There were more laughs, hoots, and groans. Aside from Fran, who was going steady, none of them had a weekend date.

Everything was shining and new. Life was indescribably

beautiful. At six o'clock I had to report for work, and at five o'clock the alarm in my room went off. I listened to it ring like some liberty bell, then reached in the cold morning darkness and shut it off, a feeling of glorious excitement washing over me. It was morning, and I was young and alive and free. I rose in the darkness, dressed, and walked the seven blocks to work, wanting to sing loud enough to wake up the whole town.

I glanced at the darkened houses as I passed. Did the people on this street really appreciate what it meant to be free, to get up in the morning and wear short sleeves or long, to say damn if they pleased, to plan their own futures? I hoped as I walked past them in the morning darkness that they did, and that it made their lives happy.

In the evenings I came home to a houseful of girls, eating, chatting, and running one another's affairs.

"Come on and have a snack with us," Freckles called one evening when I came home late from work, I glanced at the clock in the hallway. It was past ten.

"I better not," I said. "Thanks anyway, but I've got to get up at five in the morning."

"Ug!" said Freckles. "That sounds like my summer job."

"Where do you work?"

"On a lake steamer, up around Holland, Michigan."

"Hey, I know somebody who lives near there, in Zeeland."

"Guy or girl?"

"Guy."

"I thought you didn't know any guys."

"Well. I really don't know him, but I wanted to once."

"Tell us," said Wilma, chewing a cracker. "This sounds good."

I did tell them, about Gordon's visit, his letters, the fight, the frustrations, and my final choice.

"Golly," Wilma said sadly. "Did you ever write back to him?"

"No, how could I?"

"You can now."

"Oh, I can't. Not after this long. He's probably forgotten me."

"I'll bet he hasn't," said Fran. "You're probably still haunting his dreams, and I think you should write to him."

"I'm embarrassed. Somebody will have claimed him by now."

"It doesn't have to be a love letter," Fran insisted. "Just tell him you're away from home and free. If he's married, he'll get rid of the letter fast enough. If he isn't . . ."

"Oh, come on, I dare you!" Wilma said excitedly. That was all I needed.

That night before I set the alarm, I took out a sheet of paper and a pen. I sat on the edge of the bed wondering why he had not come that night and feeling the sharp stab of chagrin. Oh, well, that was long ago and in another world. John had probably killed the whole thing with his letter, but now that I was starting over again, I might as well make a fool of myself. Everything was up for grabs.

Dear Gordon,

> *You may have forgotten me. I am the girl you wrote to in Kentucky at the Galilean Home. That was almost two years ago, and a lot has happened. This may surprise you, but I have left home. One thing that has bothered me all this time is that I never answered your letter. I wanted to, but was told that if I did I would be disowned and must leave home. I was afraid, and chose not to write. But as I said, many things have happened, and my life has changed. I am on my own now, living in the town of Wheaton, where I plan to go to college next semester.*

I paused, trying to search in my memory for the address. If he was still at the same school, it would be Zwemer Hall. Or was it Zwymer Hall? Or what if he wasn't there at all? Just for insurance. I scrawled across the bottom, IF MOVED, PLEASE FORWARD. Then I lay it on the chest and went to bed, wondering if I had been foolish to accept the dare. After all the hell I had been through in the name of religion, did I want to re-establish contact with someone who was dabbling in theology? They said that daughters tended to repeat their mothers' mistakes. Did I want some God snob descending on me again, creating rules and friction, and destroying the freedom I cherished so deeply and had fought so hard to gain? I fell asleep still wondering, but the next morning on my way to work I dropped the letter in the mailbox by the railroad tracks.

It's only a letter, I said to myself. *I'm not signing my life away!*

I puzzled over a guarded letter from Anna in Birmingham, of all paces, and then Mr. Haas came to take me out to dinner. He gave me a quick once-over: the short haircut, the new makeup, and the clothes and shoes borrowed from the girls on Washington Street until I got my first paycheck. He nodded his Dutch uncle approval.

"You're doing fine," he said. "Now we'll get a G.E.D test for you and check up on some scholarships. What do you hear from home?"

"Just one letter from my mother, who's in some rest home in Alabama. It was written in such a guarded way, and the handwriting was so shaky, I could hardly figure it out. What's all this business about Birmingham?"

"To tell you the truth, I intended to get up here and see you a lot sooner, but I drove to the home and got very involved in trying to help them sort out their problems. John is in a rest home on Judge Thorn's advice. Orders, you might say."

"Wait a minute. Back up. What happened the day I left?"

"Okay, let me see if I can give you a bird's-eye view of what's gone on. Soon after you headed north, your mother called Bob Long, the big minister in Corbin, and asked him to get in touch with the doctor. The doctor, of course, didn't spare any words in describing the situation to him. Long drove out to the home immediately, to find John screaming and raving, putting on a real heavenly tantrum and trying to get God to strike down all his enemies and accusers. So Long and the doctor arranged for him to be taken to a psychiatric hospital in Knoxville."

The irony of the situation struck me, but I let him talk on.

"The doctors there sedated him and kept him for several days. I understand that when they started to question him, they thought he was quite a case. They asked him about his occupation, and he said he worked for God. They asked him about his family, and he told them he had ninety children, and they all lived on a thousand-acre tract of land in Kentucky, with several million dollars' worth of buildings and equipment. You can imagine! They thought he was suffering from delusions of grandeur!"

I shook my head, laughing wryly. "Where did you get that story?" I asked.

"Straight from the doctor," Haas said. "You see, my connection lately has been more or less official, and I had to talk with him frankly to get the true state of affairs."

"I understand. Okay, go on."

"Well, then, John began to talk about his enemies, the county officials who were out to get him, the disloyal members of his family who had betrayed him, such as you, and the lies that were being fabricated against him. You can imagine what they said."

"Paranoid." I sighed. "The whole thing would be funny if it weren't so tragic."

"The real tragedy." Haas continued, "is that after he had been there a few days the hospital received a long-distance call. We still don't know if it was from a friend trying to free him or an enemy wanting to get at him, but this call came asking if John was there. The caller said he was a lawyer, so they told him that John was in their custody, and that he was a dangerous psychotic. The caller said, 'Listen, all that man has told you is true. He does have ninety kids, and he owns a thousand acres of land. He's an important and powerful man, and no one ever tangles with him and comes out clean. If you know what's good for you, you'll get him off your hands as fast as you can.'"

"So what did they do?"

"They released him. They had been warned that there might be a legal battle and they would get caught in the middle while they were deciding if he was sane or insane. So rather than risk getting involved, they let him go."

"So he's loose again?"

"Loose, and a complete maniac. He wrote a letter to that poor abused Carlita, blaming her for breaking up the home, causing his mental breakdown, and scattering the children. He asked her to come back to him 'under the terms arranged'. The letter was turned over to Long, who has been Carlita's guardian until this is all settled. Her natural father is completely baffled. You can bet if there's a court case, John's letter will be used as evidence. He has no intentions of changing."

"Does it look as if there's going to be a court case?"

"Not as long as John stays out of the state. That's where the rest home came in. When John was released from the hospital, he immediately called Judge Thorn to ask if it was safe for him to return. Thorn told him to stay away, and to get to a rest home as fast as he could. As soon as your mother heard it, she offered to go down and take care of him."

"So who's running the home?"

"For a while we hoped that things could be patched up, that a few men like Long and Sanders and I could form a committee to keep the place going. At first Nada cooperated, but now I have a feeling she's re-established contact with John. She acts aloof, as though I'm trying to intrude. She seems to be carrying out some command. John remains head of the organization, and if he goes down the whole place goes down with him."

"But that's suicidal! What about all the kids?"

"I have a feeling, you know, that your father has never cared primarily about those kids, or any other human being. He is still obsessed with proving he's in touch with heaven."

"But doesn't he understand that the lives he has wrecked will in the end be the ruin of his dream?"

"I don't think he has ever faced that yet," Haas said as the waiter brought our steaks.

"But Birmingham," I said, still trying to fit the pieces of the puzzle together. "What made him go to Birmingham?"

"You remember the Swanns?"

"Of course!"

"When your father was released from the Knoxville hospital,

he did not go to a rest home as the judge suggested, but put a call through to Floyd Swann in Birmingham. Swann met him at the train station and took him home. They took care of him like a brother. He demanded their attention day and night. He was terrified in the dark alone, and asked Mrs. Swann to sit with him. Floyd took him on long drives to soothe him, and John confessed a lot of things to him that he's not admitted to anyone else. I guess he's sorry about that now."

"Why?"

"Because the Swanns tried to get him to accept help, to make amends to Anna, or simply to stay clear of Nada and Carlita. But he got angry at them. He made Mrs. Swann call Judge Thorn again to ask if he could come back to Kentucky."

"What did Thorn say?"

"He was furious. He told him to stay the hell out of the state! He said if the case came up in court and he tried to hand down a decision in John's favor, he would be lynched! He said his whole political career was down the drain if John ever showed his face in Whitley County, and he warned John that if he ever crossed the state line, there would be people waiting to arrest him and take him before the grand jury."

"Wow," I breathed, thinking of how he had set all this up for himself. "So now, he's left the Swanns?"

"Left them in a storm, and went to the rest home where he is now. "He considers the Swanns his mortal enemies because they're sitting on evidence that could put him behind bars."

"And my mother is down there caught in the middle of all this. No wonder her letter sounded guarded!"

"Your little mother, God bless her heart, has tried to stick with him and start all over again. I don't know . . ."

I poked at the expensive steak, suddenly feeling full. I had left all that trouble behind to find a new life, and yet it was not so easy to get rid of. Its shadow still threatened my bright new world.

I wondered what had made Anna follow him, and how long it would last, and if she were in any danger of physical harm from him. I tried desperately to push the whole problem into a section of my mind where it could not dominate me, to think of something that would reverse the wall of darkness reaching out for me again. All I could think of was the hastily scrawled letter, written on a dare, and dropped in the postbox by the railroad tracks.

CHAPTER THIRTEEN

I climbed the stairs to the tiny room on Washington Street after a day full of laughter and bantering flirtations at the student center. I was a little in love with the whole world and everyone in it, even stray cats and the old woman who operated the dishwashing machine in the kitchen. It was amazing what a remarkable place the world was, how uncomplicated people were, how free. Next to John's dream world, reality was a solid relief.

I tossed my jacket on the bed and saw an envelope and a packet on the chest. The packet was from home, and the letter from . . . There it was, just as I somehow knew it would be, addressed in the handsome scrawl complete with brown ink. I stared at the return address, almost afraid it would disappear before my eyes. Then I pounced on the letter and tore it open with unsteady fingers. This can't be happening, I thought. I'm in the real world now, not in John's world of miracles.

Dear Lenore:

I didn't know what I was seeing when your letter came. I couldn't believe my eyes! It's been a long time since we saw each other, but I certainly haven't forgotten! Your father wrote me a very strange letter, and I felt terrible that you were caught there under his power, but I didn't want to cause you any trouble by writing back or interfering. Let me tell you that I think breaking with the home has been a most important step in your life. Would you think it too forward on my part if I drove down to Wheaton to see you? In two weeks I have a class break, and perhaps we could spend a

weekend together and get acquainted. Please let me know if
it's okay to come.

Sincerely,
Gordon.

It had been a long time since I stood with a letter from Gordon in my hands. Almost everything in my world had changed, but this one feeling was the same. I wanted to see him, no matter what happened. I *had* to see him. I read the letter again, trying to focus his image in my memory. To my consternation I could not remember a single feature of his face. All that was left was a feeling of rightness that tugged at me whenever I thought of him. But his face was gone.

When I laid the letter aside and opened the package from home to find a box of cookies and homemade fudge from Max and Aunt Kay, I thought of them for a moment, pulled between love for the old and the new, the past and the future.

The night he came I was an absolute wreck. He was due at seven, and I started getting ready at four. I had had my hair up since morning and had shopped for a week trying to choose the right outfit on my sixty-five-cent-an-hour paycheck. Also I was torn between announcing my independence and wanting to please him. If a man was studying theology, what would he want a girl to look like? Bland, probably, with soft clothes and a simple hairdo. Makeup? Light pink to disappearing. Would my skirt and sweater be right? Would the pullover sweater be too tight? Then I looked in the mirror and thought, 'You ninny, what are you trying to do? Get on the gospel bandwagon again? Wear what you want, do as you please, paint a red streak down the middle of your nose, and if he doesn't like it he has a lousy sense of humor and you might as well get rid of him. What are you doing, building another cage for yourself?

But at seven o'clock sharp, when the town hall clock struck, I heard his footsteps on the porch and trembled. The whole house seemed to shake. I gathered up my purse and coat and started down to meet him. He was standing at the foot of the stairs, in the flesh, looking up at me as if he wondered what in the world he had gotten himself into. It was eerie to see a face on somebody else that mirrored so clearly what I was thinking.

I was so nervous I could hardly tell if I remembered him or not. He was a big man, towering over me, dressed in a charcoal gray flannel suit. He helped me with my coat while we chatted uneasily, then quickly left the house.

Once in the car, we both relaxed, I scooted to the middle and sat beside him, putting myself at his mercy, and we began to talk, gradually opening up to each other, breaking the dam of the long silence between us.

We drove to a candlelit restaurant in a nearby town and sat at a table for two. I watched his face in the flickering candlelight, and it began to come back to me, the chiseled features, the shadowed eyes touched with mystery and vulnerability, the white teeth, and the deep voice. I gazed at him fascinated, unable to believe that this was really the man I had dreamed of for so long, the face that had broken the spell John had cast over me. I saw again that everything about him was clean and direct. He was refreshing and open and strong. He even drank white milk. He was a part of the real world, a man who respected his family and his traditions, a man who had gone through the proper channels to get the training he needed for life. Three years older than I, he had gone to a public school and a good college.

He told me about himself, but most of the time he asked me about the home, about what had happened and why I had left. His voice was caring as he lifted the story out of me, and when I cried at the rotten parts, he reached over and gently touched my hand. Bit by bit I began to understand things that had been a scramble to me when they happened, because he understood. I watched his eyes, shining in the candlelight, and knew I had a friend.

The house rules stated that all girls had to be in by midnight, which still gave us an hour. The town was quiet; there was no place to go; so we bought two crunchy apples and walked around the streets, scuffling our feet in the leaves. We were like two people newly born, delighted to be alive, amazed that our hands locked so perfectly, that my shoulder slid under his arm as though it had been made to fit. We watched our feet scuffling through the leaves, astonished that they seemed to be dancing by themselves. I glanced up at his eyes, even more mysterious now in the streetlight. He seemed so sure of himself, so strong.

"Do you date a lot around campus?" he asked.

"Some . . . football games and skating parties and such. Nobody in particular."

"Me either."

"I think it's important for me to be exposed to a lot of different people, don't you? I mean after not dating at all?"

I waited for him to disagree with me, but he didn't.

"Maybe you're right, you should," he said, tightening the arm around me. "But I don't think I'll date anymore."

I glanced at him, wondering what he meant, but not daring to pursue the subject.

Punctually at five minutes to twelve we were back in front of the house. It was cold, and we could see our breath in the night air. Gordon paused in the shadow of the hedges, looking huge and lovable in his overcoat. I looked up at him, wondering what he wanted to say. He was looking down at me, a quizzical expression on his face.

"What is it?" I asked.

"May I kiss you good night?"

I hesitated for a moment, hoping he knew I didn't kiss just anybody. In fact I had avoided this good night ritual with everybody.

"I guess so," I said unsurely.

I felt his lips, strange at first, then deep and sweet. We stepped back and looked at each other, a little stunned, then said good night.

I watched him walk to his car, then stumbled upstairs and sat on the edge of my bed in a daze. Maybe miracles did happen, even in the real world. Who by the farthest stretch of imagination would have thought I would ever find him again, that both of us would be free, that we would meet in this strange place?

I heard the town hall clock chime every hour that night as I recalled every moment and gesture of the evening, the caring in his voice, the gentleness in his hands, and the fire in his kiss.

Gordon wrote to me every day for a month, and I answered every day. The mailbox on Washington Street became a hallowed spot, and Saturday was the best day in the week because I was home when the postman came. His letters were warm and entertaining, always containing at least one sentence that made me catch my breath and read it over, but neither of us mentioned the word "love." We were careful to avoid a word too powerful to be used lightly.

At Thanksgiving he came back, and we talked more seriously. The first evening he was in Wheaton we sat in the car in front of the house, sharing our ideas about life. Suddenly he reached across me, opened the glove compartment, and took out a small black book. I thought for sure he was going to start reading the psalms to me, and I nearly fell out of love. But it was something different, a slender black book with an open hand, and figures dancing in the palm.

"Have you ever read The Prophet?" he asked.

"No. Is it a religious book?"

"That depends on what you mean by religion. Let me read you his section on love and see how you like it."

He bent toward the window to catch the glow from the streetlight, and I listened carefully.

> *Love possesses not, nor would it be possessed: for love is*
> *sufficient unto love. When you love you should not say,*
> *'God is in my heart,' but rather, 'I am in the heart of God.'*
> *And think not you can direct the course of love, for love, if*
> *it finds you worthy directs your course.*

He paused, waiting for my response. I was counting to ten desperately, trying to think of red circles and purple squares to keep myself from bursting into tears. When I got to ten the flood broke loose and I was completely undone. He laid the book down and put a gentle arm around me.

"I love you," he whispered. "You can always cry with me."

"I love you too," I confessed through my sniffles.

"Do you really?"

"I really do."

He rolled the window down and took in a deep breath of air. "Wow, does that ever feel better," he said. "Now we can say it. I love you! I love you!"

"And I love you. I love you!"

He started the motor, and we drove through the streets of the town repeating the magic words as though it were the first time two people had ever said them to each other.

Then he was gone, and I was back in a workaday world, punching the clock and wearing a uniform with his picture in the pocket. Campus was no longer green or even gold but a chilly wet gray, and I waited every day for the letter in brown ink and feasted on it. The freedom and flirtations on campus now seemed dull, like child's play. I tried halfheartedly to enter into the social life around me, and I even accepted a few dates, thinking I should not get tied down so soon; but I was bored when I went out with some undergrad to eat pizza and listen to a jukebox. My belated flaming adolescence had lasted two months, and it was over.

The book I'd sent to the Chicago publishing house so long ago had finally been published. I paged through it, realizing how much smaller than life it was, how much more there was to say now. In one year I had grown a lifetime, yet there in that book I was, with a year ago's thoughts and values frozen into print. It was embarrassing. But it prompted a letter from John Maloney, the *Saturday Evening Post* author who had written the article on the home.

My dear little friend.

As one writer to another, I salute you! Don't let this be anything but the beginning of your career. There is a streak of genius in you, and you must develop it. Try to be less direct when you talk about religion. Read Pearl Buck. She was good at that.
Maloney

P.S. I just tore this letter open to remind you to thank your teachers. Those good women at the home must have worked hard to teach you so much. Your Friend,

J.M.

Mr. Sanders wrote and asked if I would like to come home for Christmas. He offered to pay the plane fare from Chicago to the London, Kentucky, airport, and to meet my plane. I had planned to spend Christmas with Gordon, and I was unsure about what to do. But when I placed a long-distance call to Michigan, I discovered that everyone in Zeeland was named DePree. Finally I remembered that his father's name was Adrian, and got the right number. Luckily, Gordon was home.

"Sure, why don't you go!" Gordon said. "And the day after Christmas I'll drive down to Kentucky to meet you. You can give me a personalized tour of the grounds."

"I'll take you all the places nobody's ever been!" I promised.

It was my first flight, but then it was my first everything that year, so I took it in stride. Getting off at the London airport, I saw Mr. Sanders scanning the passengers. I waved at him, but he kept looking past me at the door of the plane.

Finally I came up and touched his arm. "Mr. Sanders!" I said, laughing. "Here I am!"

He turned to face me, and gave me a look that was hard to

interpret, as full of approval and scorn as if an angel had fallen from paradise and become a Broadway star.

"Why, is that you?" he spluttered. "God damn it, you look just like all the rest of them now!" And then his face dissolved into his buttersoft grandfatherly smile. He couldn't have said anything that pleased me more if he'd tried.

The home was strangely quiet, still filled with crowds of children but curiously subdued. John and Anna weren't around, and Nada was in charge. Money had continued to trickle in from donors who had not heard or not believed the situation. But funds were low. Aunt Kay had moved into our house and was looking after the girls, but everything there was strange too. Aunt Kay slept in John's room; and Anna's bedroom, the room with the floating white curtains, was empty. It seemed the only place in the house where I could relax, and I chose to sleep there, rather than in the downstairs room with its frightening memories. The blue morning glory plaque was still on the wall announcing, IN QUIETNESS AND CONFIDENCE SHALL BE YOUR STRENGTH, and I wondered how far these qualities were carrying her now, alone with John in Birmingham.

I fell asleep, trying to dream of Gordon, but my mind was filled with unnamed fears. During the night I was wakened by the sound of a motor, then rolled over and went back to sleep, thinking it some stray traveler.

Suddenly in the half-darkness the bedroom door opened, and I could see a form that looked like Anna's. I thought I was dreaming. I rubbed my eyes and sat upright. "Mom?" I called, half terrified.

"Lenore ! What are you doing here?" It was her real voice.

"I'm here for Christmas! Are you alone, Mom?"

"Yes. Your father can't come home. He can't ever come home again."

Anna undressed quietly and climbed into her big bed beside me. She lay down with a sigh and covered her eyes with one arm. I could feel her tiredness beside me, and her desperation.

"How's it going, Mom?" I asked sleepily. "How is he? Is he sorry?"

The only reply was the sound of quiet sobbing. I put my arm around her, as I had done when I was a little girl, trying to love her and protect her from hurt.

"Why did you go back to him?" I asked.

"I'm trying," she whispered. "I'm trying so hard to make it work. I went there with such high hopes that maybe it would happen this time. I really hoped that we could finally go away, just the two of us, and start all over again. I told him I would work, that I didn't care what he did for a living, that we would forget it all, and just do some simple kind of thing—be honest people and start over again . . ." Her voice was lost in tears.

"You mean he wouldn't accept even that—your throwing yourself at his feet like that?"

"I don't know how to reach him, how to get to the person locked inside him. He still has all these wild ideas. He wants to come back here. He can't realize he's finished. He still spends all day writing official letters to Nada."

"Not again!"

"And Carlita, and Judge Thorn. He's still . . ."

I waited a moment, for her to be able to speak.

" . . . he won't change. Maybe he can't change."

"Why do you say that?"

"No matter where we are, he does the same things. He carries the trouble wherever he goes."

"What do you mean?

"After we left the rest home and moved to this apartment hotel, I got a job at a department store. We'd meet at a cafeteria every day for lunch, I'd go back to work, and then we'd meet to go out for dinner. But one day I went to the cafeteria and he wasn't there. No message, no anything. By dark he still wasn't home, and by midnight I was furious and half scared. It was three o'clock in the morning before he came sneaking in."

"Where had he been?"

"Nada had called him up and asked him to meet her. He had

spent the day and the night with her in a motel."

I felt the old stab of anger, the urge to kill. "The same stupid thing!" I said, sitting up in bed. "Are you going to put up with this nonsense all your life? Haven't you been a sucker long enough? Why don't you drop him? He's a lost cause!"

Anna was quiet.

"Once more," she finally said calmly. "I'll try once more. I've got a job now, and a social security number for the first time in my life. I know I can survive. I'm not staying with him because I'm afraid to leave. If I really come to the place where I know it can't work, I'll go."

On Christmas afternoon, immediately after the annual dinner at Mr. Sanders', she left for Birmingham.

The afternoon Gordon arrived it was warm for Kentucky in December. His sporty two-tone Ford pulled up in the parking lot, and I ran out to meet him and gave him a warm kiss in full view of all the shocked onlookers. We walked together down the old familiar gravel path, and I felt that all good things were coming together at last. The children clustered around us, curious to see this fabled prince who had stolen me.

After visiting with Aunt Kay, Maxine, and the others in the Vogel house, Gordon and I went for a walk in the woods. We took the path that led through the pine forest to the river. It was beautiful in the crisp December day, and I felt proud that my woods were showing off so well. Deeper and deeper we went into the brush, down through the cliffs and over the sage grass to the footlog that crossed Whippoorwill Creek. We followed the creek to the bend in the river where a deserted house stood, weathered and broken to a shell among the trees.

"I used to know the old man who lived here," I told him. "Once when I was a little kid, afraid to go home through the woods in the dusk, he told me, 'You know, as long as you keep singin', the boogerman can't get you.'"

We leaned against the wall of the old gray house, listening to the river on the shoals beneath, and I told him the story of when I wanted to die because life had seemed so hopeless.

"Ummm, I'm so glad you kept on singing until I found you!" he said, pulling me close. "Because one of these days I'm going to marry you. We're going to have a great life together, you and I!"

I listened to the river dashing against the rocks below us, wondering if I had heard him right.

"What . . . what did you say?" I asked, confused.

"I said I'm going to marry you!"

"Well, I guess I'm going to marry you too then!" I said happily.

He swung me up in his arms, and we did a whirling joy dance in the weathered old shack.

Supper was in the dining hall, and I felt proud to be walking in with Gordon, past the table where I had tried not to look at him two years before. All the boys and girls were curious to see him. Gram came from behind the cafeteria counter and gave him her stamp of approval. Aunt Kay and Maxine thought he was the greatest, and even Stumpy grudgingly shook hands with him. He was accepted by my family.

One big difference was that most of the girls had gone away to boarding school in Taccoa, Georgia. Carlita, Pearl, Zula—the whole singing group had been disbanded and packed off. Since Nada was running things—and it had always been the older girls who were a threat to her—the new policy was that all girls over fourteen got sent away to boarding school. It used to be the boys. Except for Stumpy . . . but then everything was changing. Old Nada herself looked subdued, a mere shadow of her former glory. There were dark rings around her eyes, and she seemed so discouraged even her bust line sagged.

She eyed me with the old malice that I somehow found more comfortable than her pseudo friendship.

"I always used to think of you as tiny," she said sweetly, "but you're really quite a big girl, aren't you?"

"It depends on how you look at it," I said politely. "I guess as people like you get older, they start to shrink."

Gordon drove back to Michigan after our arranging to meet in mid January, and, at Grams suggestion, Max and I took a Greyhound bus to Birmingham to visit John and Anna. As we wound down through the Smoky Mountains, we wondered what it would be like to see John in exile, John stripped of his power. Would he be sad and broken, somehow softened? We decided to be forgiving and to try to start again, like Anna.

In the Birmingham hotel we buzzed at a door on the third floor. John opened it. He looked nervous and worn, restless, like a king without a kingdom. Although he seemed delighted to see us, it did not take us long to realize that nothing had changed.

"Where's Mother?" I asked. "Is she still at work?"

"Your mother left," he said. "Didn't you see her in Corbin?"

"No, I thought she was here!"

"You must have passed each other on the road."

"What happened?"

"She just left,' he repeated stubbornly.

"But why?" I insisted.

As usual, he did not answer me directly. "Everybody wants to help me," he said angrily. "But nobody wants to help me the way I want to be helped. They're all the same. Haas wants to run the home. Long wants to crucify me in public. The doctor wants to protect everyone else at my expense. They all want me to be what they've always tried to make me be, to strap me with committees and budgets to run my family."

"I wouldn't worry about committees and budgets anymore if I were you," I said. "And what did you do to Mother?"

"All I asked her to do was deliver a letter for me, and she blew up."

"What kind of a letter, and to whom?"

No direct reply.

"Now the organ will be silenced," he said tragically, "and the voices of the girls will not be heard again. A huge principle was at stake. The Glory of God was on the line, and it has all been destroyed."

"But you destroyed it!"

"The doctor and the judge could have covered for me. Long had no business shooting off his loud mouth."

"But can't you see that you were wrecking at least two lives, and destroying the freedom of so many people? Can't you see?"

"A principle was at stake. What were one or two lives compared to the truth I was demonstrating? Now the world will never know what could have been accomplished by prayer!"

I sat with my mouth open, looking at him, wondering as I often had lately if he were rational and evil or insane and innocent. I felt my eyes clouding, my hands wanting to reach out to him.

"So many people wanted to help you," I said. "Why won't you be helped?"

"Nobody wants to help me. They're all trying to destroy me."

"Mother tried. I know how much she wanted you to start over together."

The bitter look on his face hardened. "All she wanted to prove," he said, "was that she was finally right. She was always against children's work, and if she thinks this is the perfect moment to drag me back, slobbering and repentant, to that damnable clan of hers, she's mistaken!"

It was a no-win situation. I changed the subject to something cheerful and told him about Gordon.

"It doesn't surprise me," he said with a half-grin. "I knew if you two ever got together, that would be it."

"Aren't you happy for us?"

"If you like stuffy Dutch Calvinists. I suppose he's not bad."

I saw it was useless to try to get through to him. He was oblivious of the people who had trusted him, the thousands of dollars he had been given in good faith, and the children placed in his hands for safekeeping who had been wronged. His only thoughts were for himself and the great indignity that had been done him.

"Shall we leave soon?" Max said. She was, understandably, feeling uncomfortable.

"Don't go by yourselves." John said. "I'm driving up as far as Tennessee, and I'll take you along."

"Why are you doing that?" I asked.

"I have to meet Gram and Nada. We have some business to transact, and we're meeting in a motel in Jellico. I'm not supposed to come back to Kentucky, but I can legally run the organization from across the state line. Might even be able to slip home some nights. Its only twenty-two miles from the border to home. But whatever you do, don't say anything about it, because if that bastard Bob Long gets wind of it, he'll have me dragged into court."

"So now we've disposed of Mother, and we're free to meet Nada in motels. How convenient."

"Gram will be there."

"Playing chaperone? At least you have a new one now. Are you planning to marry Nada and make an honest woman of her?"

"Whatever gave you that idea" He chuckled, the old smile tipping up the corners of his mustache.

I gave him a long hard look. His face was soft and decadent and his features seemed to run together. He had gleaned no wisdom from his ordeal. I was glad Anna had left him, whatever the reason, and I hoped he would marry Nada. In all honesty, I could not think of anyone who deserved him more.

But what had been the final straw for Anna?

It was not long before that piece of the puzzle fell into place. I was no sooner back in Wheaton than a telephone call came from Chicago.

I heard Anna's voice, dry and a little bitter, as though she had cried all her tears. "Lenore, could I meet you somewhere?"

We met at a greasy-spoon restaurant in Wheaton, both of us too poor to go to a nice place. I was living on my wages, and Anna had nothing but what she had borrowed from her sisters.

"What was it?" I asked curiously. "What finally did it?"

Anna took a long breath and poked at her food. I had never seen her so thin. "It was getting hopeless, she said. "Not only was it impossible for me to help him, he was trying to implicate me in the mess."

"How?"

"The day I left Sanders', I drove all night and got back to Birmingham in the morning. At noon we went out for lunch, and as soon as we sat down at the table he took out an affidavit he had prepared stating that Carlita had lied about everything she had told the doctor and the minister in Corbin, and that she had spread these lies only in order to escape from the home."

"No!"

"Yes! And he wanted Nada and me to go to Carlita's boarding school in Georgia and force her to sign it."

"Of all the dirty... What did you say?"

"What could I say? I told him that I had spent my whole life teaching kids to be truthful, and I was not going to be a party to his lie!"

"I'll bet he didn't like that."

"Of course not. He got up and stormed out of the cafeteria and stood on the street corner in one of his tragic poses. I paid the bill and walked out. I saw him standing there on the corner, and I walked past him as though he was somebody I had never known. I didn't even turn around. I just kept walking straight to the bus station. That was a walk I'll never forget as long as I live. It was as if all the lights inside me had finally gone out, and everything was as black as hell, and there was no turning back. I had a feeling I'd never see him again. A whole section of my life was over, and I was walking to the Birmingham bus station."

People in the small narrow restaurant were glancing at us, hunched over the table talking as though our lives depended on it, but I didn't care what anyone thought. I felt proud of Anna.

"Don't worry, Mom," I said. "You've done the right thing."

"I haven't told my sisters yet how bad things are," she said. "I've just told them John is sick. I'll have to go back to Kentucky once more and see if I can help... or collect my things."

I wondered if she knew John might be sneaking home nights, from his hideaway across the Tennessee border.

The February term opened, and I was enrolled as a freshman. I had taken the G.E.D. tests, and whatever our high school experience lacked in social content, it must have been adequate in academic skills, because I scored in the 90 percent range in everything but math. At long last I was a college student.

Then Maxine arrived, having traveled all the way from Kentucky on a bus. She had a large suitcase and looked fragile as a refugee. We found a room for two closer to the college. I helped her get a job, introduced her to a friend named Jim, and they started dating. Everyone thought Max was cute, and it was great to have a sister around again. We got along fabulously, as usual, each earning her own money and sharing the rent. Life was good, and we tried not to think of the ferment at home.

But Max had brought some news I wanted to hear. "A lot of kids are leaving," she said. "Their relatives are taking them out. My mother came and got Julie and Winston. Ernie left on his own."

That was the least of what she had to say. As I suspected, John had not been content to stay across the state line and run his operation at a distance. In spite of all the warnings, he had become increasingly daring, and one day he came back in broad daylight and announced to the children that their "daddy" was home again. His return seemed to go unnoticed for a week, but then Bob Long, the Corbin minister, called the county attorney. He tried to locate Carlita but, failing that, did find Pearl, brought her before the grand jury, and got her to testify. John was indicted and released on a $ 10,000 bond, pending trial.

"Who in the world had that kind of money to put up for him?" I asked Max.

"I think it was . . . No. I really don't know," she answered. "I don't really remember hearing anybody's name mentioned."

"When is the trial?"

"April, I think, but you never know when it will be really. There are all sorts of deals going on behind people's backs. He's trying to get them to drop the charges."

It was March, still cold and snowy. Gordon was coming, and I was happy. From my minuscule paycheck I had bought him a present, a tie-clip and cuff links engraved with a bird in flight.

He accepted them tenderly, then patted his coat pocket and smiled at me. "I've got a present to give you too. Would you like it now or later?"

"Later," I said, guessing what it might be.

Driving around Chicago, we paused at the airport and watched the planes go in and out.

"Do you ever think of going to another country?" he asked. "Of seeing the world and learning about different ways of life?"

"I'm just learning about this country for the first time," I reminded him. "I don't know how much more I could absorb."

That night, on the observation platform of the airport, he slipped a sparkling diamond on my finger. We went to a pancake house and gazed at each other, the dark corner lit by the sparkling gem and its significance.

"How long do you want to go to school?" he asked.

"I don't know. You finish this spring?"

"Right."

"Then what?"

"I think I'll go into the Army. I've taken an Army chaplaincy training course, and I'd go in as a second lieutenant. I can't see myself in the role of a small-town minister. I want to learn more about the world and other people, get some experience. Doing a few years in the military might be a chance to travel."

"When do you plan to go into the Army?"

"June."

"I'm going with you." I decided.

At Easter I went to Zeeland, Michigan. His mother had put new geraniums on the front porch to welcome me, and his father shook my hand with a warm little smile. They gave us the family car as an engagement present. Gordon and I walked the small-town streets where he had played as a boy—the streets I had gazed at longingly from the coach window. We went to his grandmother's house, and met his aunts. Everyone loved Gordon, and Gordon loved me. How could life be so beautiful?

It was still March when Anna called. "I'm at Della's house." she said. "I'm in Chicago to stay. How are you making out?"

"Mom. I'm doing great! You haven't even seen my diamond!"

"I haven't even seen your man! When are you getting married?"

"Either June or August."

"Oh, heavens, not June! That's too soon! Let me at least have a chance to work this summer so we can give you a nice wedding."

After she hung up, I wondered how we would word the invitation. John would not be there, that was for sure, and would not be walking me down the aisle. Weddings were one of the things he did not believe in.

All summer Aunt Della's house served as our headquarters. Gordon had four weeks after school before reporting to his first post, in, of all places, Fort Knox, Kentucky. He took a summer job in Chicago digging ditches for a heating company. I got a flunky job in a downtown Chicago bank, and Anna found one caring for an elderly man who was ill. We began to plan for the wedding. It was remarkable that Anna was excited about Gordon and about our marriage, considering her own experience. She bragged to her sisters endlessly, and they all agreed that the long years of solitary confinement had not blunted my good sense. My marrying Gordon was considered the marvel of the century.

Evenings, he and I walked or sat along the Lake Michigan waterfront discussing the future.

"Just think of it," Gordon said. "This time next year we could be in California, or Germany, or Japan."

"Or stuck in some mudhole in Alabama or Georgia," I laughed.

"No, I think we're promised at least one tour of duty overseas," he said. "Wouldn't that be exciting?"

We were married in August, in a traditional Dutch church wedding, and I felt that I had come back to the world of my ancestors. There was a pipe organ, and a dominie, and for all I knew, there might even have been a few peppermints.

The days immediately before the wedding were unreal. Aunt Kay came north and stayed at Aunt Della's house to sew my wedding dress. Six years before, this same house had been the scene of cousin Ramona's wedding, the congregating place for relatives, the place where long silky bridesmaids' gowns had hung from the doorframes and I had vowed never to get married. Now the wedding was mine, the second one I would attend in my life, and I was being swept toward it, fitted, pinned, as I counted off days on a calendar. The Swanns had come up from Alabama, and Gordon's parents drove down from Michigan, and all our worlds were converging on one spot. The intensity was overwhelming.

On my wedding day I was in a state of shock. Gordon looked nervous. The rest of his family were due to arrive from Michigan with the wedding cake, which his aunt had baked, and he was sure something would happen to it. There were cousins all over the house, getting dressed as flower girl, ring bearer, and bridesmaids. Anna was running around frantically, checking the church to see that all the arrangements for the reception were in order. John was hiding out in Kentucky with a $10,000 bond over his head. I went upstairs and fell asleep.

At six o'clock Aunt Della woke me up and told me to get ready. I was in a stupor, unable to shake myself awake. I showered and got dressed mechanically, as though I were watching someone else who was another me. I went to the church basement, slipped out of my old clothes and into the lovely white dress, and looked at myself in the ladies' room mirror as if I were in a dream. Was this *my* wedding day? The clock said seven-thirty, and the music began. I stood at the back looking at the church, splendid with orange and yellow flowers, and wondered who was getting married. Then Uncle Henry took my arm, and I walked down the aisle to join the tall dark man who held out his hand, hoping to God he was Gordon. I repeated what the dominie said, softly and willingly. Gordon's kiss was vaguely familiar, and I felt reassured. At the reception I smiled until my face hurt, and spilled coffee on my wedding gown. I wondered whom all the presents were for, and if we should have brought one. Finally, mercifully, someone told me to change my clothes and whisked Gordon and me into a friend's car that took us to our own car, parked on a side street. Suddenly we were alone.

Gordon turned to me, radiant happiness on his face. I felt his happiness spreading to me, awakening me from my daze. It was the first time I had recognized him all night.

"Sweetheart, you're my wife!" he whispered, hugging me so hard he knocked my hat off. I looked into his eyes, and we both cried for pure joy.

The bridal suite at the Hilton . . . trying to pick up our room key as if we had been married forever, with bits of confetti falling out of our hair . . . the knowing smile of the bellboy. Undressing shyly in the bathroom while Gordon stared pensively out the window at the Chicago skyline. It was going to happen, for the first time in my life. I was going to bed with a man. Oddly enough, I was joyful and unafraid.

He had reserved a cottage on a clear blue lake in Upper Michigan, where the peaceful woods were reflected in the shining water and the mountainous dunes rose up to the blue sky. We spent the days exploring—mind, body, spirit. Everything seemed right, to flow together. It was right to think, to make love, to be reverent and irreverent, to swim in the cool water and bake in the warm sun. There was no room for evil, because the world was too crowded with good. Everything we touched was full of love, full of hope, holy.

We swam in the lake and drifted toward the shore where the

clear water washed the colored pebbles gleaming like gems under the surface. We lay on our stomachs in the ripples, collecting pebbles to save forever. Forever we would touch hands and smile into each other's eyes and kiss.

We climbed the dunes, scrambling in the sand, higher, higher, higher, until we could almost touch the blue sky, climbing until there was nowhere higher to climb. Then we stood close together scanning the horizon. What would come over the farthest hill, the farthest arc of the sky? Let it come. We were filled with the power of love, the fearlessness of being whole. We would search the horizon and beckon it on, walk toward it hand in hand, choose all the highest mountains to climb, the deepest lakes to cross. We had conquered our first battle, finding each other against impossible odds. What could be too hard for us after this?

As we lay in the sand, content to be, I felt the urge to thank somebody.

"Oh, God," I whispered.

"What did you say?" Gordon asked.

"Nothing. I'm praying."

"I'm sorry. Go ahead."

"I'm finished," I said. "What more do you say on a day like today after you've said, Oh, God? I don't want to mess anything up."

He rolled over and gave me a look, and it was enough. We had come on very different paths from opposite directions, but somehow we were searching for the same thing.

I gazed across the mountains and lake and sky. The blue had been unbroken when we sat down to rest, but now there was a small cloud forming at the horizon. I brushed it out of my mind.

That evening Gordon dug in his suitcase and brought out the small black book. "Let's see what our friend the Prophet has to say about marriage," he suggested.

We snuggled on the couch, with a small candle flickering on the coffee table. Gordon read, his voice deep and resonant:

*"You were born together, and together you shall be forever.
.. But let there be spaces in your togetherness... Love one
another, but make not a bond of love: Let it rather he a
moving sea between the shores of your souls. Fill each other's
cup but drink not from one cup. Give one another of your
bread but eat not of the same loaf... Give your hearts, but
not into each other's keeping. For only the hand of Life can
contain your hearts... And the oak tree and the Cyprus
grow not in each other's shadow."*

There was silence for a moment when he finished reading. I
stared at the candle, thinking of the small white cloud in the blue
sky.

"How do you like that?" he asked.

"I don't like it," I said. "It scares me."

"It is a bit threatening," he said thoughtfully. "I don't identify
with it as much as with his writing about love. The words are
beautiful, but they're frightening too. I guess right now I don't
feel we could ever be too close."

"And I *want* to give my heart into your keeping!" I protested.

"And I *want* to feed you from my loaf," he added.

"And I *want* love to be a bond!" I declared.

"And I *want* you to drink from my cup!"

We paused and fell laughing into each other's arms.

"Screw the Prophet," I said. "He probably had a rotten
marriage!"

We were driving through Kentucky. It was September. I sat beside
the handsome lieutenant, my husband. He had to report for duty,
and we were on our way to our first apartment off the base.

"I think it might be a little easier for us to get started in a
small apartment of our own instead of living on the base," he said.
"I hope you won't mind that I've already rented a place."

"Anyplace with you is great," I assured him.

"But it's . . ."

"I don't care what it is. If you're there, it will be perfect."

We arrived in Vine Grove and drove down the main street. We stopped in front of the best-looking house in town and turned into the driveway.

Gordon hopped out. "I'll go in and check if the apartment is ready." he said.

I sat in the car waiting for him. What taste! The best in town. Impeccable. If only they could see me now. Green lawn, red tile roof, white siding.

"It's all set," he said, coming to the car.

We collected our luggage and started in. Then I saw the tastefully lettered sign in the front yard: NELSON EDELIN FUNERAL HOME.

"Gordon!" I gasped. "Are we living in a funeral home?"

"I tried to tell you . . ."

"But won't we feel creepy?"

"No, the whole upstairs is apartments for young Army couples. It has nothing to do with the funeral part. You never see them."

I picked up my suitcase full of honeymoon lingerie and gulped.

"I'll protect you from the ghosts," he promised, laughing.

I laughed too and started up the stairs. "Well, why not?" I said.

And Gordon was right. Any fearsomeness in the approach was more than compensated for by the apartment itself. It was a good place to be alone, to learn to live together. Together we made the tiny rooms a place of coziness and warmth, a place we loved to be.

In the morning he put on his Army uniform and boots, and I stood by the door, choked with love for him, hating to see him go. He would glance at his watch, throw caution to the winds, and come back for one more long embrace. Then he would be gone down the long flight of stairs, and I would stand listening to his footsteps, my heart aching with happiness.

Oh, God! Oh, God!

I tidied up the apartment, walked to the nearby town, bought food, made a new couch cover, tried to cook. I burned half of it, but he ate it all valiantly.

The young couple in the apartment next to ours were already into their second marriages. She slept all day while he was gone, and five minutes after he returned in the evening the laughter began. It sounded as if he were tickling her to death, loud hysterical whooping laughter. Sometimes we looked at each other and shrugged. Oh, well, downstairs they were dying, and upstairs they were living it up. To each his own. We were safe in our little cocoon. Let the world do as it pleased.

One afternoon I climbed out the kitchen window and sat on the red tile roof gazing over the town and feeling so happy I could have exploded. All at once I began to sing: *"Tra-la-la-ta. Tra-la-la-la. There is joy, oh, there is joy. Oh, there is joy, oh, everywhere!"*

There was a hasty knock on the door, and I climbed in the window to see who was there. It was Mr. Nelson, the funeral director from downstairs.

"Excuse me. Mrs. DePree," he said solemnly, "but we're having a funeral in the parlor, and your singing doesn't exactly fit the occasion."

On Sundays I watched Gordon officiating in uniform in the chapel. A gray-haired Catholic priest, having celebrated mass, was removing the crucifix, and the bare gleaming Protestant cross stood in its place. For the second mass they would switch again. The fearful suspicion between Catholics and Protestants seemed unreal in this room they shared. I sat in the pew as the service went on, thinking my own thoughts. *So you have your joyous Green God, your guiding spirit, your nameless one. But what formal expression of your belief will you accept? People either believe in God or they don't, anal if you do, you have to give your belief a name, line up in somebody's queue to heaven. You can't just go and shout, Oh, God!,from the rooftops. Half the people will think you're crazy, and the other half will think you're swearing. People who belong to nobody's camp are always suspect.*

I looked again at Gordon's face during his sermon, as he talked seriously to the other young men. He was what I could identify with deeply, a person with a clear mind, a gentle heart, a sense of integrity, and a love for life and people. He had no axe to grind, no demands to make of heaven. The world might not be full of people like him, but knowing one was enough to heal the hurt. One good man was enough to prove that God was not a lie.

Gordon's company had to stay out in tents for a week on a field maneuver. I packed his duffel bag mournfully, wondering what I would ever do without him.

"They gave us some papers to fill out this morning." he said. "Would you rather stay in the Army for two years or three?"

"No more than two, if they're going to do things like this," I said ruefully.

"Okay, then I'll put in for two years, Mrs. DePree."

I watched him go, thinking of how long the nights would be. And it was indeed a Godforsaken week. I roamed the town like a lost soul. I was not young and free as I had been a few months before, sniffing the dawn and shivering with excitement. I was Mrs. Somebody and my husband was gone. I had given my heart absolutely, and its keeper had gone camping. I ate at strange hours of the day, slept fitfully. I fell asleep and dreamed, the past and the present hideously scrambled, and woke in a panic of guilt and confusion.

One night just before Gordon returned I heard a knock on the apartment door. When I opened it, there stood Gram, her tiny face drawn and her big blue eyes frightened. She was like a visitor from another world.

It took her hours to come to the point, while we chattered excitedly and I told her all about Gordon.

"Don't you miss Gramps?" I asked, able for the first time to comprehend what the death of a mate could mean.

She smiled and drew herself up to her full five feet. "Will was a good man," she said proudly. "And I'm glad he's gone and at peace, that he never had to see what is happening to your father."

"Was that what you meant when he died?"

"Yes, I could see it coming long before that. I tried to warn John, but what can you tell your son when he's a grown man over forty?"

"It must have been awful for you. What's happening now?"

"The trial is scheduled for two weeks from now."

"What is the charge?"

"Statutory rape."

"Oh. Gram, poor Gram. How can you stand it?"

"I don't know. I don't know what went wrong. I tried to bring him up right. He was always such a good boy. I tried to teach him all the right things, and he seemed to learn. He was such a good man, and I was so proud of him. And now this."

"Oh, Gram!" I put my arms around her, her tiny head coming under my chin. "Oh. Gram. I wish I could help you!"

She took off her glasses, wiped them, and looked at me.

"Your father thinks you could help him," she said.

"How?"

"He wants you to come to the trial and testify."

I felt a cold stone in my stomach, an icy weight. "I'm sorry, Gram. Anything I would have to say in front of a court wouldn't help him, and I don't want to hurt him any more than I already have. Tell him I said no."

Gram stayed the night and left.

The weather turned bitterly cold, and Gordon's company came back from the field maneuver two days early. It was five o'clock in the morning when I heard his key in the lock, heard him whisper, "It's me!" and tiptoe across the floor.

He pulled off his fatigues and crawled into bed in his longjohns, shivering with cold. I snuggled close, delighting in the wonder of

299

having him back, and I lay still, hardly daring to breathe until he fell asleep. What was it, this new uneasiness that tormented me? Was it really safe to be this vulnerable, to love someone this much? This beautiful love stirred the deepest of all the terrors I had lived through. What would I do if something took him away?

CHAPTER FOURTEEN

Pulled between worlds, balancing marriage and statutory rape in my head, love upstairs and death downstairs . . . What was the news from Corbin, and what should I cook for dinner? Was he acquitted, or should we have roast beef? He was guilty as hell, and he knew it, even if pork chops were cheaper. No, that wasn't somebody hysterically mourning a loved one downstairs, it was Mary next door getting it again. Oh, well, so what, that's life. Come home, Gordon, let me feel you close to me. You're the only person who makes sense in this screwed-up world.

He called that afternoon from his office on base.

"Have you started dinner yet?" he asked.

"No, why?"

"Don't fix anything. Let's go out tonight, okay?"

"Okay! What's the occasion?"

"We'll celebrate being together."

I hung up feeling warm and loved, with just a touch of apprehension.

The mail brought a letter from Anna and a note from the Swanns. Anna's big news was that Max and Jim were getting married and would have a December wedding. Both Max and Anna had been living in Wheaton and working in the student center. It seemed to be the accepted underground escape route for defectors from Kentucky.

The Swanns' brief note enclosed a clipping from the Corbin Times. The note said, "Dear Lenore and Gordon: We've been called as material witnesses in Pearl's trial, and we're here in Kentucky.

Be glad you didn't come. Thorn has disqualified himself, but has chosen the jury. We feel that this is highly irregular."

The newspaper clipping reported the first day of the trial.

> *PREACHER ON STAND IN MORALS CHARGE*
> *Williamsburg, Ky. October 11. John Vogel, a mountain preacher accused of criminally assaulting a former ward of the children's home he founded, has taken the stand in his own defense. Vogel denied forcing the girl to be intimate with him from the time she was fifteen until she left the home last year. The girl told the jury Vogel had warned her she would go to jail for five years if she told anyone of the incidents that occurred over a four-year period. A letter introduced at the trial described Vogel as a sex maniac . . . The former ward testified that Vogel told her. "Ordinarily this would be wrong for the rest of the world but not for us." Special Judge Albright told the jury that Vogel, if convicted, could receive a prison sentence of from five to twenty years.*

I stopped reading and shook my head. *Wrong for the rest of the world, but not for us. We are the chosen, the special agents of God.* How often I had heard those words, how glad I was I had never been altogether pulled in by them. Sometimes I had horrible nightmares in which Gordon and I were making love, and he turned into John. The guilt I awoke with must be the same guilt Carlita and Pearl were feeling now. But somehow I had miraculously escaped, had never been able totally to believe John. If I had, not only I but everyone else would still be in his power. The whole blow-up had been a blessing in disguise. It was freeing the people who needed to be free, and destroying the oppressors. I laid the letters aside and forced my thoughts back to Gordon and the life we now lived. It was like waking from a nightmare to a real world, a good world.

When Gordon came home that evening, we dressed to go out. He selected his tie with extra care and shined his shoes while I watched him feeling inexplicably troubled. We drove to a beautiful old mill that had been turned into a restaurant. There we dined by candlelight, warm and cozy as rain came down outside.

"You're quiet," Gordon said. "Are you thinking about the trial?"

"Its hard not to think about it," I said. I had noticed that he too was unusually quiet. There was even an air of sadness about him that he could not quite hide.

It had begun to rain harder. We dashed to the car, and I settled in close to him. He began to drive, the sadness growing around him.

"There's something I have to tell you," he began. "I don't know what you'll say."

"What is it?"

"Please don't be angry."

"Why would I be angry you?"

"My orders came through today. Do you remember when we decided to sign up for a two-year period?"

"Yes."

"The unit has been divided. All the three-year people are going to Germany, and . . ." He paused, his voice suddenly hoarse.

"Where are we going?" I asked.

"I'm being sent to Korea," he said.

"You? Just you?"

"Yes, I have to go alone."

"But why? You promised . . ."

"I know, but its up near the border, in a no-dependents area. I can't take you with me."

"Oh, Gordon, no! For how long?"

"About eighteen months."

"Eighteen months! That's a year and a half! Oh God!"

"Sweetheart . . ." He put his arm around me and drove slowly. The rain was pelting on the windshield as though the whole sky were crying. The windshield wipers were doing a crazy dance, blurring the drops. We stopped at a red light, and I stared at it, the redness sending a deep bloody gash down the black wet highway.

"Aren't you going to say something?" Gordon asked desperately.

I opened my mouth, but nothing came out except a deep

animal moan. Frightened, Gordon pulled over to the shoulder. He shut off the motor and turned to me.

"Sweetheart, what's the matter? Say something! Say you understand! Tell me you're not angry with me. Please. I don't want to go either. I don't want to leave you. Please don't turn against me. Please say something. Tell me that you still love me."

I saw him bending over me, a dark shape in a darker world. There was no light, nothing but words and darkness.

You should have known it, something down inside me said, *should have known better than to love someone so much. Love is dangerous. Did you think you could touch such holy fire and not be scorched?*

When I finally made a sound, it was not words. It was a long strangled cry, a primitive death wail that ripped up from my guts and would not be stopped. Gordon held me, quietly crying, trying to help. "Don't, sweetheart, don't. The time will pass. Nothing can hurt our love. We've found each other now, and nothing can ever separate us. Remember the day on the dunes? Be strong, sweetheart. It's not as if I don't love you or you don't love me. It's just another waiting period. It's nothing we can't overcome together."

"But you were the last real person in my world!"

"I'm still in your world. I'm still real. I still love you, more than ever. Nothing has changed."

We drove home slowly through the rain.

From then on everything was tinged with despair. We had until February to be together, but now love was pain, and our happiest moments were the saddest.

Bit by bit, news of the trial reached us. Then the Swanns sent us a complete report, and reading their letter I could visualize every scene, feel each nuance of the battle that had taken place.

I could see the Whitley County courthouse, the old square stone building set in the middle of the little town sprawled along the Cumberland River. I could see the gnarled trees shading the patchy grass around the courthouse, and the old men sitting on the benches whittling and spitting and gossiping about what was going on inside.

And John. It was almost laughable, certainly tragic, to think of John rolling into the dusty little river town in his gleaming Super-Dura-Liner and broad-brimmed Stetson, followed by his flock of children, ready to prove his innocence in this rustic American court of justice. I could see him going through the big doors on the west side of the courthouse, down the long corridor where the lawyers had their offices, and up the creaking stairs to the dusty old courtroom. It was the same courtroom where I had sat several years before and watched Judge White take two of John's children away. John had sworn vengeance, and now White, as county attorney, was prosecuting the case against him, the case that was bound to cast a shadow on the rest of his life regardless of what this court of law decided. I could see the jury, plain men and women from the hills, sitting in judgment on this man, my father. They were the hill folk he had come to serve, and in the end had prostituted.

> Neither John, Gram, nor Nada would speak to us [the Swanns wrote]. John would not look at us at all. He knew that he had told us the truth, and he was set on denying it. Nada stared straight ahead. She looked terrible, as though she had really sold her soul to the devil. We wonder how Gram is bearing up through it all . . . The appalling thing was the hatred on the faces of the children. They had been brainwashed like an army of small political prisoners. They were brought to the trial to create sympathy, but we suspect this strategy backfired. When the witnesses against John stood up to testify, the children stuck out their tongues and shouted aloud in the courtroom. 'I hate you!' This also occurred in the hallways outside the court, causing some to wonder if the children had received such superior teaching as they had previously assumed . . .

> Some of the children seemed to have been forced to testify,

and were confused as to what they should say. For instance, Christina took the stand, and was asked if Pearl was ever alone in the study with John. Thinking to help him and blame Pearl, she blurted out, "She was in there a lot more than she should have been!" Pearl herself was an entirely different girl from the one we had known at the home. Her eyes were clear and bright. She was a good witness, told a straight story, and could not be shaken at any point by cross-examination. The defense attorney tore her apart. He tried to prove that she was immoral and a liar. He worked on the jury's sympathies by telling them that if this low girl were allowed to undermine this fine home, scores of children would be left homeless . . .

It was this last plea that resulted in the hung jury. The jurors knew that John was guilty, but were swayed by the plea of 'What will become of these poor little children?' Indeed, one does shudder to think what might happen to them if they are left with John and Nada. But in the end it was declared a mistrial, and as such is rescheduled for January. It seems that John is working behind the scenes to have it delayed until public opinion cools down.

I laid the letter aside: the whole ghastly mess was more than I could bear. John was let off. John would lie, and in January he would be acquitted. And in February Gordon would be taken away.

I closed my eyes and breathed deeply. No, that wasn't the way. John was guilty, and Gordon would never be taken away. What did Anna used to say? *Things are not what they seem.* Think, girl, think before you lose your nerve. Fight. Get back some of your old spunk. This is no time to go soft. You finally have someone worth fighting for!

Direct and straightforward as ever, Gordon decided to face the problem head on.

"How would you like to drive to Corbin and visit everyone there before I have to leave?" he asked.

"Why should I do that?" I asked, feeling it would be salt on my wounds.

"It just might help us get things in perspective."

The more I thought about it, the better it seemed. John no longer had any power over us. I was married, and there was nothing he could do.

"Do you think he'll be angry that I didn't come to his trial?" I asked, dreading a scene.

"He didn't come to our wedding either. What can he say? Let's drive down. I don't even know him, and he's my father-in-law."

"Maybe you should stop while you're ahead," I said, and laughed. I realized it was the first time I had laughed in several days.

Old Route 25 was being torn up, and Sanders' restaurant was blocked off from the main flow of traffic. The main street of Corbin looked the same, although one or two stores had changed names. At the south end of town there was a new motel. We stopped for coffee and to reserve a room.

"There's a guest room out at the home," I said. "We can stay there."

"I'd just as soon be able to say we've got a reservation in case things get touchy," Gordon said uneasily. "Let's leave our bags here too."

We drove down the Bee Creek road and through the flat woods to the entrance. The grounds looked seedy and forlorn. The grass had not been cut, and no one had taken the flag in for weeks. It hung crazily at half mast, looking ragged and mildewed. A few children played listlessly around the Vogel house, and no one came to the parking lot to meet us.

We knocked on the door of the Vogel house, and Fanny, the little lady who had accompanied me when I'd gone to make the sketches across Whippoorwill Creek, came to the door.

"Oh, its you!" she said, clutching her blouse and batting her eyes as if we were ghosts. "C-come in! I'll call the boys' dorm. I think your father is there."

I stood uncomfortably, a guest ill at ease in the house that once was home. The children were there—Phyllis and David, Marcie and Geneva—all the little ones who had no name, the ones who were not supposed to have been born and now had no place to go. Christina was there. She was the new organist, her musical ability having finally been recognized. She looked much older and was slightly stooped, as if the world had been laid on her young shoulders.

"Why don't you leave this creepy place?" I whispered to her as we waited for Fanny.

"Maybe later," she said. "Daddy needs me now."

She was probably flattered, I thought angrily. It was the first time in her life that he had ever needed her, that she had even been worth his notice.

"Leave!" I whispered. "Mom is in Wheaton. Take the bus. She'll meet you. There are jobs. We have a way . . ."

Fanny was coming, and we changed the subject.

He was at the boys' dorm firmly in Nada's power. She bustled around, energy revitalized and tits afloat. She was the old Nada, but with an even darker power. She was no longer the mistress, she was the prospective wife.

John was nervous and smaller than I remembered him. His face was red and blotched, and there was an evasive look in his eyes. He received us coolly, looking Gordon over thoroughly and seeming to shrink even smaller. As usual, his speech contradicted his actions.

"Let's go out to dinner," he said grandly, "and we can talk on the way. I never go to that damnable city of Corbin anymore. So many of them have turned against me. I never know if I'm welcome or not. Some of my closest friends have become my bitterest enemies. But I don't worry about such things. God has seen my misery and has vindicated me. You knew I was found innocent at the trial?"

"We heard it was a mistrial," Gordon said.

"Well, a mistrial, if you prefer, but they could not come to any conclusion, which leaves me innocent until convicted, if I understand the legal system. At least I won't be thrown behind bars for twenty years, as some people hoped—not even after some of my children lied on me. You should have heard the lies that dirty little whore Pearl told on me, things I've never even heard of. Where she got all that garbage I'll never know. She was with her father a few weeks before the trial, and I suppose he pumped her full of that poison to spew out in front of the judge. I live in fear of those Powers girls' father. I have had to hire a bodyguard."

I looked straight at him. "Was everything she said a lie?" I asked.

He dropped his eyes, avoiding mine.

"She got it out of those medical books she was studying, he said. "All that stuff about examining her for a pregnancy. She didn't even know what a pregnancy was until I let her have those fool nursing books. But I can hold up both hands to heaven and swear that I never raped or forced myself on any of those girls."

I could see Gordon shift in his chair. I was embarrassed. It was not what one would call a choice topic of conversation. I tried desperately to change the subject. "Why did Thorn disqualify himself as judge?" I asked.

"Oh, that was another of God's provisions that the devil tried to destroy. But God rescued me. One thing I've learned finally through all of this. After testing Him for years, I know now that God will protect me, will come to my aid if I but call on Him. One of the most blatant witnesses against me just died in an accident on the Corbin pike. His head was actually severed from his body."

Gordon glanced at me and at his watch. John caught the exchange and was on his feet in a flash.

"Come on!" he said energetically. "Let's drive to Somerset. It's only forty miles from here, and they treat me like a human being instead of an ex-convict. There's a nice restaurant on a lake. Why don't you invite Nada to join us?" he asked me. "She's not sure she's welcome when you're here, and I think an invitation from you would set her at ease."

Same old games. Same old bullshit.

"And I'd like to take Fanny along too," John said, "so you could get to know her. She's been a real mainstay over at the house with Gram. They all left me—Miss Smith, Kay—but when everyone else forsook me, Fanny stuck with me. She's a deeply spiritual woman . . . But then on second thought, if Nada's going, maybe Fanny had better stay home with the children."

I groaned inwardly. We were playing musical wives again. Anna would be divorced. Nada would be married, and Fanny would be the next mistress. She probably already was, in Anna's bedroom. I wondered if the blue morning glories were still hanging on the wall. There was only one comfort in the thought. It served Nada right. I hoped he did it under her nose.

Nada drove the Cadillac, and we went at least fifty miles with the four of us trapped in the car. Gordon and I crowded together in one corner of the back seat. John sat next to Nada and turned around toward us, talking non-stop. He asked us nothing about our lives, which in a way was a relief. Life for him had become a battle, a fight to prove the unprovable, which, knowing him, was quite in character.

"Maloney was at the trial," he said, "and has promised to write an article in our defense. He has great prestige as a writer."

"An article in the Post?" I asked.

"Well, I'm not sure where he'll publish it. We might just send it out to our mailing list. Even that would sway public opinion."

"Someone said that Bob Long has a statement from Carlita now." I said. "Does that mean there will be another trial even after this retrial?" I could see John's neck stiffen in the darkness, and heard him take in his breath.

"That two-faced snake, Long," he said bitterly. "He forced that statement out of her, God knows how, and he'll try to use it against me before this whole thing is over. But I'm going to fight its being introduced in court. I have friends. Not everyone has turned tail and forsaken me. You knew it was Sanders who put up the ten-thousand-dollar bond for me?"

"No, I didn't know."

"Now there's a man with Christ-like compassion, not like these Job's comforters who smile to my face and knife me in the back. Sanders doesn't ask what I've done. He's my friend, the only true friend I have left. God will bless him abundantly."

"I was talking to Haas," I began. "and I think he really wanted to help . . ."

"Haas!" John breathed. "Don't mention his name in my presence. That dirty rat wormed his way into my confidence, hoping to see me fall and then swoop down and take my power in his own hands! He wanted to help me, all right. He wanted to relieve me of my life's work! Don't tell me you've had anything to do with him! If you're a friend of his, don't come around here associating with me."

He fell silent and did not say another word for the rest of the trip. We arrived, ordered our meal in strained silence, and ate in misery. The drive home seemed an eternity, an empty three-way exchange between Nada, Gordon, and me.

"We'll have to be leaving now," Gordon said as we finally pulled into the parking lot at the home. "Thank you very much for the dinner."

John revived. "No, you can't leave." he said. "I won't hear of it. You'll stay here in the guest house tonight."

"But we have a room reserved in Corbin," I told him.

"How would that look? My own daughter comes to visit me, and she stays in a motel in town. That will be grist for the Corbin gossip mill, don't you forget it!"

Gordon took over, and I stood gratefully behind him. "Thank you very much," he said, "but I'm sorry. We really do have to be going. Our room is reserved and our bags are there. Thanks for the drive. It's been interesting." He extended his hand.

"Goodby, Dad." he said.

Outmaneuvered, John took the extended hand. "Goodby," he said meekly.

It was the end. I never wanted to see him again. Once I had cared deeply, had winced at his blind wickedness, but something had snapped, something had died beyond raising. I was still not sure whether he was mentally ill and innocent, or rational, clever, and evil; it would always be a double-edged question in my mind, but now I no longer cared. Or perhaps not caring was only to say I had given up, that I could no longer relate to this man who had fathered me. I only hoped that he would not go on hurting others, tricking, robbing, and raping in the name of God.

Gordon shook his head as we went into the motel. "What a shame," he said sadly. "The home is definitely going downhill. It was such a beautiful place the first time I saw it. What do you think it might have become if your father hadn't had this strange flaw?"

"That's hard to say," I answered. "But I think the flaw was built into it from the beginning. The whole value system . . . ideas were more important than people. That always scares me."

"I guess it's just as well I never came there to work," he said. "Although there was nothing I wanted more, at one time. I think I would have come to blows with him before long. How did you ever live through years of that and stay sane?"

"It wasn't easy!" I laughed.

But Gordon was right about the visit giving us perspective. It made me thankful that even though life might be giving me a boot in the tail I was at least moving in the right direction. Going back had reminded me that I might have been stuck there forever instead of married to Gordon with only eighteen months to wait.

We stopped the next day at Sanders' on our way through North Corbin. The old man eyed Gordon curiously, looking at his shoulders and long legs as though he were prize beef. We asked about his business, and he looked worried. "Damn road's being rerouted," he said. "I've been wearing a path up to Frankfort but I don't seem to get anything done about it. Tied up in some Interstate business. If things get any worse here, I'm going to fold up. Might have to take my fried chicken recipe and go on the road, try to sell the franchise. But listen here, you young folks don't want to hear an old man's troubles. Have you been out to see your father?"

"Yes, just yesterday."

Sanders shook his head sadly. "They ought to get off his back," he said. "A man's human. A man makes mistakes. But doggone it, it's the juiciest gossip in the whole goddamn world when they catch a preacher with his pants down!"

We were in the car in some nameless stretch of Indiana. It was Christmas Day. Anna had spent the holidays with us, and now we had packed up everything and left the cozy apartment. It was snowing, and the car motor had suddenly conked out. Gordon was walking to find a gas station, and Anna and I were huddled in the cold car.

"You know you're welcome to live with me," Anna said. "Will you be going back to school?"

"Not now. I can't even think straight."

"Will you get a job?

"Gordon says it's up to me. He'll send me money to live on."

As I said it, I realized John would never send her anything. She would be on her own. I told her I was sorry.

"Don't feel sorry for me." She laughed cheerfully. "I'm happier than I've been for twenty years. I might not have much, but at least I'm free!"

I thought about her words. Were love and freedom opposites, or seldom found together? Did love have to be shadowed by pain and fear? Was being alone the only way to be free?

I thought of The Prophet. The words were beginning to make sense. Perhaps there could be a kind of love that did not press so close as to extinguish the flame with its own fear.

Before the tearing apart we had one more month to live. We

spent it in Michigan. Gordon's parents were kind, his mother warm and thoughtful.

Sometimes she squeezed my hand, and her dark eyes were moist. "We're going to miss that man, aren't we?" she said. "Now you come and stay with us as much as you like. The room upstairs will always be ready for you."

Thoughtfully they left us to ourselves most of the, time. One evening when we were alone, curled up by the fire, we were talking about the days ahead.

"I wonder what our wise man the Prophet has to say about hard times?" I asked.

Gordon got up and looked in the bookcase where all his books were already standing, waiting his return. He came back with the familiar volume and began to page through it. I nestled my head on his sweater and listened as he read:

> "Your pain is the breaking of the shell that encloses your
>   understanding
> And could you keep your heart in wonder at the daily
>   miracles of your life,
> Your pain would not seem less wondrous than your joy:
> And you would accept the seasons of your heart . . .
> And you would watch with serenity through the winters of
>   your grief."

The day he left he drove me to Wheaton and settled my things in Anna's room. Anna went out, and we sat helplessly in the small rented room, too sad to do more than stare at each other, feeling the moments tick past, paralyzed.

Then we drove to the Chicago airport, and I saw him to the plane. Just before the plane door shut for take-off, a long khaki-clad figure came running down the ramp. In a moment he was beside me, his arms around me.

"I just had to kiss you one more time," he said breathlessly. "Don't be afraid. I'll come back just as I am, all yours. I'll love you every day I'm gone. Don't worry about anything, sweetheart. Be strong."

The stewardess was on the steps frantically motioning. He ran up them, the door closed, and the plane moved down the runway. I watched it go until it was a tiny speck in the distance.

Back to Wheaton, back to the stuffy little room, back to Anna. A year and a half to wait. The campus across the street was filled with life, with young people carrying books, going in and out, dating, but now it seemed further removed than ever. They were like children preparing for life. I had skipped to the back of the book and plunged into life. Going backward was a waste of time, almost impossible.

Every day I received a long letter filled with love, and I wrote every day. We began to discover facets of each other that we had never known, began to probe deeply into ourselves for more to give each other, recording and exchanging a constant diary of our lives. And we both felt ourselves growing. We were developing separately, yet there was a togetherness.

I read to Anna those parts of Gordon's letters that were not too personal to share:

> "Today I went to the village of Nulla-ri. There's an old bearded Korean there who looks For all the world like Jesus Christ with slanted eyes. He has a little group of Korean war orphans he's taking care of, and he needs help. I'm going to try to get the guys in our division interested in scrounging up clothes and money to give them. There are so many G.I.'s who are bitter about being here, far away from home and the people they love. If I can get them to think about helping someone else, it might make the time go faster for them (and for me!)."

Some letters I did not read to Anna.

So many guys get messed up here. A young married fellow
came to me today, guilty as hell because he'd been to the
village and had a prostitute. There's a lot of that here. Some
of these guys seem to have so little to live by, so little to keep
them strong. Don't worry about me, darling. I dream of you
day and night.

Don't worry. Don't worry. American soldiers and Korean
prostitutes. John and Nada, John and Carlita. John and Pearl. John
and God-knows-who-else. Don't worry. Don't worry. Television,
the big eye in the apartment. Old war movies. Clark Gable goes
off to war and falls in love with another woman. He doesn't mean
to, of course, but he does.

No! No! No!

I fell asleep at night, tossed with wild dreams, and awoke crying,
choked by terrible fears.

"What's the problem?" Anna asked. "What has he done?"

"Nothing!" I shouted, resenting her question. Anna was
expecting her divorce papers any day. John was suing her for
desertion.

Gordon sent endless pictures. He did a snow sculpture of a
huge heart and stuck his face through it for a Valentine. I knew
I was lucky. I knew, too, that I was going crazy with fear. But
the day came when I looked at myself in the mirror, a good
hard look.

"You're nuts," I said aloud. "You've got to start using your
head. You're going to ruin a good thing by wanting to keep it so
much. Think. What can you do? When did you feel the freest, the
most unafraid?

When you had nothing, nobody. When you were at rock
bottom, broke, and naked as the day you were born. When you
were walking to work at five o'clock in the morning glad to be alive
and free. Nothing possessed, nothing feared.

Nothing possessed. Was I trying to possess Gordon, to insure
a flawless future with him? He was man, a friend, and a lover, not
a thing to be owned.

Okay, girl, back to center. You are a person. You own your own soul, not anybody else's. Love and give, don't demand. Love and hope, don't fear.

But what if something happens?

Love and let go, don't grasp. Grasping kills living things, didn't you learn that?

But what about the future?

Be grateful for the past. Be grateful for every day he was near you, for every exchange of love. Be grateful you knew him at all, and don't ask for any more. After the great love you've known, even if you never saw him again, your life is already richer, fuller, more nearly whole. You've already tasted enough love to last you a lifetime. Don't ask for anything more.

And when it's all over and he comes back, it will not be your due but a gift. A man's love is a gift.

I wrote my daily letter: "My loving Sir, keeper of your own soul, when will you return to me, the keeper of my own soul? Do you remember the day we laughed and I said, 'Screw the Prophet? Maybe he wasn't so wrong. I'm learning a lot. His writing gets wiser all the time."

One day when I searched the mailbox for Gordon's letter there was only a pale pink envelope with a strangely familiar handwriting. The return address was Mrs. R. something, a name totally unknown to me. Puzzled, I tore it open and looked at the signature. It was from Carlita. My first impulse was to throw the letter away unread, to spare myself this painful contact with the past, but the letter itself began to tempt me. I read very nearly holding it at arm's length.

Dear Lenore,

I don't know if you will he happy about getting this letter from me, but I did want to write you just once and tell you some of my feelings. It's strange, even though we grew up

together,. I never felt I knew you. You were somehow different
than me, and sometimes I wanted to know you, but couldn't.
I only hope that now this has all happened, you don't hate
me. Do you remember that night around the fire when we
were talking about thinking of oneself as good, and needing
real things to believe in? I wanted to tell the whole thing
that night, but I was so afraid. It was all so confusing to me.
I did believe in God, and I was scared I would be cursed if I
didn't listen to your father. Now that I am free of him, I
realize he was crazy. I hope I can forget all about it. I'm
married to a good man now, and I have a new baby girl. I
hope you're happy too. I wish we could have known each
other under different circumstances. I think we could have
been friends. I do love you, Carlita.

But that was not the end of Carlita's story. A few weeks later a dusty station wagon pulled up in front of our Wheaton apartment. Aunt Kay got out of the car and came up the walk. It was like a reunion to see her again. She gave me one of her warm-hearted hugs.

"Where are you headed?" I asked her.

"To New Mexico. I'm going to work with Navajo children in a boarding school near Farmington."

"Wow! You really get around! And Miss Smith, where's she going?"

"Up near Bemidji, Minnesota, also working in a school."

"The great dispersion!" I laughed. "I guess there's no going back for any of us."

"The grounds are being sold," Aunt Kay said. "The organ, the coach, everything's up for sale. A second ten-thousand-dollar bond has been put up for John in Carlita's case. Long brought her testimony before the grand jury because he's worried about the other children in their care. And they've got John for twenty thousand now, on separate counts."

"They haven't sorted out Pearl's case yet?"

Aunt Kay looked grave. "No, and I don't believe Carlita's case will ever come to trial."

"Why not?"

"Well, she's married, you know."

"Yeah. I heard from her."

"Oh, did you! Did you know her baby died?"

"No! She said she had a baby girl, but . . ."

"It was born prematurely. The doctor thinks it could have been due to the abuse she suffered at the home. It's very sad. The baby died at five weeks."

"Ohhhhh," I said, tears springing up.

"And that's not the worst of it. As soon as Nada heard the baby was dead, she went down to Georgia and warned Carlita not to appear at the trial. Nada told her that the baby's death was God's judgment on her for exposing John and ruining the home."

"That dirty old bitch! Did Carlita believe her?"

"You know Carlita. She's easily influenced, and she's guilty and eaten with fear already. Now this, and Nada's warning that there will be a further curse on her if she ever stands up in court and testifies against John. The girl is terrified."

I went into the apartment kitchen and put the water on for coffee, my hands shaking. For the first time in my life I actually did not hate Carlita. I felt profoundly sad for her.

We drank the coffee, discussing the upcoming trial.

"I think it will all pass over," Aunt Kay said. "People are tired of hearing about it. There are no new witnesses, it's been two years, and the public has lost interest. You knew it was Sanders who put up the second ten-thousand-dollar bond?"

"Again? How does he do it, and why does he do it?"

"I hear that his fried chicken business is doing very well. He's selling some franchise, and he's likely to become a millionaire. And as to why, I suppose some people can't bear to be totally disillusioned, even when what they believed turns out to be untrue."

"Maybe it's not that," I said. "Do you remember the sign that used to hang in the lounge at his restaurant?"

She thought for a moment, then smiled. "There's so much good in the worst of us." she began.

"And so much bad in the best of us," I added.

"That it little behooves any of us, to say aught about the rest of us!" we finished together.

It was August, our first anniversary. Anna and I were alone in the small apartment. Gordon was ten thousand miles away, north of Seoul. We made dinner, Anna bought flowers, and we celebrated.

The mail had brought a package from Gordon and two letters. The package contained a beautiful string of cultured pearls from Japan and a maternity dress bought at the PX in Seoul. I laughed fondly at his impatience, holding up the voluminous dress and wondering when I would use it. One of the letters was a card with six little rabbits standing at attention. In ink he had named them Lenore, Lawrence, Lulubelle, Gordon, George, and Gertrude.

> I'm looking forward to a great future, sweetheart. Just the thought of having a family of our own seems so exciting. When shall we start? What shall we have—twins, triplets?

I scanned the letter again.

> And one thing you must do is come to the Orient. I have just under a year left, and I'll be out of the Army. But we'll find a way and come back here as civilians. I want to show you the countryside, the farmers, the kids. Or, if that doesn't work, we could try to go to Japan or Hong Kong. Hey, a wild place like Hong Kong, how would you like to live there? Hold on for eleven months plus, darling, and were going to live the most exciting life anyone ever had. We're going to see the world together, and make new trails of our own. We can make life what we want it to he, and I want it to be great.

Once I had thought of staying in the Kentucky mountains forever. Now this man I loved was dreaming of living on the other side of the world. Well, why not? Once a person started questioning, the sky was the limit.

After we cleared the dishes. Anna sat sewing, hemming a white uniform for working at the student center. I was writing my daily letter.

Suddenly I laid the pen down and looked at her. It struck me as ironic, the two of us once again waiting for a man to come home. Only this time it was not Anna's man, but mine, and we were sitting not in a cabin but an apartment. The world had spun around full cycle, and I was almost the age she had been.

"Do you remember," I asked her, "that night before the home opened, when you and I were in the kitchen waiting? You were frying potatoes in the black iron skillet, and everyone was so excited."

Anna looked up from her sewing. "Do you remember that?" she asked, surprised.

"I do. I think I remember everything that ever happened."

"I'm sorry it hasn't been all good."

"It hasn't been all bad either. I've had my share of laughs, but there were some things I never understood."

"What were they?"

"Number one, why you never fought for me, why you never stood up for me."

Anna took a pin out of her mouth. "From your earliest years, I always had the feeling you were strong. Did I communicate that to you?"

I thought for a moment. How many times had Anna said to me, 'You can do it better than I can . . . You're an artist and I can't draw a straight line . . . I can carry a tune but I don't know anything about harmony . . . How do you know all these things? . . . Yes, you can bake your clay models in the oven . . . I don't want to stand in the way of genius.'

"Yeah, I guess you did," I said slowly. I had never realized it. I thought I had invented the feeling myself.

"And as far as standing up for you against your father," Anna was saying. "I decided to let you fight for yourself, to find out exactly what he was like. If I had shielded you from him, you might have idolized him, and eventually been trapped."

"We're just lucky I wasn't," I said, thinking of certain scenes she did not know about. But then it had been the feeling that I was too valuable to get messed up that had protected me at those times as well. "Yeah, maybe I can see why you left me to fight my own battles, but why didn't you stand up for your own rights? Why didn't you confront Nada, or shoot her or something? I never could figure you out. You were either a saint or a fool, and I didn't see any practical difference."

Anna smiled. "It wasn't Nada. If it hadn't been her, it would have been someone else, or ten other people. If I started shooting, I would have had to commit mass murder! Your father would never have been satisfied with one woman, no matter if she were the Queen of Sheba."

"Solomon," I laughed, "and his thousand women, plus concubines. Did you know about Carlita and Pearl?"

"And all the rest. Hallie before that, and before that every woman he could get behind closed doors. Why do you think the neighbors gossiped about him? Before he opened the home, there were at least three country girls he had his eye on. All his talk of piety and moral restraint was simply a cover for his private life."

"But how could he do that?"

"I really think he was able to separate what he believed from what he lived so thoroughly that he actually thought he was pure and innocent. He was—and is—a completely split person."

"If you knew that, what were you waiting for all these years?"

"I guess I didn't know until it happened. And then I hoped for a few short months that the trauma following his public exposure would actually be healing for him, that it would be out in the open and he could face it, somehow get the parts of himself together, in focus. But I really don't think he's capable of doing it. There's something missing in him. I pity him now. It's the only feeling I have left."

I shoved my letter away and stared at Anna. "Sometimes I still can't get it through my head," I said, "that he actually did it, that all the time he was sewing up our pockets and stitching down our bras he was screwing around, was actually doing it left, right, and hindside with people. Do you believe he actually was, or that the girls didn't know what they were accusing him of?"

"There's no room for doubt. Did you hear the tape the county attorney recorded?"

"No."

"I did. Pearl went into great detail. Even before John had her come to work in the study he began to talk to her about nursing. Then, behind the locked door, he gave her a pelvic examination and a sexual demonstration. He was afraid of a pregnancy, and that accounted for the talk of sending her away to a nursing school. If she ever became pregnant, he had an out. She would be conveniently sent away to 'school.' Pearl said very explicitly on the tape that he would use her up to the point of ejaculation, then do it on the floor and make her clean up the mess.

"Oh. God," I shuddered. "Will you please spare me the details, Mother? This is my anniversary. I don't ever want to hear about that damned mess again!"

"You're picking up a lot of coarse language."

"Some things are damned, and I believe in saying it. Would you rather have me rotting with holy schizophrenia like him?"

"Lenore, I hope this whole experience hasn't left you angry at God, or hurt your ability to believe."

I picked up the pen and doodled "I love you" on Gordon's letter. "I don't think so," I said slowly. "I think the fact that Father John failed has actually helped me clear a lot of rubbish out of my mind but hasn't destroyed anything essential. I guess I've never left as much up to heaven as he did, and that makes me blame God less when things happen. I've never had the feeling that it was God's fault if my father was an asshole."

Anna was silent. I looked to see if she was shocked, but she was still stitching, no expression on her face. It was quiet. I picked up the card with the six rabbits on it, marked with G and L names.

"Were you scared when I was born?" I asked.

"No," she said.

"Did it hurt?"

"Yes, but it was a good sort of pain."

I looked at the maternity dress and the card full of rabbits, and thought of Gordon's joyful anticipation of the future.

"It's scary to have children," I said. "It's such a terrible responsibility."

"Life is scary," she said. "But you live, or you die."

"But what if I had a kid like him, like Father John. What would I do?"

"What would you do?"

"I'd strangle it when it was born."

"No you wouldn't. You wouldn't know. He would be a helpless baby, and you would care for him and protect him. And then when he was a child, you would see all his good points, praise him for all his virtues. When he started to grow, you'd blind yourself to all his faults, always hoping for the best. No matter what he did, you'd love him patiently and hope for the best."

I thought of Gram, of the pain on her face. "I guess so," I said.

"But you can't think of that," Anna said. "You have to take what life brings you, the good and the evil. The good and the evil are like day and night, and somehow they make a life that carves out its own rough kind of justice. You asked me why I never stuck up for my own rights. It would have done no good to fight him. I knew that given time he would destroy himself, but if I had stood up and made those accusations against him in his heyday, he would have had me in a mental institution, sealed and signed for life."

"That's hard to believe now. How did we accept that bondage?"

"It's over now, thank God. It's broken, and we're free!"

I got up and walked across the room and put a kiss on her forehead. "Thanks, Mom," I said. "Thanks for a lovely wedding a year ago. I'll try to make it a good investment. Do you mind if I go out for a walk for a few minutes?"

"What are you going to do?" she asked.

"I think I'll have four children, write a book, and live in the Orient," I said. She laughed and bit off the thread. "You probably will," she said.

I went out and closed the door. It was warm and dark outside, damp with the smell of summer. Overhead the giant elms arched in a leafy tunnel above the street, and the moon struggled through the clouds to cast shadowed patches on the sidewalk. I walked slowly through the archway, feeling the light and shadow fall like rhythms on my face.

I reached the street corner and looked up at the sky. The moon was still struggling through the clotted clouds. I gazed up at it knowing that somewhere, ten thousand miles away, he would see the same night sky, the same moon, maybe tomorrow.

"Hurry home," I whispered. "I love you."

EPILOGUE

So many people have wondered, after reading the last page of "90 Brothers and Sisters," what happened next? Did Gordon come home safely from Korea, and did they have four children, and did they really live in Hong Kong?

The answers to those questions and many more are yes, yes and yes! We did it all, plus things we never dreamed of. For twenty years we lived in Hong Kong, learning language and a new culture, and then went on to spend ten years in Saudi Arabia, teaching English, writing and discovering Middle Eastern art. Everywhere we went we searched and discovered, always looking for a life philosophy that would lead us to openness, freedom, responsibility and courage.

In August 2000, Gordon and I celebrated our 45th wedding anniversary. To mark the occasion we met with our four children, their four spouses, and five grandchildren for a family weekend at Cumberland Falls State Park near Corbin, Kentucky. Part of the agenda was a trip to the old grounds of the Galilean Home where "90 Brothers and Sisters" took place.

As I walked over the contours of the land, so familiar and yet now so small and strange, I could not believe that I once took those sandy paths for the boundaries of my life. Some of the old buildings were still standing, and as our thirteen "kids" posed for a photo on the rock garden in front of the school, I looked at their wonderful young faces and thought of all the talent and variety of life represented. It flashed across my mind—if I had decided to stay in that small and restricted life, most of these people would never have been born! How strange and wonderful life is with each decision at every turn creating new possibilities and endless consequences.